MW01253325

THE COLLECTIVE IMAGINATION

Thomas Hobbes wrote in Leviathan 'those that observe their similitudes, in case they be such as are but rarely observed by others, are said to have a good wit'. I came across that passage a long time ago when researching my doctoral thesis and it stuck with me. This present work is the result of 25 years of thinking about what Hobbes said. A good number of people aided and abetted that thinking along the way. I want to thank above all Agnes Heller, to whom this work is dedicated. Agnes supervised that now-distant PhD a quarter of a century ago and among a multitude of wonderful works she wrote is one whose spirit haunts The Collective Imagination. *Her book* Immortal Comedy *fingers laughter as the instinct of reason – and humour and wit as sublime expressions of the rationality of the intellect. To that idea, and the mirthful self-irony of reason, this book is deeply in debt.*

The Collective Imagination

The Creative Spirit of Free Societies

PETER MURPHY
James Cook University, Australia

ASHGATE

Published by
Ashgate Publishing Limited
Wey Court East
Union Road
Farnham
Surrey, GU9 7PT
England

Ashgate Publishing Company
Suite 420
101 Cherry Street
Burlington
VT 05401-4405
USA

www.ashgate.com

British Library Cataloguing in Publication Data
Murphy, Peter, 1956-
The collective imagination : the creative spirit of free societies.
1. Imagination--Social aspects. 2. Creative ability.
3. Intellectual capital. 4. Intellectual cooperation.
5. Statics and dynamics (Social sciences)
I. Title
303.4'8-dc23

Library of Congress Cataloging-in-Publication Data
Murphy, Peter, 1956-
The collective imagination : the creative spirit of free societies / by Peter Murphy.
p. cm.
Includes bibliographical references and index.
ISBN 978-1-4094-2135-1 (hbk) -- ISBN 978-1-4094-2136-8 (ebook)
1. Imagination--History 2. Creative ability--History. 3. Civilization. I. Title.
BF411.M857 2011
303.48--dc23

2011053306

ISBN 9781409421351 (hbk)
ISBN 9781409421368 (ebk)

Printed and bound in Great Britain by the MPG Books Group, UK.

Contents

List of Tables

About the Author

Peter Murphy is Professor of Creative Arts and Social Aesthetics at James Cook University. He is author of *Civic Justice* (2001) and co-author of *Dialectic of Romanticism* (2004), *Creativity and the Global Knowledge Economy* (2009), *Global Creation* (2010), and *Imagination* (2010).

Acknowledgements

Parts of Chapters 3, 4 and 6 draw on material from 'I Am Not Who I Am: Paradox and Indirect Communication, or the Case of the Comic God and the Dramaturgical Self', *Empedocles: European Journal for the Philosophy of Communication* 1(2), 225–36, 2009 (Intellect); 'Systems of Communication: Information, Explanation and Imagination', *International Journal of Knowledge and Systems Science* 2(2), 1–15, 2011 (IGI); 'Creative Economies and Research Universities' in M.A. Peters and D. Araya (eds) *Education in the Creative Economy: Knowledge and Learning in the Age of Innovation* (New York: Peter Lang, 2010).

Introduction

Creativity concentrates in particular societies and geographical regions and in specific historical periods. What explains this? Why is it that some societies and some historical eras are more creative than others are? Why are those societies or periods better at galvanizing the creativity of individuals than others? And why is it that our own age is less brilliant than others? *The Collective Imagination* tries to answer these questions by probing the media of the imagination, exploring the part played by paradox, antinomy and metaphor in acts of creation. Media such as these connect the unconnected. They unite opposites. In so doing, they 'double' images, thoughts, processes and deeds in uncanny, surprising and fertile ways. They make what is different, the same, and what is the same, different. In short, they make the impossible possible. That's creation.

Acts of creation contribute immeasurably to the depth, dynamism and richness of social life. They produce social meaning and they replenish it when societies exhaust it as invariably happens. They animate scientific discovery and technological innovation. They nourish artistic insight and aesthetic pleasure. Conversely, creative media are socially conditioned and socially mobilized. So that the most startling acts of individual creativity are principally found in those periods, societies and institutions that exhibit a high propensity for inventiveness. *The Collective Imagination* examines the nature of the creative spirit – the collective generative agency – of free societies that delight in invention. It also analyses how the cultural cores of creative societies energize and animate economic, social, and political systems.

Modern high functioning arts-and-science-based economies perform by successfully capturing the patterns and paradoxes of human inventiveness. They turn these patterns and paradoxes into drivers of industrial development and social prosperity. When this happens, the imagination is transformed into an integral factor of production. Ingenuity becomes interwoven with the general sense of social well-being. *The Collective Imagination* explores the resulting scientific and aesthetic modes of production and the way in which these interact with economic, social and political systems. The point is made that it is particular kinds of societies and types of economies and forms of politics that lend themselves, on a collective scale, to the paradoxical shaping and synthesizing forces of the imagination.

The Collective Imagination begins by exploring the general character of the imagination. The imagination of individuals allows each one of us to integrate incongruent qualities. It allows us to make one common thing out of two things that are unlike each other. We discover similarities in difference. Imaginative thinking is appositional. It unites opposing qualities into distinctive, socially-powerful and coherent patterns, shapes and forms. And just as individuals have imaginations, so do societies. The power of imagination resonates in specific periods and places. Elizabethan London and late nineteenth century New York, Boston, and Chicago are classic examples. Wit exemplifies the collective imagination at work. Certain societies at certain times exhibit high levels of wit, irony, and paradox. From Classical Athens to the London of Chesterton and Churchill, the witty imagination is the classic marker of a creative society. In turn, a creative society is a free society. While free societies have many forms, all are sceptical of tyrannical thinking and behaviour. Whether tyranny is born of rationalism or irrationalism, the objection is the same. Tyrants, bores, and totalitarian dictators are the special target of the witty imagination.

Conversely, creative societies nurture personalities with a gift for creative doubling. These societies encourage social 'acting'. Social actors create fictional identities. They wear inventive masks. They impersonate and parody themselves and others. Peak creative societies – the ones that produce a Plato or a Shakespeare – are dramaturgical in spirit. In these societies, truth is communicated indirectly. It is relayed by paradox and dialogue and irony. Such truths are enigmatic. They are mysterious. Yet they convey powerful appositional conclusions. Appositional thinking, the power to unite opposites in interesting and memorable ways, lies at the heart of creativity. Societies that are good at stimulating appositional thinking are creative. Appositional thinking is the rarest form of human cognition. The most common form is information. The second most common is explanation. We generate information analytically – by distinguishing objects in the world and attributing characteristics to them. Explanation, on the other hand, provides knowledge through discourse, narration, logic, rhetoric and other forms of discursive elaboration. Intellectual discovery in contrast relies on a third system of communication and cognition. This is the imagination. The imagination is rooted neither in analytic distinction nor systemic elaboration. Rather it relies on intuition and analogy.

The imagination waxes and wanes historically. It rises and falls as we move between societies. In short the social capacity to produce high levels of creative work varies across space and time. Often when a society is most voluble about creativity, it is least creative. Observing the nineteenth and twentieth centuries we see artistic and scientific creation grow and then shrink. There were some very remarkable art works produced in the early twentieth century. High Modernism in the arts, and quantum and relativistic physics, were very good. Yet the prevalence of kitsch art and kitsch science in the twentieth century, especially in the late twentieth century, underlines that the creative peak of the collective imagination is difficult to sustain. Kitsch is a good proxy for the absence of the imagination's enigma. Albert Einstein once observed (1935/2007) that the 'fairest thing we can experience is the mysterious. It is the fundamental emotion that stands at the cradle of all true art and true science'. Such an emotion (the emotion of enigma) is difficult to prolong. The power of the imagination, the capacity to think in ironies, appositions, analogies and other kinds of doubles, is sometimes socially encouraged and sometimes not. When doubling in art and science falters, much more does as well. This is because we inhabit a world where the arts and the sciences are a force of production. While that coupling was widely commented on in the second-half of the twentieth century, it is ironic that the high point of the contribution of art and science to modern economies was probably 1870. Saying something is not the same as doing something.

Social creation varies over time. In modernity there is a pattern of long waves of expansion and contraction, creative peaks and abatements. Each of these waves tends to favour different cities and sometimes different nations. Such variability has a crucial economic significance. Modern economies flourish because of the application of art and science to economic processes. Yet there are productive periods and fallow periods, and better and worse places for the arts and sciences. This is reflected in institutions that sustain the arts and sciences, notably universities. Their quality rises and falls. In the latter half of the twentieth and on into the twenty-first century, it has been more a case of falling rather than rising. High-level creativity, discovery and invention contribute to industrial innovation and economic growth via the difficult medium of appositional thinking. Such thinking is not common-place, and when it wanes, economies flatten. The second half of the twentieth century was a period of massive expansion of universities globally, followed by much heated talk about industrial innovation and technological creation. Research universities and corporate science labs both claimed to change economic and social dynamics – and for the better. They both claimed to be the key to social prosperity. But the record of what they actually did was considerably more meagre.

While universities matter, of all of the social contexts of creativity, it is cities that matter most. Historically a handful of cities have been the key crucibles for the appositional thought and paradoxical irony that mediate the act of creation. These cities produce cultures rich in dramaturgy, wit, and analogical thought. They weave this in subtle ways into their material fabric and background ethos. Some of these cities are large, some are small; all have the capacity to surprise with their energy and drive. They do not always win popularity contests and their reputations to begin with are often rough hewn, garnering recognition for their works and achievements only with the passage of time. *The Collective Imagination* asks the question then: which contemporary cities have the greatest capacity for invention and discovery? Which cities structurally embody irony and paradox? Which ones are capable of antonymic works and analogical processes of the kind capable of sparking large and interesting economic and social leaps? In which places, today and tomorrow, is appositional thinking concentrated?

If the city is the natural home of creativity in general, nations are the peculiar locus of political creativity. Nations are the great purveyors of political ingenuity and political imbecility. Without good, great and interesting politics, not only nations but cities wither and waste away. Economies crumble and social prosperity fades. Thus *The Collective Imagination* concludes with a look at that most mysterious of all things, the creative political system. These are systems that accommodate high levels of appositional thinking. Apposition, the mark of free societies, is partly a function of opposition. It is born of free-spirited debate, disagreement and contradiction. But like all acts of creation the interesting political system turns antonyms of opposition into synonyms of apposition. This is difficult to do – consequently unintended ironies abound in political life. What often passes for a free spirit in politics is actually out-and-out dogmatism. Self-declared liberals more often than not are conspicuously illiberal. Toleration is a cover for stifling control; manifestoes of openness are signs of closed minds. Talk of creativity is a sure-fire guarantee of being in the company of dim-wits. Only when irony becomes conscious, and political actors manage a gleam in their eye and turn opposition into apposition, is this reversed. Like imagination in general this is rare. But what is rare does exist. To its existence, we tip our hat.

PART I
The Media of Creation

Chapter 1
Imagination

To Take One Thing for Another

The idea of wit is an old one, though not so old. It precedes the age of the Romantics, but post-dates the Greeks, the Romans, and the rise of Christianity. It is neo-classical in spirit, an artefact of the sixteenth, seventeenth and eighteenth centuries. The idea of creativity, as we understand it now, owes something tacitly to all of these – the ancient, the Christian, the neo-classical, and the Romantic. It is its own archaeological dig. For the Greeks and Romans, to create was to make. Creation proper, *creatio*, was a Christian coinage. God was the creator. Humankind made things rather than created them. It was not until the Romantic age that the artist was thought to create 'as if' God. Yet even then the production of an object (be it an artwork, a book, or a building) was still the end-point of creation. From nothing came something. Creation was an act of objectivation. The creator was a maker. In this way, all creation was a function of wit.

The New Critics, William Wimsatt and Cleanth Brooks, summarized the history of the word 'wit' neatly (1957: 229–3). Etymologically the term meant the faculty of knowing in general. About the time of Shakespeare it came to mean smart knowing, joking, repartee, invention or ingenuity. Especially in the guise of the idea of ingenuity – the metaphysical *discordia concors* – wit was practically equivalent to poetry and synonymous with imagination and fancy. As it was defined in the seventeenth century, wit was the faculty of seeing resemblances between unlike objects. It was a faculty of synthesis rather than one of analysis. Correspondingly, and in contrast to wit, the faculty of analysis was called 'judgement'. Thus conceived in this manner, imagination is the seeing of resemblances whilst judgement is the seeing of differences. Francis Bacon stated the essence of this intellectual division in his *Novum Organum* of 1620. Bacon does not use the terms 'wit' or 'judgement'. Nonetheless he does describe the two powers – one of perceiving resemblances and one of perceiving differences.

The same distinction is artfully depicted in Thomas Hobbes' *Leviathan* in 1651 and in John Locke's *Essay Concerning Human Understanding* in 1690. For Hobbes, wit consists principally of two things. First, the 'celerity of imagining (that is, *swift succession of one thought to another*)'; second, the '*steady direction to some approved end*'. The second of these is more properly a definition of reason rather than wit. That said, though, Hobbes neatly captures the essential difference between wit and judgement. He does so in these terms:

> … those that observe their similitudes, in case they be such as are but rarely observed by others, are said to have a good wit; by which, in this occasion, is meant a good fancy. But they that observe their differences, and dissimilitudes, which is called distinguishing, and discerning, and judging between thing and thing, in case such discerning be not easy, are said to have a good judgment.[1]

Forty years later Locke drew essentially the same picture:

> For wit lying most in the assemblage of ideas, and putting those together with quickness and variety, wherein can be found any resemblance or congruity, thereby to make up pleasant pictures and agreeable visions in the fancy; judgment, on the contrary, lies quite on the other side, in separating carefully, one from another, ideas wherein can be found the least difference, thereby to avoid being misled by similitude, and by affinity to take one thing for another.[2]

To take one thing for another is the major part of creation. It is what happens in all acts of creation. Wit, it might be supposed, is the swiftest or quickest form of creation. It is very likely that all creation happens in an ineffable instant. Working through the implications of an act of creation, however, is laboured. Such labour is the mark of reason. What is captured in a snap in the imagination is patiently and steadily, and sometimes tiresomely, unfolded by the faculty of reason, ordinarily understood. Reason in this prosaic sense is what steadily leads us in the direction of some approved end. It is what the sociologist Max Weber called means-ends rationality. In everyday settings, we call this problem solving. Analytic capacity and good judgement is very important in such reasoning. Yet it has its limits. For it assumes that both the means and the ends of our actions already exist. When we reason, we fit the two together. But if our means or our ends are inadequate, and necessity calls upon us to invent new means or new ends, then for that we need more than good judgement. We need wit.

The same spectre haunts our proofs. We make statements and we propose theses. We mobilize reason in support of them. We reason by marshalling evidence that we patiently connect to principles and axioms. But as the child quite reasonably asks, where do those axioms and first principles come from? Even if we adopt the posture of the radical empiricist, and dismiss principles as puffery, and claim that all we need is the evidence of our eyes, we still cannot avoid invention. Observation is not innocent. The astronomers who looked at photographic plates of distant stars beyond our solar system had first to draw the audacious connection that Doppler effects – those small changes in the colour of light when a star moves toward or

1 *Leviathan*, Chapter VIII.

2 *Essay Concerning Human Understanding*, Chapter XI.

away from the earth – might be caused by an orbiting exo-planet.[3] Where do such connections come from, pray tell? Wit, again, I'm afraid.

In 1744, Corbyn Morris in the splendidly titled *An Essay towards Fixing the True Standards of Wit, Humour, Raillery, Satire, and Ridicule* observed that wit is 'the Lustre which results from the quick Elucidation of one Subject, by the just and unexpected Arrangement of it with another Subject'. The unexpected nature of the combination of subjects is certainly a prime characteristic of humour, as it is of literary simile or scientific metaphor, as it is of everything that arises from an act of creation. If we expect something, then it is part of routine life. It is not creative. What happens unexpectedly happens quickly. Wit is distinguished by its swiftness. The witty mind is fast. We observe this in repartee, raillery and ridicule. These depend on a very quick response, in verbal exchange for example. Creative acts or imaginative insights take place in a flash. To take one thing for another, to observe similitude, to see resemblances between unlike objects – all of these things happen very fast.

The critic William Hazlitt probably had the best go at separating the species of wit from the genus of imagination. He suggested (1818/2004: 436) that imagination was:

> the finding out something similar in things generally alike, or with like feelings attached to them; while wit principally amounts to a momentary deception where you least expected it, viz. in things totally opposite.

In Hazlitt's account, wit is the most radical instance of the imagination. It produces what is least expected and stimulates in an audience not only the feeling of what is unexpected but also a feeling of deception in connection with it. We have all experienced that momentary feeling of deception. It is present whenever anyone grasps a joke. But the same feeling is also present in the case of any far-reaching act of imagination. The response to an imaginative act is a feeling however fleeting of being tricked. 'Is our leg being pulled here?' is the reaction, even if it amounts to only a flicker of disbelief. This is properly so. Given the proximity of humour to intellect, there is a strain of the circus acrobat in any imaginative leap. The art of the cognitive acrobat is to pass over the yawning gap between distant opposites by negotiating the slender tight-rope that connects them.

Wit, imagination, ingenuity, invention, joking and smart knowing are all related to each other in ways that analytical dissection simply confounds. The very point of wit and imagination is that they are faculties that combine rather than separate. The act of combination ironically subverts their status as faculties. The analytic mind parses. It differentiates and separates out objects. The imagination

3 Doppler spectroscopy was first proposed by the astronomer Otto Struve in 1952. The first astronomers to detect an extra-solar planet were Michel Mayor and Didier Queloz at Switzerland's Geneva Observatory in 1995. The planet they found orbits the star 51 Pegasi.

in contrast synthesizes rather than analyses. That means it finds resemblances between unlike objects. It also does this with astonishing speed. Partly because of its swiftness, and partly because of the unlikely nature of the conjurations it makes, it defies our expectations and produces thereby the unexpected. It forges unusual congruity out of manifest incongruity. It combines opposites such that we do not know, and cannot tell, where one finishes and the other begins. It creates similarities out of differences. All of this is startling work.

The imagination is through and through uncanny. This is reflected in its basic nature. Its agency is both individual and social. It is a psychological and an institutional phenomenon. It is expressed in unique genius and in statistical regularity. It is existential and sociological in the same breath. Consequently, there are imaginative nations, exciting historical periods, and audacious states as well as brilliant artists, inspired statesmen and far-seeing founders. Some individuals are especially adept at the imaginative ability to see something as being what it is and other than what it is. A handful of individuals have a breathtaking ability to do this. Practically every second line in Shakespeare has a simile or metaphor of some kind. Notwithstanding that, all human beings are born with the capacity to understand jokes and metaphors. Imagination – whether it happens to be imagination in reception or imagination in conception – is a very pleasurable act. Much the same is true of societies. Few societies can extinguish invention entirely. The most successful in that are the most tyrannical. It is equally evident though that some societies, in some historical periods, are much more imaginative than others. The varying concentrations of inventiveness in the arts and the sciences across time and space are an unimpeachable indicator of this. But the reason why this is the case is less clear. Just as it is not immediately evident why it is that some people are very witty and others are not, or why some have extremely quick senses of humour and others, alas, do not sparkle.

That the imagination is an incongruous faculty, individual and social at the same time, means also that we do not know, and cannot tell, where the individual imagination finishes and the collective imagination begins. This reminds us that analytic distinctions in general, useful as they are, are always parlous and invariably a little misleading. From the stand-point of our species being, and that is not a stand-point we can easily dispense with, there is not an implacable distinction between the individual and society. Winston Churchill (1909: 79) put this rather neatly when he observed that:

> It is not possible to draw a hard-and-fast line between individualism and collectivism … The nature of man is a dual nature. The character of the organization of human society is dual. Man is at once a unique being and a gregarious animal. For some purposes he must be collectivist, for others he is, and he will for all time remain, an individualist.

Individual and society are implicated in the other. Just as one self always interpolates another self, each one of our selves interpolates the thing called society. Thus

'*I* am always not *me*'. This is true in the sense that *I* carry within *myself* thoughts, feelings and experiences of my own along with the expectations of particular significant others and also of the generalized other that we call society.[4] Each is translatable into the other. I am singular. I am a multitude. My singularity is many. At the same time, I am a super-singularity. My individuality carries within it the collective impress of society, while that collective impress is refined over time by individualities that aspire to generality.

Thus the work of the imagination is not just the work of individuals, though there are many smart, witty, and ingenious individuals. The point is not that there are not clever individuals but that wit and imagination are species-capacities. Human beings, as a species, display a collective capacity for wit and imagination. If anything, it is humour that distinguishes humankind from the animal world. Dogs do not tell jokes. With witty aforethought, we anthropomorphize dogs. But they do not canine us. Animals have one nature. Human beings have two natures. We live both in a first natural nature and a second artificial nature of our own making. We extend membership of that second nature to some of our animal friends. Dogs, all things considered, have a pretty cushy life. Yet that does not mean that dogs have the peculiar capacity of human beings to see resemblances in what is different. Sometimes we find profound resemblances in what is radically different. Thus we domesticate animals. Some of us even find some of our animal friends, cats among them, more companionate than most of our own species. Nevertheless, they do not cheer us up with jokes. That is a species-specific ability. We are the humourous species.

The fact that the imagination is a capacity of the species means that it manifests itself socially as well as individually. In fact, what is social and what is individual, although distinguishable, are difficult to distinguish with any finality. The social 'me' and the individual 'I' are wound together in uncanny ways. Their relation is eerie. The apprehension of such eerie relations is itself a function of the imagination. The species that imagines readily leaps over any analytic boundaries, whether between 'I' and 'me', or any other distinction (perceptual or linguistic) that is made. While the making of analytic distinctions is powerful, equally powerful is the imaginative capacity to override them. The larger point is that all oppositions, at a certain turning point, become unions, fusions, blends, and mergers. In acts of imagination, antithetical elements coalesce into one entity and yet continue to exist concurrently.[5] This occurs in the course of what Hegel called sublation or *aufheben*, the simultaneous cancelling and retaining of things.[6] Hegel's term

4 George Herbert Mead (1934) made roughly the same point.

5 See for example the description of this in Cleanth Brooks (1947: 213–14).

6 'To sublate, and the sublated … constitute one of the most important notions in philosophy. It is a fundamental determination which repeatedly occurs throughout the whole of philosophy, the meaning of which is to be clearly grasped and especially distinguished from nothing. What is sublated is not thereby reduced to nothing. … "To sublate" [*aufheben*] has a twofold meaning in the language: on the one hand it means

is a potted description of what happens in the act of creation. Things (events, deeds, words) are cancelled and retained at the same time. Differences become similarities or similitudes that are both simultaneously the same and different. Although this is an odd thing, it is not so odd because it is deeply embedded in human cognition. It is how the human species apprehends the world.

The philosopher Cornelius Castoriadis observed (1987: 127–31) that individuals and societies apprehend the world in imaginary and symbolic ways. In the most general terms, the imaginary powers the symbolic. The imaginary is inarticulate, invisible, intuitive and primary. The symbolic is articulate, visible, discursive and secondary. Whilst different, the imaginary and the symbolic share something profound in common. This is the capacity to *see in a thing what it is not* such that 'what it is not' is 'what it is'. Thus we consider a thing (event, deed, word). We 'see' it for what it is. We 'see' it for what it is not. We equate the two. The equation is the act of creation. Creation is circular. What A is, is 'what it is not' is 'what it is'. What that describes among other things is the act of metaphor. This is the capacity to say 'You have seen/Sunshine and rain at once; her smiles and tears'. What the Gentleman does, when he describes Cordelia's behaviour to Kent (*King Lear*, IV.3), is a species capacity. And what a remarkable capacity it is. It is the possibility and at the same time the necessity, as Castoriadis (1997a: 242) puts it, of *thinking A by means of non-A*. This is what gives the human species its ability to invent and adapt and create. It is also what gives human beings the capacity to make meaning. It is what makes the human being the being that imputes significance and insignificance to things. Put simply, creating, valuing and signifying are Janus-like processes. Each involves seeing, saying, attributing, or implying in two directions at once. It is as if two worlds are conceived together. That is the way the critic William Empson (1947: 226) described it. The conception of two-worlds-as-one is at the heart of poetic meaning. It is, as Shakespeare's Richard II declared, as if language sets 'the word itself/ Against the word'.[7] In a beautiful discussion of four lines from a fragment of Sappho's poetry, Castoriadis (2007) meditates on the Greek word *hōra* – with its several senses of season, day, hour, and point in time. In the middle of the night, the poet says that the *hōra* passes. With this single word, the poet evokes multiple and contrary meanings that are folded beyond easy distinction into each other. Season, hour, and the fading of youth – cyclical time, periodic time, and biographical time – congeal in an ineffable synchrony.

---

to preserve, to maintain, and equally it also means to cause to cease, to put an end to. Even "to preserve" includes a negative element, namely, that something is removed from its influences, in order to preserve it. Thus what is sublated is at the same time preserved; it has only lost its immediacy but is not on that account annihilated' (G.W.F. Hegel 1812–1816/1969: 107). In English, sublation has acquired the senses of abolish, annul, destroy, cancel, suspend, keep, save, preserve, hold, overcome, transcend, lift, and raise-up.

7 *Richard II*, 5.5, 13–14.

It is such concentrated congealing or impaction of meanings that gives things significance. The more that meaning is enfolded upon meaning, the greater the significance of a thing. This is why, in the case of great works of creation, we can endlessly return to them without exhausting their meaning. What makes this possible is the fact that whenever we look at something, whether it is an event, a deed, or an object, we see it and 'we see it other than it is'. Castoriadis (1987: 12) phrased it perfectly. To see *it* other than *it* is involves intuitive imagination and articulate wit. We imagine in the media of silence and invisible depiction. We are witty in speech and visual imagery. In each instance, we unify what is dual. We make one out of two. The 'it-in-itself' and the 'it-other-than-itself' are different and yet resemble each other. Shakespeare's line 'the ship ploughs the seas' comes to mind.[8] The line assumes that we can distinguish between a plough and a ship *and* imagine them as being one and the same.

Distinction and union are intrinsic to all forms of invention, not just linguistic invention. Winston Churchill took a keen interest in developments in military technology. In his study of the Duke of Marlborough, he observed (1933/2002: 564) that, in nearly every great war, there is some new mechanical feature introduced which confers important advantages. In Marlborough's age, the role of infantry on the battlefield changed decisively. The change was sparked by the invention of the ring bayonet which was fastened around the muzzle of the musket instead of blocking it by being screwed inside it. This technological adaptation permitted a key tactical innovation. It allowed the infantry soldier to become at once pikeman and musketeer. This capacity of the human being to be one thing and another lies at the core of the human condition. Just as words have multiple meanings, so technologies have both utility and beauty. The first tools that human beings created were ornamented as well as useful. The same remains true today. The best technologies have qualities akin to artworks. Their power is explained in equal measure by their aesthetics as by their science. It is less important that we are a tool-making and tool-using species (though that is very important) than it is that our tools, like all experiences including our use of those tools, are double coded. Experience is singular but its meaning is multiple. The double coding of what is singular powers our invention. It gives the world around us the unfathomable meaning that it has. Things have significance because in their very singularity they are double.

I do not mean by this that the human species is beset by cringing ambivalence. It is not Nietzsche's sick animal. Dire uncertainty, no matter how well it is disguised, is a sign of a society or an individual that is on the edge of suicide. Suicide is an indicator of a symbolic order that has gone awry. In such a case the individual draws from its natural ambidexterity nothing more than confusion and uncertainty. In contrast to this, self-confident societies and robust individuals are those that cope splendidly with the presence of two opposing ideas, attitudes and emotions because they can perfectly well interpolate each one in the other at the same time.

8 *1 Henry IV*, 1.1.7.

This is the intellectual acrobatics of the human species. It is so constituted to do this. Each human being is born into a world where everything potentially stands for something else and everything is potentially a symbol of something else. The apprehension of this world is first and foremost pre-linguistic. That is why the individual act of creation is so often referred to as an intuition. Intuition is simply a word for the intellectual capacity to relate and merge successfully and productively two opposing ideas, attitudes and emotions at the same time. Upon intuition is grounded more explicit cognitive abilities such as wit and paradox. They make explicit what is implicit or tacit in intuition.

Intuition accompanies the world of symbols into which all human beings are born. Thus to be human is to be born into an order in which everything (always already) represents something else. Every A that is in the world is also (potentially, actually, latently, explicitly) not-A. Everything (act, utterance) is also (potentially, actually, latently, explicitly) a symbol, metaphor or figure of something else and a reference, referral, and deferral to something else. Everything in the human world is double coded. More than that, it is both 'one' *and* 'two' at the same time. That makes possible all things interesting including Myth, Religion, Love, Friendship, Justice, Freedom, Art, Philosophy, and Science. Everything in human experience is latently symbolic, even if normally trivially so. Thus everything is a kind of being-at-one-with. The human world is one and whole. Yet it is also double and divided. So the meaning of anything points in more than one direction while its significance emerges from its implicit unity and is comprehended as a single entity. Importance or consequence, i.e. meaning, is forged from the (seeming) impossibility of this. Meaning – that is to say deep resonant lasting meaning which has moment and magnitude – arises from the experience, cognition, understanding, and at the bottom the intuiting that 'one' and 'two' are different and same at the same time, just as a pair of lovers (two) are united in love (one). Every word we utter is itself *and* (implicitly) another word.[9] Every deed we do is understood in its own terms ('in itself') and in the terms of what it stands for ('for itself'). Meaning, including linguistic meaning, arises because of that condition.

When I look up a dictionary I find that word 'A' means 'not-A'. Because of the nature of language, I can begin the day by 'rising and shining' and going off to work to find that my efforts are 'a drop in the bucket' surrounded as I am not only by work mates who are 'salts of the earth' but also by those who are 'thorns in my flesh'. Engaged with the latter in tedious battles, I periodically 'lick the dust' and escape their claws 'by the skin of my teeth', but despite all my trials I still somehow manage to grow 'from strength to strength'. All of those descriptors come from the *King James Bible*, whose translators created some of the

9 As the hero, Denis Stone, in Aldous Huxley's *Crome Yellow* remarks (Chapter XX), 'One suffers so much from the fact that beautiful words don't always mean what they ought to mean'.

best-known idiomatic expressions in the English language.[10] What such expressions underscore is the fact that nothing in human experience is ever exactly itself. Forget words – pre-discursive experience is no less storied. Is this not confusing for us? Certainly it would be dizzying if we could not bracket the impulse to always see something as something else or always *re*-present what we experience in terms of other experiences. If we did that all the time, we would be paralysed. Yet also to do it too infrequently is stultifying and deadening. To do it sometimes is very powerful. The Janus-like nature of the human species has given it enormous evolutionary advantage. For a start, human beings can think ahead. They can calculate, anticipate, and strategize. Dogs do not strategize. They do not hold war councils. The direction or goal of human action is provided by the imagination. The imagination intuits what is not there. We know where we will end before we begin, and where we will arrive before we embark. In the imagination, we can synchronously compare beginning and end, start and finish. The imagination deals with what is virtually existent, with what exists and does not exist at the same time. It manipulates imaginary time and space – in front, behind and above us. It projects where we were, where we might be going to, and how high and far we aspire to go. It looks upwards from beneath, outwards in front of us, and glances behind us as we move through the world.

Imagination permits us to see around corners in time and space – to see what is not there. There are many modes of 'seeing' what is not there. 'Seeing' itself is a metaphor for hearing, feeling, touching, and animating what is not there. Memory and anticipation are not exactly imagination but they are complicit in the imagination. Imagination does what the historian does. As Kant observed, history is the past made present. Imagination is the coalescing of past and present, present and future. Spatially, it is the way we have of looking up beyond the visible sky and down deep below the visible ground. Such uncanny cognition allows the sense of the artistic and the sacred to emerge along with the historical.

---

10 *Isaiah 60:1* Arise, shine; for thy light is come, and the glory of the Lord is risen upon thee.

Isaiah 40:15 Behold, the nations [are] as a drop of a bucket, and are counted as the small dust of the balance: behold, he taketh up the isles as a very little thing.

Matthew 5:13 Ye are the salt of the earth: but if the salt have lost his savour, wherewith shall it be salted? It is thenceforth good for nothing, but to be cast out, and to be trodden under foot of men.

Corinthians 12:7 And lest I should be exalted above measure through the abundance of the revelations, there was given to me a thorn in the flesh, the messenger of Satan to buffet me, lest I should be exalted above measure.

Psalms 72:9 They that dwell in the wilderness shall bow before him; and his enemies shall lick the dust.

Job 19:20 My bone cleaveth to my skin and to my flesh, and I am escaped with the skin of my teeth.

Psalms 84:7 They go from strength to strength, [every one of them] in Zion appeareth before God.

Emergence is the correct word. The creative significance of this is enormous. As imaginative power and symbolic capacity expands, it becomes possible to manipulate in the mind endless morphological possibilities and to anticipate the unknown. This allows human beings to travel across huge distances, to forgo immediate gratification for the promised returns of long-distance trade, and to enjoy long-term social relationships extending beyond an immediate life-span or the life-time of an off-spring into the venerable, imperishable span of endless past and future generations. Progress and permanence are two sides of the same coin of the imagination.

The two sides of Janus, the Roman god, sum up things. To imagine something is to be able to imagine its opposite kind. The imagining of something is not the negation of something, nor is it simply the structural pairing of opposites. Rather it is the super-positioning or consubstantiation of them. Thus we imagine the end of the year in the light of the start of next year. We imagine the worst of days in and through the image of night-time; we imagine the greatest freedom in and through the image of necessity. We face our most terrifying nightmares in the harsh light of day, and we are freest when we act in a self-disciplined way. Homer's Odysseus, the great adventurer, could imagine locales in the far distance because he could imagine a return home. The human mind analytically separates near and distant, home and away, beginning and end, only to unite them in the imagination. Castoriadis called this uncanny fusion *union/separation*. He observed that the schemas of union and separation are not possible without each other (1987: 399; 253, 256). They require one another. Each emerges due to the fact that the other also appears. It would be meaningless, he noted, to say that they are the same. Rather they inhere, and are mutually implicated, in each other.

In the same spirit, the Queen of the United Kingdom is neither a peer nor a commoner but a sovereign who sublates both commoner and peer without being either one of them. Permit me to coin a word for this. The word is *sepion*. It is a compound of separation and union. All systems, all arrangements, are set in motion by a sepion. This is Aristotle's unmoved-mover. It is Einstein's space-time. It is creation itself. Here, though, I part company with Castoriadis when he says that creation is something that arises out of nothing, bewitching as that might sound. Creation, rather, is the super-positioning of something *and* nothing, their poietic, which is also their poetic, compounding. Here we reach the limit of language. There is not a singular word for the 'something-nothing', any more than there is one for 'space-time' or the 'unmoved-mover'. Hegel (1812–1816/1969: 107) was tremendously excited by the fact that the word 'sublation' had antipodal meanings. '… it is certainly remarkable', he said, 'to find that a language has come to use one and the same word for two opposite meanings. It is a delight to speculative thought to find in the language words which have in themselves a speculative meaning …'. Yet, as Hegel also implies, this is very rare. So while *sepions* exist in our intuitions, for the most part they do not exist as discrete words in our language. So we have to adapt. Human beings resort to irony, humour, and paradox, in other words to a certain kind of artful absurdity, where-in sense teeters on the edge of non-sense, in order to communicate the weighty and overwhelming and yet virtually inarticulate sense of the intuitive sepion.

The act of creation is a making sense of non-sense. The faculty of wit is the mediator and facilitator of this. Wit permits the uncanny combination of worlds. It allows distinctions to be thought together as a seamless whole. In the flash of wit, as in the foundation of philosophy, as at the peak moments of high politics, contrary worlds are conceived together. Those who think and live and function in such worlds simultaneously are able to scale the heights and explore the deep, deep depths of existence. They also, it must be said, make very good jokes. That latter aptitude is no accident. It is a certain kind of absurdity that is pregnant with the most weighty and enduring meanings. The intensity of sense arises out of what appears, on first encounter, to be devoid of sense. From that paradoxical event arises all that is brilliant, profound and mysterious in life and thought. For this, we are impossibly indebted to the faculty of the wit.

The Civil Wars of Troublesome Metaphors

Wit appears to us suddenly and unexpectedly. Any surprise sprung by the imagination is best leavened by a respect for the sobriety of reason. While irony is the enemy of pomposity, equally it is the friend of constancy. In human affairs, the steady direction to some approved end has much to recommend it. That is reason's work. Yet the reason that seeks to attain goals and realize values is also habitually the cause of its own undoing. At times reason can be very unreasonable. The ironic faculty of the imagination is often animated by a sense that what is stable in life, far from being supported by reason, is threatened by reason. Reason aspires to faithfulness but routinely disappoints in two ways. Reason's work often is stale and vacuous. It readily descends into the minutiae of rules. Alternately, it becomes infatuated with giddy change. Either way, its faith proves quite faithless. The imagination in response does pirouetting leaps. It does this either to reverse reason's terminal bland inertness or else because reason has become drunk on its own rationality. The pathos of reason is that it cannot move in interesting ways without being set in motion by acts of imagination. Reason's own internal regulator of motion produces either a dull kind of soporific methodological doggedness or else a countervailing propensity to lurch about uneasily, unsecured by any transcendent purpose.

The surprises of the witty imagination are often born out of a sense of reason's betrayal of faith. The idea that reason is unreliable and needs to be anchored in the imagination is the converse of the view of the great English philosopher Thomas Hobbes. Like many of the philosophers and critics of the seventeenth century, Hobbes underestimated imagination and overestimated reason. Reason is methodical. Our regular plans assume that 'A follows B follows C' in some logical, inferential pattern. A succession of thoughts in our mind models this. Hobbes called this the 'train' of the imagination. The succession of human thoughts, Hobbes observed, *can* be constant. In such cases, the succession of one thought followed by another is regulated by some overarching desire or design. However Hobbes further observed it is in the nature of sense, at least human sense, that in the case of *one and the same thing perceived, sometimes one thing and sometimes another, succeeds it.*[11] Hobbes took exception to this. Indeed he thought that, at the root of things, the unregulated, bifurcating succession of thought, i.e. the branching of the 'train' of imagination, was the cause of civil war. The simplest way of understanding that proposition is to suppose that the imagination inspires the wars of metaphors which animate, stimulate and falsely legitimate the baleful battles of subjects and citizens. A terrifying chaos reigns where a pleasant order once did. Hobbes assumed correctly that meaning is connection. He further assumed, perhaps less correctly, that, for the sake of certainty, one word must connect with one word only. Where unrestrained semantic branching occurs, and one word connects with many words, allowing figures of speech to flourish, uncertainty will prevail. In the most radical of such cases, the synonym of a word will turn out to be its antonym. The shadow of paradox haunted Hobbes.

Hobbes understood brilliantly what wit, imagination and metaphor were. Yet he also held them up as villains. Metaphor, to him, was the root of the political agonies that tore England apart in the seventeenth century. There are two types of eloquence, he insisted.[12] One is the elegant and clear expression of conceptions of the mind. In such cases, words have their own proper, definite and singular signification. The second (bad) kind of eloquence derives from the metaphorical use of words. Hobbes' condemnation of this was serial. Metaphors are a function of the passions. They arise from received opinions rather than from true principles. Metaphoric speech belongs to the art of rhetoric rather than that of logic. Its end is victory, rather than truth. At the heart of truth is 'the right definition of names'.[13] Those who reason from wrong definitions fall into error and worse. Hobbes is very clear about what constitutes the wrong definition of names. The foremost culprit is paradox. He cites paradoxical definitions – as for example 'when men make a name of two names, whose significations are contradictory and inconsistent: as this name, an *incorporeal body* …'.[14] Hobbes rails against what he considers the absurd and false connecting of names. He complains about inconstant signification: what 'one man calleth *wisdom* … another calleth *fear*'.[15] He remonstrates against the failure to begin reasoning from settled definitions. He protests the propensity to name things paradoxically: to give the name of bodies to accidents or the name of names to bodies, and so on. In general, he objects to the use of metaphors, tropes and other rhetorical figures 'instead of words proper'.

11 *Leviathan*, chapter III.

12 *De Cive*, chapter X. See Hobbes,1972: 253–4.

13 Hobbes, *Leviathan*, chapter IV ('Of Speech') and chapter V ('Of Reason and Science').

14 *Leviathan*, chapter IV.

15 *Leviathan*, chapter IV.

If securing the proper foundation of reasoning in settled, non-paradoxical, non-figurative definitions is one problem, then reasoning itself and its failure to achieve a 'good and orderly method' of proceeding from definitions to conclusions is a second problem. If one or other problem occurs, political disorder follows. As far as Hobbes is concerned, the unregulated succession of thought is the symptom of a wild raging mind. Semantic raging gave rise to dangerous comparisons. The air of his own century, he thought, was thick with garish notions that encouraged warring that in turn bred further lurid and scandalous ideas. In such moments, he mused,

> … the thought of the war introduced the thought of the delivering up the king to his enemies; the thought of that brought in the thought of the delivering up of Christ; and that again the thought of the thirty pence, which was the price of that treason.[16]

While it is highly doubtful whether any participant in the English Civil War ever imagined themselves as Judas, this age nevertheless did indulge plenty of extravagant political similes. It was in this era that the medical term 'crisis' became a metaphor for the social condition. Yet the irony of all of this is that Hobbes himself was a supreme master of metaphor. It is he who compares the sovereign with a leviathan. It is he who likens the state of society without a sovereign to one that is short, nasty and brutish, and its fate to a war of each against all. Hobbes is part of a brilliant tradition of literary language that extends from Shakespeare to Pope and from Gibbon to Churchill. If metaphor is a culprit, then all of these characters, Hobbes included, are guilty of inciting war by metaphor. But is metaphor the guilty party?

There is no question that the mind is capable wild rages. But while the mind may rampage, the imagination leaps. Both motions have political implications. Both have cognitive consequences. Each is very different in nature. Rage is painted in the palette of banality. The works of tyrants are pitiful. Extremity breeds mediocrity. Tyranny smothers opposition. This does not prevent tyrants acting with great caprice. A tyrannical regime may change its mind at any time. By doing so it wilfully manufactures uncertainty. Uncertainty induces fear in others. It terrifies and cripples them. The act of creation commingles one thing and its contraries. Tyranny permeates all things with fear and dread. Tyranny unsettles everything via the medium of terror. It knows only one pseudo mode of creation. It presses the stamp of violence and trepidation on anything in its reach.

During the 1980s the Argentine was convulsed in a dirty war. The ruling military dictatorship caused many of its opponents to disappear. Women were detained, raped and their babies sold for profit. This monstrous conjunction of birth and violence had first to be conceived as a paramilitary policy before it was carried out in practice. How is such a thing to be understood? Was this not a

16 *Leviathan*, chapter III.

conjunction of the imagination in the same sense that the man-bird or the mermaid creature is a projection of the mythical imagination? I do not think so. Rather what we have to distinguish between are an act of imagination and a contrivance of evil. What imagination and evil superficially share in common is that both defy expectation. That is why intellectuals who are easily charmed by the imagination are also easily charmed by evil. Hannah Arendt was correct. The mind-set of dictatorship is banal not imaginative.[17] Tyrants defy expectations. They do so not by leaps of imagination but rather by behaving with devastating arbitrariness. That is the basis of all terror. Even the most stupid person is capable of an act of infernal terror simply by violating any one of the basic moral norms that a child is supposed to learn.[18] To do this, no intelligence whatsoever is required. Rather those who are best equipped for wicked acts are those who are deficient in the faculty of sympathy. A 'lack of sympathy' is another way of saying a 'lack of imagination'. The imagination that allows us to see one thing as another also allows us to imagine our own self in the place of another person. I feel *as* you feel, I suffer *as* you suffer. This cannot be literally true, but we can nonetheless up to a point feel, think and act '*as if*' we were someone else. Torturers and rapists, like the regimes that orchestrate torture and rape, cannot and do not do this. They lack the faculty of sympathy. When they concoct infernal systems, like gulags or the sale of babies conceived in rape, what transpires is not the transcendental surprise of the imagination but rather a shocking surprise that is born of a violently arbitrary will. The diabolical conjugation of impregnation and violence, the perverse bonding of birth and commerce, is born of a pathological desire to violate basic norms. This is sheer wickedness. It is not the imagination's elevated fusion of semantic nuclei but rather the morbid will to the gutter, the will to transgress anything and all that is sacred, elemental, and decent.

Friends and relatives gather to celebrate the wedding of a young couple. The suicide bomber wreaks havoc. The peaceful scene is wracked by devastating surprise. The surprise is shocking. The shock is dependent on the violation of an elementary norm. The imagination *also* surprises, perhaps shakes, and even

17 '[Eichmann] began by stating emphatically that he was a *Gottglaubiger*, to express in common Nazi fashion that he was no Christian and did not believe in life after death. He then proceeded: "After a short while, gentlemen, *we shall all meet again*. Such is the fate of all men. Long live Germany, long live Argentina, long live Austria. *I shall not forget them*." In the face of death, he had found the cliché used in funeral oratory. Under the gallows, his memory played him the last trick. He was "elated"; and he forgot that this was his own funeral. It was though in those last minutes he was summing up the lesson that this long course in human wickedness had taught us – the lesson of the fearsome, word-and-thought-defying *banality of evil*' (Arendt 1963/2006: 250).

18 Catalogues of these norms include 'the ten commandments' (*Exodus* 20: 2–17). For anyone who has forgotten them, the most instructive of that list of ten are 6–10, viz. that 'You shall not murder', 'You shall not commit adultery', 'You shall not steal', 'You shall not bear false witness against your neighbour', and 'You shall not covet your neighbour's house or neighbour's wife'. A person can do a lot worse than obey these norms.

on occasion shocks. But it does so without violating the basic norms of human intercourse. The imagination is not irrational. Rather it is sceptical and ironical. The ironic intellect satirizes norms. It lampoons practices. In doing this, though, a superior wit supports rather than subverts social order.[19] It seeks out the transcendent thread in that order. It seeks to enrich and embellish and uphold it. In so doing, it mocks evil doers and ridicules stupid behaviours – and it does this in a particular way. Wit operates through the media of reversal. It communicates via transposition, inversion, transfiguration, and consubstantiation. The ironist says one thing and means the opposite, and sometimes teasingly means *both* things, though in acutely knowing and selected ways.[20] At the same time the ironist more often than not is provoked into action by the ironies of the world. Irony is an inversion of the world's own inversions – and an attempt at reversing its perversions.

I use the term perversion here in the same sense that Winston Churchill did when he upbraided the Nazis for their perverted science.[21] Churchill always chose his words very carefully. The horror-kitsch science of warped medical experiments represents exactly what the imagination is not.[22] Even if at times the sinister dreams

---

19 The philosopher Jean-Paul Sartre (2010: 263), after a fashion, was correct in the observation that he made in his 1943 essay on George Bataille when he noted that 'revolutionaries, who are the most convinced of the insufficiency of the commanding heights, are the most serious people in the world. Satire and pamphleteering come from on high. Conservatives excel at it; by contrast, it took years of labour to build up a semblance of revolutionary humour. And even then it looked less a direct insight into the ridiculous and more a painful translation of serious considerations'. Sartre himself ended his life ignominiously supporting Mao Zedong's Cultural Revolution, a ruthless nihilistic movement that ruined the lives of millions of Chinese. Revolutionaries at the commanding heights, it would seem, are not only humourless but exceedingly dangerous people.

20 This is akin to what Johannes Climacus does at the end of Kierkegaard's *Concluding Unscientific Postscript*. Johannes retracts everything he has said. Yet he adds the teasing disclaimer that to say something and then to un-say it is not the same as not having said it in the first place.

21 'Hitler knows that he will have to break us in this Island or lose the war. If we can stand up to him, all Europe may be free and the life of the world may move forward into broad, sunlit uplands. But if we fail, then the whole world, including the United States, including all that we have known and cared for, will sink into the abyss of a new Dark Age made more sinister, and perhaps more protracted, by the lights of perverted science'. (Churchill 1940, *Never Give In*, hereafter *NGI*, 2004: 218).

22 These 'experiments' were truly sickening and insane. Martin Small recounts one, the handiwork of the Nazi Security Service Dr. Wichtmann, who in 1942, experimented with hammer blows to the head: 'When I realised what I was seeing through the window, my stomach turned inside-out. I put my hand to my mouth as if trying to muffle my own outburst. I nearly vomited. Now, more than sixty years later, I cannot erase the vivid terrible image from my mind. I felt like I was bursting inside and at the same time I wanted to run far away. But there was nowhere to run. Inside this structure, in a little room, sat a young boy of eleven or twelve, strapped to a chair so he could not move. Above him was

of tyrants are mistaken for the imagination, it is instructive to understand why the two nevertheless get to be confused. I am drawing here a firm distinction between the tainted dreams of tyrants and authentic acts of creation. Both conjugate. Both entail forms of condensation. But one yields ugly, crude, brutal works in which the underlying conjugation is invariably anchored in transgression. This is the dream-cum-nightmare condensation of norm and crime, rule and dictate, virtue and terror, objectivation and arbitrary will.[23] The perverse conjugation of crime and pseudo-creation has proved itself, time and again, to be seductive. Intellectuals especially love it. When they think of a norm, they always think of the exception. They idolize the exception as the norm. In their eyes, *the rule* is to violate the rule, and *to rule* is to break the rule. One can think of situations where such behaviour is appropriate. Yet why then are the dreams of intellectuals so often so shabby? One answer is that these dreams lack wit. In case you had not noticed, intellectuals frequently lack a sense of humour, especially humour that is directed at their own precious selves. This is a manifest deficit, not least because creation is a function of wit. In some circumstances the best rule *is* to break the rule. Equally the mirthless pursuit of trespass ends in the slave camps of North Korea.

Not all intellectuals are drawn to the criminal conjugation, thankfully. One of the exceptions to the perverse rule of the exception was Castoriadis. He spent most of his life in philosophy puzzling about the nature of the imagination. He was a shrewd observer of the many evils of the twentieth century and the habitual

---

suspended a mechanised hammer that every few seconds came down upon his head. The boy had been driven insane by the torture. Over and over and over this hammer came down upon his head; it was inhuman. Dr. Wichtmann, the tall, fair-haired family man who, not too many days before, generously saved us from an Aktion, kept this boy alive to be tortured, slowly, endlessly, mercilessly. Tears running down his cheeks, his face red and swollen, his eyes mere slits, his moaning was reduced to a dying, wounded animal's whimper. I dropped to my knees in sickness and disgust and I trembled' (Small and Shayne 2009: 134–5).

23 Robespierre (1794): 'If the strength of popular government in peacetime is virtue, the strength of popular government in revolution is both virtue and terror; terror without virtue is disastrous, virtue without terror is powerless. Terror is nothing but prompt, severe, and inflexible justice; it is thus an emanation of virtue; it is less a particular principle than a consequence of the general principle of democracy applied to the most urgent needs of the fatherland. It is said that terror is the strength of despotic government. Does ours then resemble the one with which the satellites of tyranny are armed. Let the despot govern his brutalized subjects through terror; he is right as a despot. Subdue the enemies of liberty through terror and you will be right as founders of the Republic. The government of revolution is the despotism of liberty against tyranny'.

George Orwell, *1984* (1948): Then the face of Big Brother faded away again, and instead the three slogans of the party stood out in bold capitals:

WAR IS PEACE
FREEDOM IS SLAVERY
IGNORANCE IS STRENGTH

seduction of intellectuals by tyrants.[24] In response to both, Castoriadis suggested that the imagination is equally capable of the creation of immense horrors as it is of good and great works.[25] That is a plausible idea. Yet, in the end, I think I disagree with it. When Stalin sent 14 million people to the gulag labour camps or forcibly deported millions of members of ethnic populations to new territories or murdered the kulaks in order to collectivize agriculture or withheld grain to create mass famines – were these acts of imagination or acts of tyranny? True, Stalin's

24 Martin Heidegger (1935): 'The violent one, the creative one who sets forth into the unsaid, who breaks into the unthought, who compels what has never happened and makes appear what is unseen – the violent one stands at all time in daring … the violence-doer knows no kindness and conciliation (in the ordinary sense), no appeasement and mollification by success or prestige and by their confirmation … For such a one, disaster is the deepest and broadest Yes to the Overwhelming … Essential de-cision, when it is carried out and when it resists the constantly pressing ensnarement in the everyday and the customary, has to use violence. This act of violence, this decided setting out upon the way to the Being of beings, moves humanity out of the hominess of what is most directly nearby and what is usual'.

Jean-Paul Sartre (1974): 'Solzhenitsyn represents someone who has nineteenth-century ideas … so he's an element harmful to development … He experienced the camps and so he was completely immersed in Soviet ideology'.

Michel Foucault (1978): 'During my entire stay in Iran, I did not hear even once the word "revolution," but four out of five times, someone would answer, "An Islamic government." … One thing must be clear. By "Islamic government," nobody in Iran means a political regime in which the clerics would have a role of supervision or control. To me, the phrase "Islamic government" seemed to point to two orders of things. "A utopia," some told me without any pejorative implication. "An ideal," most of them said to me. … With respect to liberties, they will be respected to the extent that their exercise will not harm others; minorities will be protected and free to live as they please on the condition that they do not injure the majority; between men and women there will not be inequality with respect to rights, but difference, since there is a natural difference. With respect to politics, decisions should be made by the majority, the leaders should be responsible to the people, and each person, as it is laid out in the Quran, should be able to stand up and hold accountable he who governs'.

Baron Giddens (2007): 'As one-party states go, Libya is not especially repressive. Gadafy seems genuinely popular'.

Slavoj Žižek (2008): '… crazy, tasteless even, as it may sound, the problem with Hitler was that he was not violent enough, that his violence was not "essential" enough. Nazism was not radical enough, it did not dare to disturb the basic structure of the modern capitalist social space (which is why it had to invent and focus on destroying an external enemy, Jews)'.

25 He suggested (1997b: 273) that the Greek-Western imagination, 'while it has produced democracy and philosophy, both the American and the French Revolutions, the Paris Commune and the Hungarian Workers' Councils, the Parthenon and *Macbeth*, it has produced as well the massacre of the Melians by the Athenians, the Inquisition, Auschwitz, the Gulag and the H-bomb. It created reason, freedom, and beauty – and it also created massive monstrosity'.

rearranging of the face of a country and its peoples occurs on a sublime scale and its methods are totalitarian. Yet its motive is still tyrannical. A great statesman sees his country simultaneously for what it is and for what it is capable of. Realism and idealism meld. The tyrant cannot perceive his own country as something that it is not except insofar as it can be warped and twisted. The art of the dictator thus is not an art at all but instead a kind of anti-art, a horrible demented kitsch in which society's tacit aesthetic form is buckled and bowed, collapsed and shrunken by real and symbolic violence.[26]

Let us suppose that the term uncanny does describe the human mind's propensity to see everything in another guise. It is possible then that the creepiness which all astute observers experience when they visit dictatorships and totalitarian states is a result of the encounter with the evil uncanny.[27] I think though that, in the end, this misstates the nature of tyranny, no matter how vast are the ambitions of the tyrant. The sinister is not the dark equivalent of the uncanny. Tyrannies are much less interesting than that. The work of the Gulag Archipelago and the work of J.S. Bach are incommensurable. In the hands of Shakespeare, Richard III is a profound character. But what the dramaturgical figure of Richard III personifies is not the imagination but rather the seductive nature of evil. Evil can be charming.[28] Seduction and charm are not the same as imagination. Richard III was not the

---

26 The palaces, courts, offices, residences and ante-chambers of dictators and their bestial broods habitually evoke the lurid style of brothel kitsch.

27 This creepiness is perfectly captured by the journalist Christopher Hitchens (2010: 113–14; 2001) in reports on two visits one to Cuba in 1968 and one 30 years later to the morbid slave state of North Korea.

28 The epitome of seductive evil is Richard of Gloucester's courting of Lady Anne, Anne Neville, whose husband, Edward of Westminster, has been murdered by Richard. Richard's explanation is that murder is exculpated by his love for Anne. Seduction is a play upon such perversity. Wickedness (murder) is justified by goodness (love).

GLOUCESTER
I know so. But, gentle Lady Anne,
To leave this keen encounter of our wits,
And fall somewhat into a slower method,
Is not the causer of the timeless deaths
Of these Plantagenets, Henry and Edward,
As blameful as the executioner?
LADY ANNE
Thou art the cause, and most accursed effect.
GLOUCESTER
Your beauty was the cause of that effect;
Your beauty: which did haunt me in my sleep
To undertake the death of all the world,
So I might live one hour in your sweet bosom.
Act 1, Scene 2, *Richard III*.

Poet Laureate of the Plantagenet state. Neither was Stalin the Pushkin of his age. Yet both were capable of charm of a particularly disturbing kind.[29]

The case for the proposition that tyrants have no great imagination can be made by examining the counter-case of Winston Churchill. Without question Churchill had a remarkable imagination. This is borne out in part by his prescience. Prescience is a very rare quality. When duly armed, imagination allows human beings the occasional opportunity to see around corners in time – to see what is coming in the otherwise unknowable future. The rarity of this is underlined by the fact that social prophecy is almost always a waste of time.[30] Donkeys make better predictions on average than most experts do who predict the future on the basis of today's trends. This is futile – for time and history, as Shakespeare endlessly depicted, switch in the blink of an eye, just as the faculty of wit does. Both move with lightning speed having not moved for a long time. To anticipate time's turning points requires an acrobatic mind, not the prophetic touch. Churchill illustrates this to a tee. He was prescient because he was imaginative. In the 1890s, he observed that, if not for modern technological science, Europe would fall to the onslaught of militant Islam (1899a: 240–50). In one of his first parliamentary

---

29 A generation or two of intellectuals was charmed by the perversity of Stalin. Stalin engineered a genocide-famine in the Ukraine in the 1930s. Between 7 and 11 million people were killed by it. The pioneering study of this murderous famine was Robert Conquest's 1986 study *Harvest of Sorrow*. One of the side-stories in Conquest's mournful excavation was about the role played by Western intellectuals both conniving in and covering up Stalin's handiwork. The motivation of the intellectuals in such cases is tediously consistent: extreme wickedness in their eyes is perversely sanctified by some ethereal good. It seems to take very little to seduce them. The journalist Askold Krushelnycky in 2003 summed up the events of the 1930s observing that '… the most influential role in the cover-up was *The New York Times* correspondent Walter Duranty. A drug addict with a shady reputation, Duranty was also an avid fan of Stalin's, whom he described as "the world's greatest living statesman." He was granted the first American interview with the Soviet leader and received privileged information from the secretive regime. Duranty confided to a British diplomat at the time that he thought 10 million people had perished in the famine. But when other journalists who had travelled to Ukraine began writing about the horrific famine raging there, Duranty branded their information as anti-Soviet lies. Conquest believes that Duranty was being blackmailed by the Soviet secret police over his sexual activities, which reportedly included bisexuality and necrophilia. The year before the famine, in 1932, Duranty won the Pulitzer Prize, America's most coveted journalism award, for a series of articles on the Soviet economy … Duranty died in 1957 an impoverished drunk … when details about the famine finally came into the open, Duranty was credited with coining the famously callous phrase, "You can't make an omelette without breaking eggs"'. Conquest relates the saga of the egregious Duranty in *Harvest of Sorrow*, 304, 309, 318–20.

30 The Victorian-era Conservative politician Lord Salisbury remarked (Cecil 1931) on 'the proved futility of theorists to whatever school they might belong; the worthlessness of forecasts based on logical calculation; the evil which has repeatedly been wrought by the best intended policies; the hopeless incongruity between aim and result which dominates history'.

speeches in 1901, he foresaw the carnage of the First World War, more than a decade hence.[31] As soon as that war ended, he warned of the evils of Bolshevism.[32] In the early 1920s, Churchill foresaw the coming of the Second World War.[33] In the early 1930s, almost alone he warned of the hellish rise of Hitler.[34] And in the middle of the Second War World, he was already anticipating what was to become the Cold War with the Soviet Union.[35]

Churchill's most controversial prognosis still haunts us. In the 1930s he opposed Britain granting India independence.[36] Even his most ardent admirers

31 'I have frequently been astonished since I have been in this House to hear with what composure and how glibly Members, and even Ministers, talk of a European war. I will not expatiate on the horrors of war, but there has been a great change which the House should not omit to notice. In former days, when wars arose from individual causes, from the policy of a Minister or the passion of a King, when they were fought by small regular armies of professional soldiers, and when their course was retarded by the difficulties of communication and supply, and often suspended by the winter season, it was possible to limit the liabilities of the combatants. But now, when mighty populations are impelled on each other, each individual severally embittered and inflamed – when the resources of science and civilization sweep away everything that might mitigate their fury – a European war can only end in the ruin of the vanquished and the scarcely less fatal commercial dislocation and exhaustion of the conquerors. Democracy is more vindictive than Cabinets. The wars of peoples will be more terrible than those of kings' (Churchill 1901; *NGI* 10–12).

32 During a speech to his constituents in Dundee in 1918, Churchill declared that 'Russia is being rapidly reduced by the Bolsheviks to an animal form of Barbarism ... Civilization is being completely extinguished over gigantic areas, while the Bolsheviks hop and caper like troops of ferocious baboons amid the ruins of cities and the corpses of their victims' (Gilbert 1975/1990: 227).

33 In 1922 Churchill observed: 'What a disappointment the Twentieth Century has been. How terrible and how melancholy is the long series of disastrous events which have darkened its first 20 years. We have seen in every country a dissolution, a weakening of those bonds, a challenge to those principles a decay of faith an abridgment of hope on which the structure and ultimate existence of civilized society depends ... And only intense, concerted & prolonged effort among all nations can avert further & perhaps even greater calamities' (Gilbert 1975/1990: 915).

34 'Now the demand is that Germany should be allowed to rearm ... Do not let His Majesty's Government believe that all that Germany is asking for is equal status ... That is not what Germany is seeking. All these bands of sturdy Teutonic youths, marching through the streets and roads of Germany, with the light of desire in their eyes to suffer for their Fatherland, are not looking for status. They are looking for weapons, and, when they have the weapons, believe me they will ask for the return of lost territories and lost colonies, and when that demand is made it cannot fail to shake and possibly shatter to their foundations every one of the countries I have mentioned, and some other countries I have not mentioned' (Churchill 1932; *NGI* 101).

35 In 1943, Churchill warned the Americans of 'bloody consequences in the future. Stalin is an unnatural man. There will be grave troubles' (Hastings 2009: 388).

36 He thought the then distant 1980 a better date for Independence. He was defeated resoundingly on this and all other matters related to India.

wince at this today. Most people though forget that one of the primary reasons for his standing up like King Canute on the beach and opposing the tidal force of nationalism impelling the independence of India was Churchill's prophecy that Hindus and Muslims would end up embroiled in deadly violence, a prediction that turned out to be absolutely accurate.[37] If Churchill was pugnaciously wrong, he was also puckishly correct. The independence of India from Britain led immediately to the partition of India and Pakistan which caused, in its wake, the death of more than a million people. Subsequently wars broke out between India and Pakistan in 1947, 1965, 1971 and 1999. Pakistani-inspired terrorism in Indian cities recurred through the 1990s and 2000s. Today the single functional institution in Pakistan – the military – exists in, and because of, a perpetual state of paranoid expectation that an Indian invasion of Pakistan will happen at any moment in time.[38] Thus it came to pass that even if the imperatives of modern nationalism made the independence of imperial India inevitable, and who could today imagine anything else having happened, nevertheless Churchill's warnings about the consequences of independence proved to be no less true.[39]

37 'Side by side with this Brahmin theocracy and the immense Hindi population – angelic and untouchable castes alike – there dwell in India seventy millions of Muslims, a race of far greater physical vigour and fierceness, armed with a religion which lends itself only too readily to war and conquest. While the Hindu elaborates his argument, the Muslim sharpens his sword. Between these two races and creeds, containing as they do so many gifted and charming beings in all the glory of youth, there is no intermarriage. The gulf is impassable. If you look at the antagonisms of France and Germany, and the antagonisms of Catholics and Protestants, and compounded them and multiplied them ten-fold, you would not equal the division which separates these two races intermingled by scores of millions in the cities and plains of India' (Churchill 1931; *NGI* 98).

38 Pakistan is a perverse state. Its perverseness has a variety of Orwellian-style expressions. Amongst the most repulsive is the way in which, in this society, crime is punishment. As Christopher Hitchens (2011) observes: 'Here is a society where rape is not a crime. It is a punishment. Women can be sentenced to be raped, by tribal and religious kangaroo courts, if even a rumour of their immodesty brings shame on their menfolk. In such an obscenely distorted context, the counterpart term to shame – which is the noble word "honour" – becomes most commonly associated with the word "killing". Moral courage consists of the willingness to butcher your own daughter. If the most elemental of human instincts becomes warped in this bizarre manner, other morbid symptoms will disclose themselves as well. Thus, President Asif Ali Zardari cringes daily in front of the forces who openly murdered his wife, Benazir Bhutto, and who then contemptuously ordered the crime scene cleansed with fire hoses, as if to spit even on the pretence of an investigation. A man so lacking in pride – indeed lacking in manliness – will seek desperately to compensate in other ways. Swelling his puny chest even more, he promises to resist the mighty United States, and to defend Pakistan's holy "sovereignty". This puffery and posing might perhaps possess a rag of credibility if he and his fellow middlemen were not avidly ingesting $3 billion worth of American subsidies every year'.

39 'Democracy is totally unsuited to India. Instead of conflicting opinions you have bitter theological hatreds'. Churchill's speech to the Indian Empire Society, May 25, 1932.

It is not foresight alone, though, that characterizes Churchill's imagination – even if his foresight far exceeded, as it indeed did, the historical scope of Stalin's not inconsiderable cunning. What makes the imagination imaginative is not the capacity to make the absent present, but rather the 'syn-antonymic' act of taking one thing for its opposite. Please forgive this awkward locution but no word exists for what I want to say. In this case, we need a concept for a case where absence and presence are *both* separable *and* identical.[40] Churchill's imagination was not a function of his foresight, extraordinary as that was, but rather that foresight, that uncanny peering into the future, was a function of the imagination's syn-antonymic structure.[41] Churchill thought, composed and spoke habitually in antonymic pairs with a relish for reconciling them. Syn-antonymic thinking is a mirror of civilization. It is the mental interior of civilization's material exterior. Imagination is the ghost in the machinery of civilization. Civilization, conversely, is the apotheosis of the human double act. Everything in the human world has a latent imaginary or symbolic dimension. Everything that we encounter is 'one' and 'two' at the same time, even if only tacitly or latently. This double nature, this uncanny or enigmatic character, is what makes all that is most interesting and most compelling in human existence. We can encapsulate all that is humanly interesting in one word: *civilization*. This includes Friendship, Justice, Love, Freedom, Happiness, Myth, Religion, Art, Philosophy, Technology and Science. All that is fascinating in life has an uncanny double edge. I do not mean that everything that is fascinating or absorbing is ambiguous.[42] Rather, more simply,

---

40 Hegel was one of those who pointed out that there is nothing really in isolation. One of his analogies for this, outlined in the *Science of Logic* 1812–1816, was the idea of mathematical ratio: a ratio holds two distinct things in contrast, and yet a ratio is a single thing that binds two quantities into one. In 1918 Walter Benjamin (1996: 106) produced a non-Hegelian formulation of this. In a then unpublished critique of Kant's separation of freedom and experience, he suggested the idea of 'a certain non synthesis of two concepts in another'. He elaborates thus: '… besides the concept of synthesis, another concept, that of a certain non synthesis of two concepts in another, will become very important systematically, since another relation between thesis and antithesis is possible besides synthesis'.

41 'You have no doubt noticed in your reading of British history and I hope you will take pains to read it, for it is only from the past that one can judge the future … that we have had to hold out from time to time all alone, or to be the mainspring of coalitions, against a continental tyrant or dictator, and we have had to hold out for quite a long time: against the Spanish Armada, against the might of Louis XIV, when we led Europe for nearly 25 years under William III and Marlborough, and 150 years ago, when Nelson, Pitt and Wellington broke Napoleon, not without assistance from the heroic Russians of 1811. In all these world wars our Island kept the lead of Europe or else held out alone' (Churchill 1945; *NGI* 392).

42 Kierkegaard observed that ambiguity results from contraries that do not coincide. In a society of reflection, there is no real opposition, there is just ambiguity. We can say then that in contrast to ambiguity, the uncanny results from contraries that *do* coincide. Sigmund Freud wrote a very interesting essay on the concept of 'the uncanny' or, in German, the

what I mean is that great ideas and edifying practices arise as and when and because the human imagination is able to present something and *re*-present that thing *as* something else. Those ideas and practices arise firstly as intuitions and then as artefacts and images, and finally, and only belatedly, as discourses. From the standpoint of linear time, this is a long historical process. It is an agonizingly slow one, punctuated with occasional startling breakthroughs such as in Greek antiquity. The sum consequence of this process is civilization. The imagination is the natural ally of civilization.

And so it was with Churchill. Pugnacious and puckish, he was equally – and eminently – at home with caustic jokes and fine liquor along with the ingenious technologies of modern industry and the delicate brushstrokes of the landscape painter. Hitler in stark contrast set in train not the work of civilization but a sequence of monstrous deeds. Nevertheless Hitler did not have a monstrous imagination. This is only because he had little imagination at all beyond the repetitive conjugation of norm and crime. There is scant evidence in his case of even an abject or gothic imagination. Look at Hitler's paintings. They are stilted, inexpressive, post-card-kitsch banalities. In contrast, Hitler's nemesis Churchill was a genuinely gifted amateur painter. This is not to suppose that world history is a contest of painterly technique. Rather what it points to is that Churchill conceived the world in aesthetic terms. In his writings he repeatedly evokes a faint deism and an explicit stoicism.[43] He talked frequently, and did so in very subtle terms, about

---

unheimlich. What gives the *unheimlich* its character is what is latent in the word *heimlich*. As Freud (1919/2011: 226) explains, '… *heimlich* is a word the meaning of which develops in the direction of ambivalence, until it finally coincides with its opposite, unheimlich'.

43 *Deist*: 'The unexpected came to the aid of design and multiplied the result' (351); 'the long arm of destiny' (356); 'the House … desired to offer thanks to Almighty God, to the Great Power which seems to shape and design the fortunes of nations and the destiny of man …' (390); 'Do not let us be led away by any fair-seeming appearances of fortune; let us rather put our trust in those deep, slow-moving tides that have borne us thus far already, and will surely bear us forward, if we know how to use them, until we reach the harbour where we would be' (345); 'Bearing ourselves humbly before God, but conscious that we serve an unfolding purpose, we are ready to defend our native land against the invasion by which it is threatened' (235); 'When one beholds how many currents of extraordinary and terrible events have flowed together to make this harmony, even the most sceptical person must have the feeling that we all have the chance to play our part and do our duty in some great design, the end of which no mortal can foresee' (298). *Stoic*: 'fortitude in suffering' (184); 'that ever-fresh resilience which renews the strength and energy of people in long, doubtful and dark days' (197); 'I have nothing to offer but blood, toil, tears and sweat' (206); 'we are ready to face it; to endure it; and to retaliate against it' (208); 'to call forth from our people the last ounce and last inch of effort of which they are capable' (209); 'Olympian fortitude' (317); 'Upon that rock, all stood unshakeable' (295); 'enduring, resilient strength' (256); 'uplifted in spirit, fortified in resolve' (304); 'stranding steadfastly together' (260); 'when we face with a steady eye the difficulties that lie before us' (274); 'common resolve' (321); 'a new scene opens upon which a steady light will glow and brighten' (321); 'consistency

the liberty of spirit, the power of necessity and the working of destiny in human lives. Each was interpolated in the other.[44] He thought freedom unimaginable without laws *and* the incessant profusion of modern laws the bane of a free society. For anyone who thought this to be inconsistent, he warned (1932: 22–30) against consistency in politics. He understood that politics was paradoxical and that history was ironical. He also knew instinctively that human beings reconcile the irreconcilable aesthetically.

The world that the human being inhabits has aesthetic shape. To bend, buckle, twist, deform and warp it is the act of a tyrant. For the most part Churchill was irreligious in outlook and yet he had a theologico-politics that seems to me to have been at least as deeply thought out as that of Spinoza. He knew that human beings only reached the exalted state of liberty and freedom through the dint of dogged necessity and arduous destiny. All of this was subsumed and reconciled in a transcendental aesthetic – an aesthetic politics – of scale, magnitude, light and colour.[45] An overarching philosophy of vista and proportion, light and colour provided Churchill with a painterly vision of the ends of politics. Of the many promises he made as war-time Prime Minister to the British people and to all the peoples who sacrificed in the Second World War, he never, not once ever, made an ideological promise. He resorted neither to the language of liberalism, nor that of socialism, which in any event he despised, nor any other 'ism'. What he evoked instead was the joyous serenity of benignant world framed by broad horizons, dotted with uplands and highroads, and bathed in sunlight. This is a world where the land is bright and a steady light glows.[46]

---

of mind, persistency of purpose, and the grand simplicity of decision' (415). All quotes from *NGI*.

44 This is contrary to Kierkegaard who argued that Hegel's philosophy alienated life on the grounds that it denied individual choice and personal freedom, not in virtue of a tyrannical impulse but because it eliminated the either/or of things.

45 The nature of Churchill's vision is best, in the sense of most unselfconsciously, captured in his essay 'Painting as a Pastime' (1932: 232–46).

46 See for example 'peace with its broadening and brightening prosperity' (194); 'breadth of view and sense of proportion' (317); 'Our qualities and deeds must burn and glow through the gloom of Europe until they become the veritable beacon of its salvation' (256); 'Westward look, the land is bright' (266); 'This is … no war to shut any country out of its sunlight' (198); 'The tunnel may be dark and long but at the end there is light' (302); 'For my own part, looking out upon the future, I do not view the process with any misgivings. I could not stop it if I wished; no one can stop it. Like the Mississippi, it just keeps rolling along. Let it roll. Let it roll on full flood, inexorable, irresistible, benignant, to broader lands and better days' (248); 'broad highroad of freedom and justice' (298); 'that joyous serenity that we think belongs to a better world' (267); 'a new scene opens upon which a steady light will glow and brighten' (321); 'I turn for one moment from the turmoil and convulsions of the present to the broader basis of the future' (322); 'I feel the broadening swell of victory and liberation bearing us and all the tortured peoples onwards

What made Churchill both seer and friend of civilization was his imagination. The art of rhetoric – the art that Churchill excelled at – is the link between imagination and history. The structure of Churchill's rhetoric emulates and imitates the act of creation. It is a mimesis of creation. His political speeches and historical writings are awash with antonyms, all of them carefully balanced, and each faintly, finely, subtly, slyly combined with their contrary. Here the inherent duality of things – the double, dual, 'two-by-two' quality of existence – is not only carefully *in*scribed. It is also *tran*scribed and interpolated. Each duality is a union. Every twin is singular. Powerful antonyms belong together just as much as they stand in opposition. Opposites attract. Every antithesis is a synthesis.[47]

This reverberates through the fabric of reality. It is not just a function of words. It is as true for the course of history as it is of the mind-set of art, philosophy and religion. Take for instance the British and allied military victory at El Alamein in October and November 1942 against the German army in North Africa. It was achieved in desperate circumstances. The victory followed upon numerous defeats – a function of the irony of history that most wars, though not won by the meek are won by the weak, that is by the weaker or less prepared opponent who, at the outset of war, looks as though they will lose the war. Churchill, like Shakespeare, knew that war, like politics, pivots.[48] When the turning point of history finally came late in 1942, the moment called forth from Churchill the observation that 'this is not the end, nay, not even the beginning of the end, but it is, perhaps, the end of the beginning'.[49] In that line, Churchill draws a distinction between two terms only then to draw a resemblance between them. Creation is the third imaginary term that binds together two contrary terms. This third term is provided by the media of creation. These media range from pairings and paradoxes through alliteration, rhymes, and echoing repetitions. All achieve the impossible. Each in its own way forges a union of the different and the same, perfectly exemplified in a phrase like the end of the beginning. Rather than sharpen the distinction between end and beginning, the act of imagination coalesces them. A grand alliance of

---

safely to the final goal' (329); 'I see the light gleaming behind the clouds and broadening on our path' (329). All quotes from *NGI*.

47 'You do your worst – we will do our best' (Churchill 1941; *NGI* 297).

48 Churchill, 'Wars come very suddenly' (105); 'Therefore, Mr Winant, you come to us at a grand turning point in the world's history' (264); 'I have taken occasion to speak to you tonight because we have reached one of the climacterics of the war. In the first of these intense turning points, a year ago, France fell prostrate under the German hammer and we had to face the storm alone. The second was when the Royal Air Force beat the Hun raiders out of the daylight air raid and thus warded off the Nazi invasion of our islands while we were still ill-armed and ill-prepared. The third turning point was when the President and Congress of the United States passed the lease and lend enactment, devoting nearly 2,000,000,000 sterling of the wealth of the New World to help us defend our liberties and their own. Those were the three climacterics. The fourth is now upon us' (289). All quotes from *NGI*.

49 *NGI* 342.

terms is created, such that the antonym becomes a synonym. What emerges from this is a super-positional entity, 'the end of the beginning', rather than two distinct counter-positional entities, 'a beginning and an end'.

Uncanny unions of this kind reverberate through Churchill's vast prose works. By dint of their compacting of meanings, such forces endow the human world with significance. In Churchill's imagination, summits were peaks to be climbed *and* conferences that might encapsulate the destiny of humankind. Like the poets, he made memorable metaphors. In the years 1940 and 1941, he became the great national poet as much as the indispensable war prime minister, a striking and enigmatic elision of roles. He mobilized metaphor in the defence of the metaphorical being and its vocation for civilization. Alone among the species, the human being has the capacity to see a thing, to see in a thing what it is not, and (conversely) to allow that thing to stand for another. One thing both exists and exists '*as if*' or '*as in*' another thing. Each thing exists 'in itself' and 'for itself'. The philosopher might say that this evokes the uncanny co-presence of space and time, past and present, present and future, rest and change. From the venerable Heraclitus to Gottfried Leibniz to Simone Weil – the echo rebounds and rebounds. The imagination elicits the enigmatic multiplicity in unity. In this elision, difference is both distinguishable and at the same time indistinguishable from sameness. It yields similitude. A strange paradoxical 'relationality' haunts the imagination.[50] Thus we, the species who brokers metaphors, can thereby imagine that what is potential is actual, and what is plural is singular. We see daffodils as symbols of human happiness and we think that relations can exist without parts. We also sense, perhaps uneasily, that in the act of creation we compound the act of copying and the act of originality.

There is a kind of yoking in all of this; we recognize in the act of creation a hint of violence. Destruction is the strange twin of creation; it is an antithesis that nonetheless bears a certain similarity to its opposite. We know full-well that wit is cruel. Often it is devastating. There was no more devastating wit in the twentieth century than Winston Churchill. Not least of all, he used his wit to mock Corporal Hitler.[51] He ridiculed the tyrant. He launched upon the Hitler regime not just the most ferocious weapons of industrialized warfare, but also the weapon of laughter. The great English philosopher Thomas Hobbes thought that the function of laughter was to belittle others. True, Churchill occasionally made use of this

50 The centrality of 'relationality' is stressed by Andrew Benjamin. See for example Benjamin 2000: 107–27.

51 'I am free to admit that in North Africa we builded better than we knew. The unexpected came to the aid of design and multiplied the result. For this we have to thank the military intuition of Corporal Hitler. We may notice, as I predicted in the House of Commons three months ago, the touch of the master hand. The same insensate obstinacy which condemned Field-Marshall von Paulus and his army to destruction at Stalingrad has brought this new catastrophe upon our enemies in Tunisia' (Churchill 1943; *NGI* 351).

function, notably against the dictators.[52] But more telling than the mockery of the ferocious wit is the compressive force of metaphor and jokes. The ability to make space time and time space has a 'violence' of its own, a ferocity, an intensity, that compounds one thing into another – a little like the end of the universe in which all that will be left of things will be the singularity into which all that is plural is compressed. Every joke is an anticipation of the end of the universe. Jokes exist because we can 'see', that is we can imagine, that things that are most unlike each other in fact are remarkably like each other. That is what the imagination does. It permits us to see what is unseen.

Accordingly, the image of 'the iron curtain', plucked by Churchill from obscurity and made famous by him, takes the strongest material and the most flimsy material (each one of them) for the other.[53] It is in this sense that history is creation. It moves at times like lightning speed. It does not move just from one thing to another. Rather the act of moving, which here is the act of creating, is possible because one thing can be conceived as another. In 1946, Churchill could clearly foresee the post-war Cold War coming because he could imagine a paradoxical political condition that had some of the characteristics of the belligerent state that engulfed the whole world in the 1940s and some of the characteristics of a benignant sunny peace.[54] When it is said that 'history is creation' or that 'society is creative' we are deploying a metaphor. What we are doing is deploying a metaphor to describe the metaphorical process of human history and the metaphorical state of being of society. We deploy metaphors not

---

52 He satirized Mussolini as 'an absurd impostor', a 'tattered lackey' of Hitler, and as a 'jackal' (*NGI* 270, 284, 290). On the other hand, he was mortified when he heard the faux-Churchillian jokes that made the rounds at the expense of his war-time partner in government, Labour leader Clement Atlee. Churchill was well-acquainted with Atlee's limitations, but he came to respect him as a loyal deputy in war-time. Pseudo-Churchill has Atlee as 'a sheep in sheep's clothing' and 'a modest man, who has much to be modest about'.

53 'From Stettin in the Baltic to Trieste in the Adriatic, an iron curtain has descended across the Continent' (Churchill 1946; *NGI* 420).

54 In his 'An Iron Curtain Has Descended' speech in March 1946, Churchill spoke on the one hand in sunny terms about the planetarian 'brotherhood of man', 'the great principles of freedom and the rights of man which are the joint inheritance of the English-speaking world', and in the coming next few years and decades 'an expansion of material well-being beyond anything that has yet occurred in human experience'. On the other hand he observed the shadow that had fallen on scenes so recently lighted by the allies. The Soviet sphere, Soviet influence and Soviet control were growing. He didn't think a new conventional war was inevitable or immanent but to forestall it would require the united strength of the English-speaking world. Twelve months before Churchill had been more catastrophic in his outlook. 'Sombre indeed would be the fortunes of mankind if some awful schism arose between the Western democracies and the Russian people, if all future world organizations were rent asunder, and a new cataclysmic upheaval of inconceivable violence destroyed what is left' (*NGI* 372).

only singularly, as the poet does, but socially as well. Conversely when the poet-statesman coins a metaphor that bears the impress of the imagination, it becomes by virtue of its compelling power the lingua franca of society. It becomes the collective self-representation of society, the singular identity of the otherwise fractious, idiosyncratic, teeming, and tumultuous members of the social world.

Churchill's imagination was a talisman of the imagination in general. It was uncanny. From its uncanny structure, it drew its literary power. I do not mean that it was literary in the sense that a novel is literary or that literary criticism is literary, though Churchill (1899b; 1939) did write one mediocre novel and the occasional perceptive literary profile. Rather and much more importantly Churchill deployed with penetrating power the resources of a language that had developed from Tyndale and Donne through Johnson, Austen and Dickens to Orwell. We are inclined to forget that Churchill was awarded the Nobel Prize for Literature in 1953. That was not just a political gesture.[55] There is no greater orator in history than Winston Churchill. He is greater than Cicero – whose words were the foundation of European education till the end of the eighteenth century. In a thousand years, Churchill will still be read, while Stalin will be remembered like the Greek Tyrants of antiquity are today, as one of a bunch of very bad guys whom no one really cares to distinguish between.

Most mid-twentieth-century intellectuals preferred Stalin to Churchill. Even now, astonishingly, a few *still* do.

But time is an unerring judge in these matters. So, while Stalin had many thoughts that would thick the blood, would anyone today wish to read his collected works?

55 He was cited, correctly, by the Nobel Foundation 'for his mastery of historical and biographical description as well as for brilliant oratory in defending exalted human values'.

Chapter 2
Wit

The Comedic Spirit of Creation

On the occasion of Churchill's inaugural speech to the British House of Commons in 1901, an anonymous scribe said about him that he had a gift for viewing familiar objects from a new standpoint.[1] It is fitting that this observation was made in the satirical magazine *Punch* not only because Churchill was an exceptionally humorous character but also because he was brilliantly imaginative when it came to the most arduous and demanding of human tasks which he disposed of with remarkable mirth. In politics and war he bore burdens that would crush most human beings, and indeed did crush most of his peers. Yet in the gravest of circumstances his wit never abandoned him. What this underlines is the double meaning of wit. Like all interesting concepts, wit pivots in two directions. It points simultaneously towards humour and intellect. It is a compound of both. Indeed the most serious thoughts and the drollest expressions share a structure in common.

Born in 1874, Churchill was not sui generis. He came from a society that produced comic wit of the first order. Churchill's generation overlapped with that Oscar Wilde (b. 1854), George Bernard Shaw (b. 1856), P.G. Wodehouse (b. 1881), and Evelyn Waugh (b. 1903), none of whom shared Churchill's politics, but all of whom, Churchill included, were comic masters.[2] Wit and imagination are not just individual. They are social phenomena as well. There are witty societies. These are societies in which the ironic rationality of the intellect plays a prominent role. This does not mean that the members of such societies are on average smarter than the denizens of other societies. Rather these are societies that are able to make unusual congruities out of commonplace incongruities. A handful of societies in specific historical periods are inflamed with the imagination. The society that produced Wilde, Waugh, Wodehouse and Shaw, in the second-half of the twentieth century also produced comic masters in Tom Stoppard, Kingsley Amis, Peter Sellers, Peter Cook, and John Cleese.

The concentration of comic talent is as good a litmus test of the collective imagination as any. This is because of the close alignment of comedy and intellect. Both take one for the other. *Rosencrantz & Guildenstern Are Dead* was

1 Anon, *Punch*, 27 February 1901.

2 Waugh initially admired Churchill but became disenchanted with Churchill's policy in Yugoslavia where Waugh served as a military officer reporting on the likely (dim) prospects for the churches under Communism.

the break-through play for Tom Stoppard. With his star on the rise, and fame beckoning, Stoppard was asked the inevitable question by a reporter: 'what is the show about?' Stoppard replied: 'it is about to make me famous'. *Da-da-ba-boom*. Stoppard's quip illustrates perfectly the nature of comedy. It is an agon – a contest or war – of logics. It is an illogical logic. Two 'logics' are simultaneously embodied in the playwright's witty answer: the logic of denotation and the logic of causality. What ensues is the agon of logics. We expect to be told that *Rosencrantz & Guildenstern Are Dead* is about Hamlet seen from the standpoint of two marginal Shakespearean characters. That is what the reporter's question sets us up to expect. The playwright's answer plays with that expectation. What makes the reply funny is that the answer shifts without warning from the expected logic of denotation to the unexpected logic of causality. Suddenly, Stoppard is telling us what effect the play is going to have on his life.

That is how intellect and comedy work. Both are forms of meta-logic – a fuzzy logic of antitheses and opposites. Agnes Heller, in *Immortal Comedy* (2005: 46, 154–5), calls this the simultaneous presentation of two contrasting rationalities. *Immortal Comedy* is one of the few systematic philosophic treatises on comedy. Tragedy has been widely studied by philosophers and by philosophically-inclined students of literature. Comedy, on the other hand, tends to be overlooked. There are some exceptions like Henri Bergson's *Laughter* (1901), Leo Strauss' *Socrates and Aristophanes* (1966) and Gilles Deleuze's *The Logic of Sense* (1969), but they are still exceptions. Peter Berger's luminous *Redeeming Laughter* (1997) is more a work of sociology than philosophy, with a nod to theology. There is also Shaftesbury's *Sensus Communis, an Essay on the Freedom of Wit and Humour* (1707) but little else.[3] This is odd considering that philosophy is often the butt of comedy. Of course that might be a reason for philosophers to be wary of the topic. Yet, in point of fact, many comedies, even ones that parody philosophers, have a philosophic undertow.[4]

---

3 Another philosophical work that thinks of itself as comedic is Sloterdijk's *Critique of Cynical Reason*. It draws on the very funny tradition of the philosophical Cynics, but manages – despite this – to turn itself into an ideological tract. Gilles Deleuze has his moments of being po-faced in *The Logic of Sense*, but these moments are redeemed by the dazzling reflections on Lewis Carroll, who emerges from the hands of French philosophy unscathed and whimsical as ever.

4 Philosophers who do take comedy seriously seem to be principally influenced by Stoic or Epicurean philosophies – or by the tradition of Cynical philosophy. That is true of Heller and Deleuze, and also Shaftesbury. So, while it is not the norm, you will from time to time come across a philosopher who has a comic touch. I am reminded in this connection of a letter that Hannah Arendt wrote to her friend Mary McCarthy. In the letter she describes some prestigious academic venue in Europe populated by visiting professors with their wives in tow busily typing their husbands' manuscripts. The image is hilarious. Forget equality of the sexes. What is rib-tickling funny is the pomposity of the professors with their inflated sense of self importance. They believe they are at work on things of world-historic significance and they have their domestic slaves chained to the enterprise.

Many comic playwrights – from Molière to Stoppard, Aristophanes to Shaw – have been well read in philosophy. Aristophanes was probably a friend of Plato. But the familiarity of the comic writer with philosophical themes also presents a problem for philosophy. This is because comedy does something that philosophy is not comfortable with. It plays with logic. It combines incongruous reasons and rationales, logics and topics. That is the soul of humour, wit and whimsy. Comedy segues mercilessly from denotation to causality, freedom to necessity, and back again. Comic writers engage in fabulous lightning-fast leaps across the abyss from the terrain of one kind of logic to another.

There are exceptions of course, but philosophers on the whole feel the need to take sides with either denotation or causality, and not with both at the same time. Philosophers, for the most part, are partisans of Right Logic. Accordingly, there is a pathway that leads from the French *philosophes* to the Terror of the French Revolution. It was Aristophanes, in *The Clouds*, who observed what it is that philosophers dislike about Wrong Logic. It creates new maxims by cunning shifts.

> UNJUST DISCOURSE
> Take me where you will. I seek a throng, so that I may the better annihilate you.
> JUST DISCOURSE
> Annihilate me! Do you forget who you are?
> UNJUST DISCOURSE
> I am Reasoning.
> JUST DISCOURSE
> Yes, the weaker Reasoning.
> UNJUST DISCOURSE
> But I triumph over you, who claim to be the stronger.
> JUST DISCOURSE
> By what cunning shifts, pray?
> UNJUST DISCOURSE
> By the invention of new maxims.
> JUST DISCOURSE
> … which are received with favour by these fools.
> (He points to the audience.)

Of course philosophers themselves create new maxims by cunning shifts. However, philosophy is curiously uneasy with what it actually does. It denies its own behaviour because it has always had a problem with 'first philosophy', its own premises. It has never been sure that these are not arbitrary confections. Its instinct therefore is to equate reason not with its own maxims but with 'discourse' or 'logic'. It is not unusual for philosophers, or for philosophically-minded writers,

---

O comedy – burst the bubble of these idiots. Make fun of them, and restore proportion to the world.

to think that they can prove anything and justify anything with a long enough 'discourse'. Some philosophers go as far as to say that philosophy is without foundation, which is just a re-statement of philosophy's embarrassment with the maxims on which it rests its arguments.

To create new maxims by cunning shifts is essentially a comic act. When a philosopher announces that *it is better to suffer injustice than to cause it*, a new maxim has entered the world, and this has happened because of a cunning cognitive shift that has taken place between the idea of suffering and the idea of causing suffering. The moral dignity traditionally accorded to the endurance of suffering is asserted by the philosopher but in the name of the less than traditional idea of alleviating suffering. While this kind of paradox lies at the heart of philosophy, its 'logic' is comic, its force is creative, and its effect is unsettling. There is, therefore, something 'absurd' about the maxims on which philosophy rests. Yet philosophy resists this idea, and quite insistently. A classic example of this resistance is the epistemology of Thomas Hobbes. Hobbes, as has been noted, uses his great literary mastery of metaphor to denounce the cunning shifts of metaphor in favour of the more methodical 'train' of mental discourse. Metaphor is bad because it casts one thing ('thought') as something else (a 'train'). In contrast, discourse and logic (those regulated but also remorseless trains of thought) are good. If we put aside the question of good and bad, the clear implication of what Hobbes has to say is that philosophy entails contrary notions of reason. There is the kind of reason represented by the enigmatic and comic maxims on which philosophy rests, and then there is the reason of 'giving reasons' and the logical procession and progression from one reason to another.

Hobbes' distinction of two kinds of reason is not to be confused with the proposition introduced by the English philosopher Peter Winch (1926–97) that multiple kinds of reason or rationality exist. Winch's influential book *The Idea of a Social Science and its Relation to Philosophy* (1958) took its cue from Wittgenstein who coined the metaphor of multiple language 'games' as a way of understanding the way language is used by speakers. Just as words were deployed in multiple language games, Winch concluded that reason was expressed in multiple forms of rationality. Thomas Kuhn's idea of scientific paradigms, introduced in Kuhn's 1962 book *The Structure of Scientific Revolutions*, was similar in type. The notion of multiple rationalities reached its apotheosis in various post-modern treatises, exemplified by Paul Feyerabend's *Against Method* (1975).

Philosophers divide, sometimes bitterly, over the question of whether multiple rationalities exist or not. Some of them – monists and positivists – insist that there is only one kind of rationality. This super-rationality tends to go by the name of science. The idea that there are several kinds of scientific reasoning – or that Aristotle, Galileo, Newton, and Einstein developed different and incommensurable models of reasoning – is an anathema to a monist. Yet other philosophers – the pluralists – love the idea that there are multiple rationalities. Effective causality and teleology, reasoning from variable conditions and final ends, are manifestly different. Pluralists ascribe a mystique to the idea of 'difference'. This mystique paved the way for the era of postmodernism (1970–2000). In this period, it became a popular intellectual conceit to think that any belief system – not excluding witchcraft or tarot card reading – had its own kind of rationality. This ended up turning into a satirical comedy. All kinds of quirky fantasies and zealous pedantries were touted as rationalities.

As is often the case, comedic ridicule is the most effective refutation of a philosophical fad. Yet it should also be noted that the impetus to treat rationality as plural rather than singular was not new. The philosopher Søren Kierkegaard divided the world into the spheres of aesthetics, ethics and religion. The sociologist Max Weber drew a firm line between religion, politics and science. Apparently neither monists nor pluralists had ever heard of comedy. For comedy makes both of them redundant.

> Valentine: Science and religion
>
> Hannah: No, no, been there, done that, boring (Stoppard *Arcadia*)

Kierkegaard comes close to understanding this. For him, comedy was the religious incognito. (Irony was the ethical in disguise.) A religious parable and comedy have in common the simultaneous presentation of two contrasting rationalities. Comedy, in a *volte face*, segues from one kind of rationality to another. It is a highly intellectual process that shifts a thought from one kind of logic to another in a snap. Comedy is not monist. It always summons up more than one reason and more than one kind of rationality simultaneously. It has the reasons of male and female, young and old, the arts and the sciences, the able and disabled all in play, or more exactly, in combat. This is a delicious, frenetic, spirited combat, in which neither side triumphs. Yet it is not an exercise in simple-minded pluralism, either. Via the dazzling swing shift, the warring sides are yoked in matrimony. They are gathered together in a third-party comic marriage. Humour unites them in a paradoxical antithetical union. It makes one out of two by adding, often by implication, a third linking term that connects the (seemingly) un-connectable. Putting all the fancy words aside, that is what we laugh at:

> William and Corker went to the Press Bureau. Dr. Benito, the director, was away but his clerk entered their names in his ledger and gave them cards of identity. They were small orange documents, originally printed for the registration of prostitutes. (Waugh 1937/2005: 284)

It was Aristophanes who first observed the agon of logics. He did so by reconnoitring and then parodying philosophers in combat with their enemies. Along with the birth of philosophy in Greece came the philosophers bandying different models of discursive reason, and trying to demarcate reason from myth and rhetoric. Philosophy invented Right Logic and Wrong Logic. You can just about imagine Aristophanes' raised eyebrow as he ponders the ambition of his friend Plato to kick the poets and their pesky gods out of the city, or to put the bad sophists in their proper place.

Comic theatre was born in response to philosophy – or rather more accurately in response to those two Greek miracles, philosophy and politics. *The Clouds* was Aristophanes' response to philosophy. The *Assembly Women* was his comedic take on politics. Politics and philosophy, at their best and at their worst, are rationalist in spirit. Comedy is their sceptical twin. It is not anti-rational or irrational. Indeed it is highly intellectual. As Agnes Heller suggests (2005: 11, 30, 60, 62, 66, 154–5), comedy is born with the instinct of reason. Nevertheless comic reason is also distinct from regular reason. The instinct of comedic reason is to take one kind of rationality – say that of denotation – and another one – say that of causality – and find the thing that, in the most unlikely or unexpected way, binds the two together. That is what wit does. It makes one thing out of two things that are unlike each other. That is also a definition of creativity. It is something that is very difficult to do because it creates an effect that is both singular and plural at the same time. Acts of creativity should not exist and yet they do exist. They are in principle impossible, but wit overcomes this impossibility by the calculated and rational deployment of absurdities that are tacitly sensible.

One of the principal functions of comedy is to deflate pretension. Mad philosophers and foolish politicos are equally the butt of comedy. But I do not want to suggest that either politics or philosophy is merely a 'bad joke'. Both can turn themselves into bad jokes when, as they sometimes do, they invent good reasons for inane and sometimes insane things, and ally themselves with mean-mindedness and cruelty. But this is not always the case. Indeed, on occasions, politics and philosophy work brilliantly. When they do, they often work best via the medium of wit or humour. They work in a comedic fashion. What I mean by this is that they work through the miscegenation of concepts and the marriage of unlikely bed-fellows.

To take just one example from philosophy: in Kant's *Groundwork of the Metaphysics of Morals*, freedom is defined as the opposite of nature. But at a certain point – as the reader reads this great tract – it also becomes evident that moral freedom is a human necessity. The actions of human beings may be determined by their appetites and other kinds of un-freedom but paradoxically nature also determines that humanity is an indeterminate being – one that acts on the pure practical reason of principles. The moment that determinacy determines the indeterminacy of human autonomy is a comic moment.

That is what comedy does. It jokes that our freedom is determined. We who choose have no choice but to choose. Conversely, each choice in the making is indeterminate, but once made (indeed in the very act of making) each choice is a determination.

> Augustus: You are not my tutor, sir. I am visiting your lesson by my free will.
>
> Septimus: If you are so determined, my lord.

Underlying the surface joke is a point of great seriousness:

> The unpredictable and the predetermined unfold together to make everything the way it is.

The quantum character of reality that Tom Stoppard evokes in *Arcadia* echoes the dual nature of all things that Winston Churchill sketched in his autobiography, *My Early Life* (1930). Churchill's view is sceptical on the surface. It looks upon human beings as free. Yet it is providential beneath the surface. It sees human beings as governed by fate and destiny. Predestination and free will, Churchill concludes, are identical. They are the same thing viewed from a different perspective (1930/1947: 28):

> I have always loved butterflies. In Uganda I saw glorious butterflies the colour of whose wings changed from the deepest russet brown to the most brilliant blue, according to the angle from which you saw them. In Brazil as everyone knows there are butterflies of this kind even larger and more vivid. The contrast is extreme. You could not conceive colour effects more violently opposed; but it is the same butterfly. The butterfly is the Fact – gleaming, fluttering, settling for an instant with wings fully spread to the sun, then vanishing in the shades of the forest. Whether you believe in Free Will or Predestination, all depends on the slanting glimpse you had of the colour of his wings – which are in fact at least two colours at the same time.

Wit and Society

> Question: Is Mr. Sartre free today?
>
> Answer (from Mrs. Jean-Paul Sartre): Ooooh, he's been asking himself that for years!

The parody of Sartre by *Monty Python's Flying Circus* illustrates the complex relationship of comedy to philosophy. It sends up philosophy philosophically. *Monty Python's Flying Circus* (1969–74) appeared in the middle of the Golden Age of twentieth-century British radio and television comedy. This great comic era began with *The Goon Show* (1951–60) on BBC Radio. It peaked with *Fawlty Towers* (1975–79) and the immortal Basil Fawlty and ended with *Yes Minister/ Yes, Prime Minister* (1980–88). The period included such classics as *Morecambe & Wise* (1961–83), *Not Only ... But Also* (1965–70), *Dad's Army* (1968–77),

Porridge (1974–77), *The Good Life* (1975–78), and *Blackadder Goes Forth* (1983–89). In spirited parallel to this mirthful fountain, Kingsley Amis' *Lucky Jim* was published in 1953, *Jake's Thing* in 1978 and *The Old Devils* in 1986. Tom Stoppard's *Rosencrantz & Guildenstern are Dead* was first staged in 1966, *Jumpers* followed in 1972, and *Hapgood* in 1988. *Hapgood*, Stoppard's play about quantum mechanics and espionage engaged knowingly with Niels Bohr's paradox that 'the answer is the question interrogated'. Peter Sellers' and Spike Milligan's absurdist treatment of time, in series 7, episode 18 of *The Goons*, is probably unsurpassable in the quantum effects it achieved with language:

> Bluebottle: What time is it Eccles?
>
> Eccles: Err, just a minute. I've got it written down here on a piece of paper. A nice man wrote the time down for me this morning.
>
> Bluebottle: Then why do you carry it around with you, Eccles?
>
> Eccles: Well, if anybody asks me the time, I can show it to them.[5]

How can we explain such an explosion of comic invention? Agnes Heller suggests that comedy flourishes when the times are 'out of joint'. She observes (2005: 37) that 'both tragedy and comedy are born in times when the order or hierarchy of values gets shaken or severely questioned; both arts come about during periods of turbulence in which previously held beliefs and ideals become uncertain, unstable and labile'. When the time is out of joint, what previously may have appeared to be natural, no longer appears to be natural.

Still, caution is required here: for the United Kingdom in the 1960s and 1970s was not embroiled in anything like a civil war or a revolution. The times – from the early 1950s to the late 1980s – were not violently out of joint. This was more modestly and even merely a 'turbulent' era. Social values were in transition. The ethos of British society shifted visibly during the period. The traditional British class system declined. Culture was reshaped by youth style and the pop arts. The social roles of men and women were rewritten. If this kind of mild social turbulence set the stage for comedy, we might ask, though, in what way? One ought not conclude that because social upheaval tends to tease out brilliant comedy that comedy therefore is a flag-bearer of such upheaval. Comedy responds to change, yet it is a conservative response to change. This points to the classic paradox of the comedic spirit. Comedy has an unusual relationship to society. It is not pious or sanctimonious. It is not saintly, good or proper. One is tempted to say that it does not uphold social norms, though that is not exactly true. In any case, comedy does not seek reform or improvement – or change or utopia – or a better world . Yet that is not exactly true either – for there are some things that

5 The episode was entitled 'The Mysterious Punch-up-the-Conker'.

the comedic spirit detests. Here we see the dual logic, the inherent incongruity, of comedy at work – or is it at play? At the very least, comedy is more conservative in spirit than it first appears to be. If comedy flourishes in times of change, it is not because it is an agent of change. I do not mean that comedy is reactionary or nostalgic for the past, or that it is a defender of the status quo ante. Rather, more simply, comedy is a defender of society's nature. Society has a nature. It has a proportionate shape. Distortion of that shape triggers a comedic response. Comedy parodies social distortions with its own comic distortions. It exaggerates exaggeration for comic effect.

Proportion is a key word. It signifies a specific relation between ontological qualities. As the ancient Greeks observed, proportion was a pleasing way of relating antitheses to each other – long and short, fat and thin, large and small. Proportion harmonizes odd pairings. Wit does the same. At its sharpest and most acerbic, it connects the (seemingly) unconnected. Conversely it rebels (if that's the right word) against disproportionate social relations. The most instantly recognizable kind of social distortion is excess. There are various kinds of excess. Firstly, there are the excesses of the intellect. Pomposity, conceit and vanity are the typical comic faults of professors. Then there are material excesses. Avarice is the typical comic failing of the wealthy. There are also the excesses of identity. The envious person wants to be someone else. The jealous person wants to control someone else. Each comic excess brings forth a deficit. Conceit encourages pedantry, avarice produces meanness, and jealousy produces emotional blindness. All these faults seem to inspire around them a lack of courage and a lack of sense. Is there anything more comically disreputable than cowardice or stupidity?

From time to time, in all societies, the social sense of proportion is lost and the inherent shapeliness of society is distorted. This is when the times are 'out of joint'. This can occur because the social norms and values that previously gave effect to the proportionate nature of society lose their credibility and need replacing. It can also occur because social actors are tempted to step over the invisible line that separates proportion from excess. In the golden age of twentieth-century British comedy, both of these factors were at play. This was an era when values were questioned and behaviour (at times) was excessive. We see a huge outpouring of first-rate comedy in this period. This was not because comedians were 'against the class system' – or anything equally lame. It was rather more simply because the comedic instinct of reason incorporates the conservative instinct for proportionality.

Peter Spence, the principal writer of the English television comedy *To The Manor Born* (1979–81), embodied that instinct perfectly. His story lines deftly weaved between the Whiggish arriviste shop-keeper values of Margaret Thatcher's Conservative Party and the decidedly anti-mercantile values of the old English Tory landed class. In the witty battles between the indebted Audrey fforbes-Hamilton and the new owner of Audrey's familial manor house, the self-made supermarket chain magnate and immigrant Richard DeVere, neither protagonist ever manages to completely trump the other. Each represents a limit for the other. Audrey has to learn economic sense and Richard has to learn the close-knit ways of village life. In a larger but similar sense, the emergence of a distinctly small-c conservative world view at the end of the eighteenth century was the result of the coalescence of Whig and Tory attitudes, a merger personified by Edmund Burke the great Whig critic of the French Revolution and conservative icon of later generations. In the twentieth century Churchill proved himself to be a similar double act.

> Churchill: 'Who are you?'
>
> Mallalieu: 'I'm Bill Mallalieu, sir, MP for Huddersfield.'
>
> Churchill: 'What party?'
>
> Mallalieu: 'Labour, sir.'
>
> Churchill: 'Ah, I'm a Liberal. Always have been.'

At the time this conversation took place in the 'Lord's Lift' in the British Houses of Parliament in 1962, Churchill had been a Conservative Member of Parliament since 1922 and Conservative Prime Minister from 1940 to 1945 and from 1951 to 1955. This clearly was no ordinary politician. The exchange with Mallalieu evokes drama, history, a stage, rhetoric, performance, consummate acting, immaculate timing, an audience, political communication and poetical meaning. Churchill, born on a grand historical stage, Blenheim Palace, into a great political family, lived his life as a brilliant actor, who, when he was a Conservative was a Liberal, and when he was a Liberal was a Conservative. He could play all the leading parts, and yet was not in the slightest a Machiavellian. He was no dissembler. Disingenuousness was foreign to his personality. Yet he was victorious in the Second World War not least because of a great secret (the Enigma code) that he shepherded. He had no guile and yet changed political sides not once but twice. He was theatrical but beneath the mask he wore was a core of granite-like substance that saved the world from catastrophe. He was an enigma.

Agnes Heller (2005: 38) put it aptly. Comedy is played out in the world of finitude, the world of limits. The nineteenth-century English novelist George Meredith explained the nature of this very well. He observed that whenever people

> 'wax out of proportion, overblown, affected, pretentious, bombastical, hypocritical, pedantic, fantastically delicate' or are 'self-deceived or hoodwinked, given to run riot in idolatries, planning short-sightedly, plotting dementedly; whenever they are at variance with their professions, and violate the unwritten but perceptible laws binding them in consideration one to another; whenever they offend sound reason, fair justice; are false in humility or mined with conceit individually or in the bulk; the Spirit overhead will look humanely malign and

> cast an oblique light on them, followed by volleys of silvery laughter. That is the Comic Spirit'.[6]

Pretty much all of the above – from pedantry to self-deception, bombast to demented plotting – are pilloried in the comic character of Basil Fawlty, the worst hotelier in the history of hospitality. In doing so, comedy does not subvert social norms. It does not encourage the transgression of norms. Instead it upholds them. But it does not uphold a particular norm – say honesty, against the act of deceit or thievery. Rather comedy upholds limits – that is to say finitude, against excess. This is a very simple norm. It does not demand piety or sentimentality, righteousness or benevolence. The only thing it requires is a sense of proportion.

The comedic norm of 'no excess' implies that other great comedic commandment 'no tyranny'. Heller (2005: 59–61) put it beautifully: comedy is the enemy of tyranny, fanaticism and cruelty. The classic comic figure is the tyrannical father who wants to prevent the marriage of his daughter or son to their beloved. Another classic comedic target is the controlling, suspicious husband who is wracked by jealously. From the ridicule of domineering husbands and autocratic fathers, comedy naturally segues into the comic pillorying of tyrannical sergeant-majors and dictatorial presidents. One explanation for political comedy is that tyranny is a form of excess. The comic distaste for bombast and lack of proportion naturally sets it against the behaviour of any tyrant.

Does this mean, then, that comedy is a reflex of freedom? Loud laughter is certainly the sign of a free society. But, remember, tyrants also possess a kind of freedom. Hegel called it the freedom of one. For a time, they are able to do more or less what they please because everyone else is not free. The arbitrariness of what they do requires everyone else to be un-free. Comedy, in response, makes fun of their addled-brained schemes. It satirizes irrational planning and delusional plotting.

> Q: What does Saddam want for Thanksgiving?
>
> A: Turkey.

But do not forget that it is not only tyrants that do dumb or crazy things. There are plenty of misjudged free acts in free societies that comedy merrily lambastes. All societies suffer from stupidity, hypocrisy, conceit, avarice, obsession, and the rest of the traditional targets of comedy. Excess and lack of proportion are human failings, period. Tyranny in a way is an exaggeration of the human vice of exaggeration. It is the ludicrous summa of ludicrousness. What comedic intuition most resists is the human predilection for obsession that leads to the fanatical

6 George Meredith, 'On the idea of Comedy and uses of the comic spirit' (1877). This was first given as a talk on 1 February 1877 at the London Institute and was subsequently published in the April 1877 issue of *The New Quarterly Magazine*.

behaviour that turns into tyranny. Human obsession appears in many guises. One of these is reason. In principle reason ought properly to be antithesis of obsession. In practice it is often little more than the sublimation of it. Without its own comic corrective, reason all too easily rationalizes extreme behaviour and fixated thoughts. Comedy is the critique of obsessive reason. Comedy cuts it short.

This cutting short is built into the very nature of comedy, its capacity for the *volte face* – the swing shift from one rationale to another. Dramatically this is symbolized by a change of identity. Trading places, the confusion of identities (*Rosencrantz and Guildenstern*), cross-dressing (*Some Like It Hot*, *Tootsie*), authors denying their authorship (*Don Quixote*), and shipwreck locales (*Gilligan's Island*) where identities are subverted in the very act of trying to maintain them – all are comic devices for exploring how the human self becomes a stranger to itself.

> Jerry (as Daphne): 'You don't understand, Osgood! Aaah … I'm a man!'
>
> Osgood: 'Well, nobody's perfect'.[7]

Swing shifts are dramatic pressure points. They are moments in which comic action pivots and turns. The swing shift is what breaks obsessive motion. When reason rushes forward – in a demonic burst – comedy breaks its momentum. You see this in political debate. The earnest speaker prosecutes the case with vehemence. The reasons pile up. Then someone from the gallery breaks the escalating force of reason with a joke. The swing shift has occurred. Other reasons can now be heard.

Radical evil arises from obsession. It is animated by an *idée fixe*. Fanaticism is the consequence.

> Churchill: A fanatic is one who can't change his mind and won't change the subject.

Comedy is the great enemy of extremism because it punctuates the train of fanatical thought and behaviour. There is no stopping, no shifting, and no swinging in the mind of the extremist. The comedic mind is the opposite. For it, the world is full of unmoved movers and necessary freedoms. It revels in the enigma of these plural singularities. The mystery of such paradoxical, deeply contradictory, seemingly impossible forms is the antidote to the pedantry, fundamentalism, and ideology of fanatics and fools.

Comics satirize buffoons who have discovered 'the key to the universe' (phrenology, global warming, etc.). Comedy dislikes one sidedness. The very structure of humour is multiple, manifold and compound. It segues from one side

7 *Some Like It Hot* (1959) directed by Billy Wilder, script adapted by Billy Wilder and I.A.L. Diamond from a story by Robert Thoeren and Michael Logan.

of a contradictory proposition to the other side, and brings its audience along for the ride. The surprising thing about humour is how universal its judgements are. It speaks in a universal voice. If you are sad, you are sad by yourself. Others may be sobered or troubled by what has happened to you, but rarely are they ever sad in sympathy with you. This is why tear-jerking in movies is a contrivance and why it produces low mawkish art.[8] Laughter, on the other hand, is naturally infectious. Tell a joke at someone's expense and, if it is a good joke, even the person who is being sent up will laugh along.

> Woman: Mr. Churchill I have travelled 50 miles to view the unveiling of your bust.
>
> Churchill: Madam, I would gladly reciprocate the honour.

Most comedies are about pairs – sometimes pairs of pairs.[9] In comic dramas and comic novels there are the pairs of father–son, father–daughter, husband–wife, master–son, and master–servant. There are pairs of lovers and pairs of clowns. There is Don Quixote and Sancho Panza, Vladimir and Estragon, Felix Ungar and Oscar Madison, Stan Laurel and Oliver Hardy, Max Bialystock and Leo Bloom, Walter Burns and 'Hildy' Johnson, Rosencrantz and Guildenstern, Audrey fforbes-Hamilton and Richard DeVere, Captain Mainwaring and Sergeant Wilson. The comic genius Evelyn Waugh, in his semi-autobiographical novel *The Ordeal of Gilbert Pinfold* (1957), created a two-in-one character – Pinfold beset by delusions and Pinfold of sound mind. So what explains the preoccupation with pairs? Think of comedy as being driven by the illogical logic of pairing. Comedy encapsulates the strange logic of marriage. The essence of comedy is that its pairings are odd couples. Sometimes what comedy is telling us is that successful couplings in life by their nature are odd, and because they are odd, they also surprise us.

In comedy, pairs begin in conflict or else in contrary status relationships. Comedy arises out of the conflict of generations, the war of the sexes, marital warfare, and so on. The warfare is verbal – though it often involves throwing things as well. It involves deep misunderstandings and contrary natures. But comedic conflict also always ends in happiness or resolution. In comedy, the most unlikely sniping pairs – Harry Burns and Sally Albright, C.K. Dexter Haven and Tracy Lord – turn out to be couples who are destined to be together.[10] The warring

8 *Immortal Comedy*, 32. Tears that are cathartic, releasing tension created by drama, are a different matter.

9 *Immortal Comedy*, 43, 53, 62. Pairs figure prominently in comic acts as well: Peter Cook and Dudley Moore, Abbott and Costello, Ronnie Barker and Ronnie Corbett, Desi Arnaz and Lucille Ball, George Burns and Gracie Allen, and many others.

10 *When Harry Met Sally* ... (1989) written by Nora Ephron, directed by Rob Reiner; *The Philadelphia Story* (1940), playwright Philip Barry, screenwriter Donald Ogden Stewart and director George Cukor.

couples do verbal battle with each other. They trade barbs in fast-talking repartee. They bang heads on a high plane of ingenuity. But, as in the warfare of Heraclitus, contrary opposites turn out to be the true complements of each other. Or to put it another way:

> Question: What happens when an unstoppable force meets an immovable object?
>
> Answer: They surrender.[11]

All comedic couples, even those who do not go to war, are odd. This is true of those status pairs who subvert status relations. The comedic spirit creates the servant (Jeeves) who is smarter than his 'mentally negligible' master (Bertie) or the amateur detective (Miss Marple) who is cleverer than the professional Detective-Inspector (Dermot Craddock). Comedy mediates and reconciles the pairs. It creates what the Zen novelist and playwright Gao Xingjian (2004: 12) called the expert amateur.

Comedy is a creature of oppositions. It produces main characters who are obscure, heroes that are anti-heroes, promises of salvation that will never arrive, communication that is egocentric, metaphors that are literal, dumb orators, and so on. As Heller observes (105–6, 115–16, 120, 156), comedy is a marrying logic. It creates sense out of nonsense. In comedy, a metaphor ('throwing someone into a bin') is enacted in a literal sense. Comedy yokes a communal request ('Do you know the time?') to a solipsistic statement ('I do'). It ties the sentimental ('Why do you love me?') to the brutally realistic ('There is no one else').

This is not just for fun. For such odd coupling is also the logic of creative science. It is Einstein's time-space. It is Heisenberg's wave-particle. It is also Socrates' learned ignorance and Aristotle's unmoved mover.

> Vladimir: Well? Shall we go?
>
> Estragon: Yes, let's go.
>
> They do not move.[12]

In light of the preceding, the conclusion then is that the latent core of philosophy is comic. It is built on paradoxes that confuse and irritate students, and many philosophers as well. Each wishes for hard-line certainty or else smug slack relativism. Comedic paradox satisfies neither. Enigmatic 'one hand clapping' double takes are neither relativist nor absolutist. Wit, though, is conservative. It has a built-in preference for proportion. It naturally ridicules exaggeration. Great

---

11 *All Star Superman* (DC Comics, 2005), issue 3.

12 Beckett, Waiting for Godot.

wit is not tempted, as philosophy repeatedly has been tempted, to replace norms with nothing and finitude with excess. It is tempted neither by nihilism nor tyranny.

No comic followed Sartre in his infatuation with Stalin and Mao – or Plato in his beguilement with the tyrant of Syracuse. Though, that is perhaps not completely true. In the 1920s George Bernard Shaw became enthralled by the European dictators.[13] The First World War embittered him to democracy. Of it Shaw quipped but hardly in jest:

> It is said that every people has the Government it deserves. It is more to the point that every Government has the electorate it deserves; for the orators of the front bench can edify or debauch an ignorant electorate at will. Thus our democracy moves in a vicious circle of reciprocal worthiness and unworthiness.[14]

Shaw did repudiate Hitler when he finally woke up to the dictator's anti-Semitism. But he remained enthralled by Stalin. Shaw liked his humourless Fabian political causes a tad too much. The ageing Shaw thus is the exception that proves the rule. His decline as a playwright partly explains his infatuation with deadly earnest causes. The earnestness of his opinions, though, equally explains his decline as a playwright. Shaw, Rattigan, Stoppard, Beckett and Brecht are the great dramatists of the twentieth century. Shaw's best work is principally concentrated between *Arms and the Man* (1894) and *Pygmalion* (1912–13), his retelling of the paradoxical myth of the statue that comes alive. Shaw's drama at its best relied on the precarious balance between earnest opinion and sparkling wit. The former got the upper hand over the latter after the First World War. Churchill, who knew him quite well, observed (1939) that his drama depended not on the interplay of character and character or character and circumstance but of argument and argument. Shaw's theatre has something of the dramaturgical character of Plato's *Republic*. When the play of ideas receded and the prosecution of arguments took over, the comic mask slipped. The wit suffered and the spirit of *The Intelligent Woman's Guide to Socialism and Capitalism* (1928) triumphed.[15] Churchill noted

---

13 In America in 1933, Shaw said: 'You Americans are so fearful of dictators. Dictatorship is the only way in which government can accomplish anything, See what a mess democracy has led to. Why are you afraid of dictatorship?' 'Shaw Bests Army of Interviewers', *New York Times*, 23 March 1933, 17.

14 George Bernard Shaw, *Heartbreak House*, 1919.

15 Reviewing Shaw's *On the Rocks* (1933) the American critic Edmund Wilson captured the problem well. Wilson observed that comedy relied on a deep social order rather than its demolition. Once Shaw could no longer tacitly draw on the invisible image of that social order, his comedy began to fail him. When the uprising in the play occurs, Shaw's characteristic methods of comedy stop working. 'He is still splendid when he is showing the bewilderment of the liberal governing-class minister: it is surprising how he is still able to summon his old flickering and piercing wit, his old skill at juggling points of view, to illuminate a new social situation … But with the shouts and the broken glass, we are made to take account of the fact that Shaw's comedy, for all its greater freedom

that Shaw came of age intellectually in the 1890s. The conceits of 'the New Journalism, the New Political Movements, the New Religious Movements', not to forget the New Woman, took hold of him and never let go. He emerged from that decade as a self-styled 'herald of revolt, a disconcerter of established convictions, a merry, mischievous, rebellious Puck, posing the most awkward riddle of the Sphinx'. As long as Shaw could pose those riddles, his drama worked. When the enigmas dried up, Fabian authoritarianism took over.

Wit in general disdains utopians and tormentors. Consequently it is normally to be found in the company of those like the colleague of Martin Heidegger who, one day, saw the Master Thinker in the street. The story is well-know. Nonetheless, like any good joke, it is worth telling again. Heidegger had just finished his term as the Nazi Rector of Freiburg University. He had taken the post in the expectation of creating his own spiritual Reich but was forced back into professorial life having failed miserably in his ambition.

> Passing Heidegger, the colleague turned to him and intoned: 'Back from Syracuse, eh?'

Wit does not like tyranny of any kind. This includes the tyranny of reason. Wit has its own reason but it is an enigmatic reason. No funny man ever created a gulag archipelago or a concentration camp.[16] Indeed jokes are among the most powerful weapons directed against tyrants. Jokes about life under communism did more to bring about its collapse in Eastern Europe than any political debate or philosophical argument.

> Question: How many times can you tell a good joke in the Soviet Union?
>
> Answer: Three times. Once to a friend, once to a police investigator, and once to your cell mate.

Even as late as 1989 a large number of intellectuals in the West still preferred the promises of dysfunctional and tyrannical communism to functional and liberal capitalism. Many of those same intellectuals in the 2000s flirted with militant Islam or apologized for it. This is an old form of behaviour. Pisistratus the tyrant of Athens and Dionysius the tyrant of Syracuse liked to have literary figures around them. The intellectuals of the day obliged – but why?

It is true that intellectuals are flattered by attention but there is also something of themselves that they see in tyrants. This, again, has to do with the obsessive nature of reason. Thomas Hobbes was right to call reason the 'train' of thought.

---

in dealing with social conditions, is almost as much dependent on a cultivated and stable society as the comedy of Molière' (see Holroyd 1991/1993: 340).

16 Many have justified them. The work of Slavoj Žižek is a classic case. Žižek is a mildly witty writer with exceedingly ideological and Leninist politics.

That metaphor captures something of the implacable nature of philosophical thinking. Often reason does not know when or where to stop. It is a train without a station. It is ironic then that enlightened despots always end up treating their court philosophers in an arbitrary way. Tyranny is always cruel. Intellectuals never learn that lesson. They don't or can't learn the lesson because reason has its own tyrannical predisposition. Intellectuals exaggerate. For them, a problem is always a crisis, and a crisis is always a catastrophe. Comedy seems to have been born as reason's corrective to tyrannical reason. Yet most philosophers are wary of the comedic antidote to their own folly.

Perhaps this is because of comedy's rival claim upon creation. The philosopher (Zeno) proposes a clever paradox that the physicist (Heisenberg) translates into serious science. Both point to the identity of position and momentum. Both hint at the comic spirit of creation. Yet intellectuals are much divided about this spirit. Some of them are attracted to ideas of incorporeal bodies and the like. Others despise such notions. The latter may want either spirit or body, but not both at the same time. It is not uncommon for these intellectuals to admire metaphors in old novels. Yet they recoil from the notion of a metaphorical world. Temperamentally, what these intellectuals want is a world that is precise, petty, and perfunctory. These acolytes of correctness admire platitudes and cannot abide that which is other than it is. More than that, they sulk publicly if they cannot get their own way. They wish upon us the world of the functionary. This is a world that is anodyne, colourless, and dull. It is a world of prosaic reason, rather than of peerless imagination.

The intellectual party that advocates for a world of reason sometimes does so with imagination. Nonetheless what is imagined is a harbinger of soft despotism. One sees this less in the philosophical arguments for a rational society than in the plans, policies and procedures that such arguments inspire. Reason being reason usually documents itself and often at tedious length. Here the poverty of reason becomes apparent. Reason unconsciously mocks reason. Its justifications are populated with bizarre locutions.[17] These interpolate atrocious metaphors in the very act of trying to avoid eloquent metaphors. The comic riposte has to barely to do more than quote these queer locutions. In contrast, in hard despotisms, when

17 Thus, explained the social worker, sex is a 'human right' and his disabled client, a virgin, was consequently entitled to state support so he could exercise his right. By such casuistry we can justify dipping into a government fund to 'empower those with disabilities' in order to send the poor fellow to the Netherlands for remedial sex. 'The girls in Amsterdam are far more protected than those on U.K. streets. Let him have some fun – I'd want to. Wouldn't you prefer that we can control this, guide him, educate him, support him to understand the process and ultimately end up satisfying his needs in a secure, licensed place where his happiness and growth as a person is the most important thing? Refusing to offer him this service would be a violation of his human rights' (Sims 2010). In a breath, fun becomes controlling, guiding, and educating, hanky-panky becomes state-authorized, secure and licensed, and happiness and growth sounds distinctly totalitarian.

the slave is told that he is free, this is not a metaphor. In George Orwell's *1984*, in the name of the doctrine of oligarchic collectivism the party-state declares that war is peace, slavery is freedom, and ignorance is strength. This is no ironic conflation of predestination and free will or paradoxical transfiguration of synonym into antonym. It is simply bald-faced lying. In a hard despotism, every word is a lie. Every definition is a piece of propaganda. Every act is monitored, every thought is scripted, and every dissent is punished. A hard despotism is far worse than a soft despotism. Nonetheless the two share characteristics in common. In both, spirit is subsumed by power, intellect by status, sympathy by office, and judgement by rules. No one laughs with them, though many laugh at them. In a hard despotism, though, one is best advised to laugh silently.

Chapter 3
Paradox

> Everything actual has a double aspect: *quid sit* (what it is), *quod sit* (that it is).
>
> Friedrich Schelling, *Notes of Schelling's Berlin Lectures* (1841/1989: 335)

> But the not self can be posited only in so far as a self *is* posited in the self (in the identical consciousness), to which it (the not self) can be opposed. Now the not-self is to be posited in the identical consciousness. Thus, insofar as the not-self is to be posited in this consciousness, the self must also be posited therein. … Thus I does not = I, but rather self = not-self, and not-self = self.
>
> J.G. Fichte, *Science of Knowledge* (1794–95/1982: 106–7)

> Everything deep loves a mask …
>
> F. Nietzsche, *Beyond Good and Evil* (Section 40)

I Am Not Myself

Aristotle noted the inherent equivocalness of being. Or rather what he said was that we say that things *are* by equivocation.[1] This does not mean that we are in a muddle when we say that A *is* B. Nonetheless the copula, the signifier of being, is a strange connector. Often when we say that A *is* B we are forced to explain that A *is not* B. If we say that the fields are alive with the sound of music, we are often then forced to explain that, no, that is not literally true. It is a figurative manner of speaking. The streams and woods don't sing, but then they do. Being is equivocal. Even less colourful turns of phrase, commonplaces like 'the sun has risen', easily fall prey to the querulous who point out that the sun really does not rise or set. It has a celestial orbit. The rising and falling is a metaphor. It has been transported from one context (our getting out of bed, perhaps) into another context (the celestial). Even – one suspects – our humble rising in the morning has its own metaphorical antecedents.

That the fields sing and the sun rises are like creation itself. They are all, creation included, analogies. Two things are compared to two things. The rustling and swishing sounds of the fields are compared to the vocalizing of the singer. Each delights us. From the comparison of two things with two things arises our sense of proportion. Analogy is Aristotle's proportionate metaphor. Not everything can be compared with everything. Like time, analogies are not reversible. At least they are not commonly reversible. The fields sound like the singer; the singer

---

1 Aristotle, *Metaphysics* Z 4.

rarely sounds like the fields. Achilles resembles the lion; the lion does not resemble Achilles. Man is like God; God is not like Man.

Once upon a time theologians used to point out that reason was dependent on faith. Wits pointed out in response and with equal theological probity that God was a joker. Zeno the philosopher pointed out that an arrow in motion presents a mind-bending problem about the nature of time. Imagine the arrow shooting through the air. Now imagine each 'moment' of time in the midst of the shot. In each moment of time that we can imagine the arrow is static. Yet we know that the arrow is in motion. How puzzling this is. The arrow moves through space but is it stationary in time? Or does time flow, and if it does, is it like a river in space? Is time then a kind of space? Is position then a kind of momentum? Is every answer we give a type of question?

God is a joker. This sets the tone for the world. Humanity is distinguished from the beasts by our ability to laugh and to make others laugh. Dogs do not laugh and cats do not make jokes. We are the funny species. Therefore it is plausible that humankind was conceived in the image of a witty God. Whether this is true or not, it is at least a tantalizing hypothesis. Let us be content to say that God is a heuristic that allows us to better understand the nature of things. But before we get too comfortable, in the warm glow of that tender nostrum, *be warned* – there is nothing simple about understanding. For what we best understand is the salutary by-product of what we most *mis*understand.

The joke exemplifies this. To make a joke, I forge a horizon of understanding with someone else – and then I smash it to pieces. I engage in the classic hermeneutic act – and then I shred it. I stamp all over it. A joke is misleading. It feigns one meaning then it delivers another, entirely different meaning. A joke is a clever deceit. It leads you on with the promise of one sense – only to ambush you with another sense that makes a non-sense of the first sense.

> *George*: Rather close line there, eh sir? That phone system is a shambles, no wonder we haven't had any orders!
>
> *Edmund*: Oh, on the contrary, George, we've had plenty of orders. We have orders for six meters of Hungarian crushed velvet curtain material, four rock salmon and a ha'pence of chips and a cab for a Mr. Redgrave picking up from 14 Arnost Grove Raintop Bell.
>
> *George*: Rather we don't want those sort of orders, we want orders to Deck Old Glory. When are we going to give Fritz a taste of our British spunk?
>
> *Edmund*: George, please. No one is more anxious to advance than I am, but until I get these communication problems sorted out, I'm afraid we're stuck.

(phone rings) Captain Blackadder speaking … no, I'm afraid the line's very cclllffffhhtttt![2]

The comic lulls the unwary audience into thinking that 'order' means a 'military command', and then pounces with a punch line. The pugilist metaphor is telling. Swift and violent body blows accompany the reversal of meaning – we feel it in our gut. Comedy is physical and startling. *Bang* – suddenly it turns out that 'order' means a commercial transaction, and not the directive of a general. Having opened up the delicious gap between ordering curtains and ordering soldiers to their death – *its curtains for you* – the comic then plays merrily with the double meanings of words. The audience is launched on a see-saw between two worlds – civilian and military – as Edmund desperately tries with the only tool at his disposal, savage irony, to avoid the mechanical ballet of death, the miserable hell that was trench warfare during the First World War. Such irony is possible because you and I never quite mean what we say we mean. Nor do we ever – quite – mean what we think we mean. Like all other things, words by nature are double and duplicitous. All communication is misunderstanding – and all truth is a lie. A moralist, I suppose, might be offended by this. But the problem with moralists is that they cannot see that every good act has a down side and that bad acts are sometimes the necessary corollary of good deeds. Oskar Schindler was one of the rare moral personalities in the morally despicable twentieth century. He was that because he lied on a grand scale. If there was ever an act of redemptive communication, it was Schindler's audacious dramaturgy of lies. He conned the Nazi brass into believing that he had productive slave labour factories so he could save the Jewish workers on his sacred list. When moralists tell you 'do not lie', remember Schindler.

This paradox of the liar is well assayed by Bob Dylan when, with the wryness of age, he growls 'All the truth in the world adds up to one big lie/I'm in love with a woman who don't even appeal to me'.[3] If I pause to think why the pop music of the 1960s and 1970s was so good, I am reminded that it was a glorious mimesis of a hundred, maybe even a thousand, demotic musics that had come before it. When Mick Jagger sings the song about the girl with the 'Far Away Eyes' in mock preachy drawling camp gospel country tones, he manages to self-consciously wink at his audience, slide between American evangelical white and black musics, send up 'the church of the sacred bleeding heart of Jesus/Located somewhere in Los Angeles, California', sing reverential even religious country harmonies about someone who cannot find any harmony in their own life, and turn mawkish country sentiment into a secular hymn of salvation. When life has become disgusting, the girl with the far away eyes will redeem you.[4] Allan Bloom, who wrote a rather good Swiftian satire

2 Richard Curtis and Ben Elton, *Blackadder Goes Forth* Episode 1 'Corporal Punishment' (1989).

3 B. Dylan, 'Things Have Changed' (Special Rider Music, 1999).

4 M. Jagger and K. Richards, 'Far Away Eyes' (EMI Music Publishing, 1978).

of American higher education, complained that Jagger was a chameleon.[5] But that is exactly what Bloom's own heroes – Plato and Shakespeare – were. That is their genius. They were, as it has been said of Jagger, a hell of a bunch of interesting characters. You never know which one you will meet at which time on which page.

What makes such a thing possible is the double nature of everything. The art of the chameleon is the nature of art. The nature of art is mimetic. The human species is comic because it can mimic. It can parody, mock, exaggerate, caricature, lampoon, burlesque, spoof, and satirize. All of these are misrepresentations, and misrepresentation lies at the core of the human ability to represent. Even the most faithful representation is a caricature. Thus faith is a comedy and faithfulness is comic because of the double nature of everything. When I was a young man, hermeneutics, linguistic philosophy and various kinds of ordinary language philosophy were all the rage. Earnest discussion of the poly-semantics of words was mandatory. But Lenny Bruce and Groucho Marx could have told the philosophers that everything is poly-semantic – or double-coded – and not just words. Comedy is corporeal, gestural, and physical – and gestures, motions and objects all come with double meanings.

Anything meaningful has a double meaning. This is because no one thing is identical with itself. Everything has a meaning. *Every*thing has meaning because *any*thing can be funny. Even mass slaughter can be funny – witness *Blackadder* – but it takes remarkable comic ability to make it so. We laugh for various reasons – some of them very serious. The condition of the possibility of laughter, though, is singular. *Any*thing in principle can be funny because *all* things are at a slight tangent to themselves. This is ultimately because the cosmos – or nature – itself is double-coded, or as the quantum physicists put it: a light wave from one observation standpoint is a light particle from another standpoint. It is in this sense that God is joker. God is the name for the gap that separates each thing from itself. Everything that exists, exists in a phase-shift.

All comedy is about doubling. This is true of comedy both in the cosmic and mundane senses. From the lamest stand-up comedian to the sublimity of Shakespeare, at the heart of comedy is the doubling of human identity. Comedy explores the gap between 'who we are' and 'who are we', or as the wonderful Viola in *Twelfth Night* puts it: 'I am not what I am'.[6] Indeed so – I am not what I am.

---

5 Of Jagger, Bloom (1988: 78) wrote that '[i]n his act he was male and female, heterosexual and homosexual; unencumbered by modesty, he could enter everyone's dreams, promising to do everything with everyone …'.

6 Shakespeare, *Twelfth Night*, 3.1
Olivia Stay:
I prithee, tell me what thou thinkest of me.
Viola That you do think you are not what you are.
Olivia If I think so, I think the same of you.
Viola Then think you right: I am not what I am.
Olivia I would you were as I would have you be!
Viola Would it be better, madam, than I am?
I wish it might, for now I am your fool.

All of us lead double lives in a world that is double coded – even if some us like Malvolio in *Twelfth Night* do not realize this and end up as the butt of humour. Great human personalities are aware that they are not what they are. They are self-aware. This does not mean that they do not suffer the burden of their double self. Viola's self-knowledge is tinged with pathos. Her concealment – the dramaturgical disguise of her own self, her playing the role of a boy – brings her close to her love but at the same time separates her from him – and she knows it. This comic pathos – the pathos of a paradox – saves Viola from being thought ridiculous or risible. She still gets plenty of laughs – but laughs that are due someone who has a distance from their own self.

The ability to distance one's self from one's self is central to both human self-consciousness and human self-understanding. It is the essential – the higher – task of humour. Yet some human beings have difficulty distancing themselves from their own selves. They are unintentionally funny as a result. We laugh at them, rather than with them. They are the ones who are least like Viola and most like Malvolio. They are the upwardly mobile amongst us – you know who you are. They are the ones who are wedded without parody to their brilliant careers. These are the souls who not only pretend to be someone whom they are not – there is nothing remarkable in that – but they also pretend not to be pretending. Most absurd of all, they pretend to themselves that they are not pretending, and so end up being pretentious prats – the typical fate of all social climbers. They cannot see that life is a game, to be enjoyed.

'I am not what I am' is a paradox. It is the uncanny truth of those who lead double lives, who are players on the stage of life. Yet it is not only individuals who double themselves. Societies do so as well. All societies have some aspect of theatricalityand all human beings have one foot in nature and one foot in society, and by default play nature and society off against each other. Yet there are a small number of societies that do this with a special luminous intensity. These are dramaturgical societies. In the modern world, the first of the great dramaturgical societies was Elizabethan England. The great later inheritor of the spirit of Elizabethan England was the United States. Both the Americans and the English faced a singular option in their history – either dramaturgy or civil war. Both chose both. Both allowed their society to slide into civil war. Yet both returned from the abyss – and rebuilt themselves as intensely theatrical societies. Both had Puritan and Romantic currents that disavowed dramaturgy in the name of morals and authenticity, and both mastered those currents.

We often think of the United States as a Puritan society, and there is an element of truth in this of course. But, in a larger sense, America is the off-shoot of a society, the United Kingdom, which had begun to stage itself, indeed to stage itself comically. Consequently, America is filled with incongruous characters – with epicurean puritans and bourgeois bohemians. In the nineteenth century the puritan religion and protestant zeal of America turned itself into something distinctly different – viz., evangelical dramaturgy. At exactly the same time, America became besotted with

Shakespeare. America's evangelical dramaturgy, from its start, was fiercely musical. In time this musicality mutated from spirituals, hymns and gospel singing into the anti-puritan pleasure-cantered headland of rock 'n roll. In the 1960s, Englishmen like Mick Jagger and Keith Richards imported this soundtrack of unfathomable ambiguity from America – only to export it again, in various, often very knowing, ways back to America. In so doing, these twentieth-century artists reprised with an added touch of irony England's earlier export of Shakespeare to America.

It is no wonder, then, that Tom Stoppard has his wonderful *Shakespeare in Love* (1998) end with Viola heading for the comic-tempest-shore of the New World in the beautiful tracking shot that ends that film. I cannot think of Stoppard and Marc Norman's dazzling screenplay without also thinking of how close in spirit it is to the tradition of American sociology. This is not an obvious point of comparison but all the more revealing for that. I am struck by the amount of dramaturgical social science that America has produced – most particularly from the 1920s onwards. I am thinking of figures ranging from George Herbert Mead, Kenneth Burke, Hugh Dalziel Duncan and Erving Goffman to Richard Schechner, Richard Sennett and Jeffrey Alexander. American sociology of the 1960s was dominated by the mammoth figure of Talcott Parsons. Parsonian sociology was a sociology of social functions and roles. The world of roles is the world of Violas. At the time, there was much snorting about this. Role players are inauthentic, the cry went. Well, *yes*, they are – that is the point. The better actor a role player is, the less important the original self is to the functioning of personality. 'Exactly', the retort came back, 'so my true self is mutilated by the roles I play. If "I am not what I am" then I am not being true to my true self'. But what self is that exactly – and what exactly is wrong with a doppelganger self?

This question touches on a basic human anxiety. If I play a role, then I do and say things that are not true. If I admit I do that then in some way I seem to be admitting that I am a dirty rotten scoundrel – or, in more flushed terms, I am saying that I am a wicked Machiavellian doing the devil's work. Most social actors, even the most accomplished social actors, the great communicators, do not want to say this – and there is no reason in any case that we would want to turn those selves or our own selves into scheming reprobates. Nor do we want a world filled with raving lunatics like Shakespeare's Leontes – for whom 'all's true that is mistrusted'. That is simply madness. Still that doesn't stop all the truth in the world adding up to one big lie either. The reason for this is the paradox of the truth teller. There is the ordinary truth of truth claims. *This* is what I am saying – and I am telling the truth. What I am saying is factually accurate, normatively correct, scrupulously honest, and so on. But human beings also lie by telling the truth. In war, the best camouflage is to leave something in plain sight. In politics, candour is a strategy safely conducted because even the most fulsome statement is selective. Every time we reveal something, we also hide something. We do that consciously and we do it unconsciously. We do it cunningly and we do it naively. Courts try and get around this by asking witnesses to speak 'the truth, the whole truth and nothing but the truth'. But that only works to a certain extent – because everything is double coded. Even the most honest person misrepresents what they are trying, with pains, to scrupulously represent. The worst witness is the eye witness.

Different from this merry-go-round is dramaturgical truth. It simply takes for granted that human beings hide things with their candour – and reveal things by communicating them indirectly. Dramaturgical truth is the truth of those who think and behave as if the world is a stage. It is the truth of the unreconstructed Elizabethans among us – those who think that everything important said and done is said and done 'in role' in the sense that Viola/Cesario played *a role played by a boy playing a girl playing a boy*.[7] When she declared 'I am not what I am', she alluded to these multiple antithetical identities – and the delicious comic confusion that they create. What is *the truth of a boy playing a girl playing a boy*? It is the truth of a paradox. It is the truth of a virgin queen. It is the truth of the Stoic who when asked 'what is freedom?' replies that 'freedom is the following of necessity'. This answer may seem puzzling and enigmatic on first hearing. It may seem somewhat 'Jekyll and Hyde' to combine two patently contradictory ideas – those of freedom and necessity – but that is what dramaturgical acts and dramaturgical societies do. They combine male and female, master and servant, old and young, high and low, liberal and conservative, republican and democrat. In a dramaturgical world, boys play girls playing boys – or if you are Tom Stoppard, girls play boys playing girls.

Truth in such a world is not spoken directly. It might not even be spoken at all. It is just as likely to be visual or gestural, historical or geographical as it is verbal or discursive. Dramaturgical truth is not newspaper truth, it is not ideological truth. It is not the truth of a moral or political 'view point' – God save us from those! Dramaturgical truth is communicated indirectly – via the surreptitious intertwining and oblique overlay of contrary roles, deed and thoughts. It is the truth of pseudonymous works. These are works – as Søren Kierkegaard (1859/2009: 528) said of the ones that were attributed to him – where

> … there is not a single word by myself. I have no opinion about them except as a third party, no knowledge of their meaning except as a reader, not the remotest private relation to them …

Something similar applies to the works of Shakespeare and Plato. Their works do not have an authorial point of view. That is what makes them great works. There are truths in them, but they are contrary paradoxical truths.

It may be easiest to explain the notion of paradoxical or contrary truth with an example. Take the case of humour. There is a type of lame humourist who thinks herself a courageous 'critic of society'. So she pillories the president or prime minister of the day – whereas a great humorist will not only criticize power but will also criticize those who criticize power. In comedy, it is a truism that 'nothing is sacred'. Nothing cannot be satirized or sent up. If you cannot give offence to all and sundry, including your own tribe, then you are not a very funny person. You

7 In Elizabethan theatre, female roles were played by boys.

confuse smarminess with humorousness – not an uncommon mistake. Yet it is also *not* true that 'nothing is sacred' in comedy – it is just that, most often in the comic vein, blasphemy is the best defence of the sacred. It will get you into trouble of course – just ask poor Salman Rushdie. Most true believers do not have a sense of humour – it is what makes them true believers. This malady is not only a function of religion. Militant secular liberals are just as mirthless as dogmatic pious throw-backs. Nothing on earth is more tiresome than earnest professors and semi-lettered journalists who have a 'point of view' – usually with a sharpened tip that they wish to drive all the way down your throat.

The answer to the self-righteous purveyors of self-certain truth was imparted a long time ago by Socrates: *All I know is that I am ignorant*. Knowledge is not transparent, and interesting truths are contrary and paradoxical. That is so not least of all of self-knowledge. For no matter what we know, we are always a puzzle to ourselves. Thankfully this is so – for if this was not the case, we would not want to know anything. Misunderstanding ourselves is the necessary condition of understanding ourselves, and we understand ourselves only insofar as we misunderstand ourselves. 'I am not, therefore I am'. That is the human condition. It is the human condition because we are a species that makes jokes. Understanding via the act of misunderstanding – crisscrossing the gap between 'what is' and 'what is', between 'what I am' and 'what I am' – is what it is about ourselves that allows us to wring sense from the world. God is the name of the gap between what is and what is. God is the 'I am that I am' that is the condition of the possibility of the 'I am not what I am'.

The former is the inverse of the latter. Both are different sides of the same coin. Everything that exists – exists in phase shifts. God, existence, being – *you choose the name* – is the indivisible common thing that divides itself remorselessly. It is the paradoxical singular that is double. The human condition, like the cosmic condition, is a paradoxical one. What is interesting is not simply that God is a joker but the nature of being – and of being human – that makes such joking possible. A simple term for it is 'mystery'. A weightier term might be the 'non identity' of things with themselves. The great Catholic convert, writer and critic, G.K. Chesterton, seemed to think that God was comical and creation was witty.[8] The reason for this was simple. Religion is concerned with mysteries – much like the detective stories that Chesterton wrote. Mystery is a comic phenomenon.

8 Chesterton's excellent biographer, Ian Ker (2011), emphasizes that humour is the thing Chesterton was most serious about. Chesterton thought that seriousness implied humour and that humour implied seriousness and that one had to be serious to be really hilarious. Why do we laugh when someone tumbles? We laugh because the fall is grave. Chesterton believed that there was something eternal in a joke and that gaiety and frivolity were central to Christianity. He had a mini-theology of laughter. This was related, among other things, to his view that the imagination enables us to see the familiar afresh.

It is what does not make sense and yet at the same time does make sense. This is the limit case of understanding. Mystery and humour share this in common. In both cases, understanding is produced by perplexity.

Religion in this sense is comical. It is comical in the same way that a joke relies on a word meaning one thing and another thing at the same time. The key word in a joke is not what it is. 'Why are there schedules if trains are always late?' grumbles the commuter. 'Because how else would we know that they were late,' replies his friend. The schedule is both the cause of things being on time and the measure of things running late. It 'is' and 'is otherwise' – at the same time. In a larger sense, mystery 'is' and 'is otherwise' at the same time. We know from detective stories that mysteries hang on what 'makes sense' and 'doesn't make sense' simultaneously. Little oddities, tiny little phase-shifts, lie at the core of mysteries – and cause the observant sleuth to recognize them, and then to solve them. The great fictional detective sees what it is that everyone else sees in plain sight – and yet concludes that the innocent gesture was in fact a malign one. The kindly old grandmother who puts the teaspoon of sugar in her nephew's cup was poisoning him. Everything has two meanings, and sometimes these dual meanings are potent antinomies. A mystery is a quantum state of being. At the heart of a mystery – or at least at the heart of an interesting mystery – is a paradox.

Chesterton's Father Brown appreciated this – and so did Shakespeare, though Shakespeare rarely talks directly about God. There is relatively little overt religion in Shakespeare's dramas, and yet there is a ton of paradox. Art or Nature replaces the figure of God in Shakespeare, yet Art and Nature have the same paradoxical, enigmatic, quality of Chesterton's God. An enigma is the product of two contrary warring qualities that are identical – or as Polixenes suggests so beautifully in the exchange with Perdita in Shakespeare's *Winter's Tale*, the paradox of nature is that nature is made by art but nature also makes art, making art and nature identical. Art adds to nature, art changes nature – but nature creates art in the first place. Thus art *is* nature.[9] Two *is* one. Correspondingly, Art-Nature *is* God. That is Plato's

9 Shakespeare, *Winter's Tale*, 3.4:
Perdita For I have heard it said
There is an art which in their piedness shares
With great creating nature.
Polixenes Say there be;
Yet nature is made better by no mean
But nature makes that mean: so, over that art
Which you say adds to nature, is an art
That nature makes. You see, sweet maid, we marry
A gentler scion to the wildest stock,
And make conceive a bark of baser kind
By bud of nobler race: this is an art
Which does mend nature, change it rather, but
The art itself is nature.
Perdita So it is.

Pre-Socratic point also – all opposition ends in union. In Hegel's terms, the Stoic God of Reason divides itself in time wholly and solely with the point of being reunited at the end of time.

Every paradox in the paradox-ridden works of Shakespeare and Chesterton says the same thing. One may talk profusely about God as Chesterton does – or only on tenterhooks as Shakespeare does. It makes no difference. One may suppose that this is so because both Shakespeare and Chesterton experienced religion in *difficult* ways. These difficulties seem to have brought out, in each, a deep sense of paradox. Chesterton was a Catholic convert in an age with little interest in religion. Shakespeare emerged from a Catholic milieu in an age that had far too much interest in religion. Conversion in an agnostic era is a contradiction in terms. Likewise to be 'Catholic in a Protestant world' is a contradiction in terms. Both are perfect metaphors for the nature of paradox. Both are instrumental in the making of someone who has a particular kind of self – a dramaturgical self. The dramaturgical self is a person who impersonates their own self. This is a *person* who becomes a *personality*. This is a self who can say, as Viola does, 'I am not what I am'.

The dramaturgical self inhabits a world of plays, of plays within plays, and of player-kings. But do not make the mistake of thinking that this is always a playful world. The dramaturgical self has a knife-edge. As when Henry V says to Falstaff: 'presume not that I am the thing that I was', cutting off all relations with the rotund rogue. A personality is a self that 'presents' itself to the world – that appears in disguise, that feigns its own reality – sometimes in very complex ways. The player-king can slip into disguise and move among the common soldiers – claiming that 'the king is but a man, as I am'. The paradox of the 'king as commoner' is redoubled later on, when the common soldier, chided by the king, chides his majesty in return: 'Your majesty came not like yourself'. *So there* – we are peers. But this exchange is not just about power or status. In fact it is mostly about the selfhood of selves in a staged world – selves who do not appear, even to themselves, to be who or what they are.

The luscious, ripe complexities of this mount up when we remember that the public staged world also has an off-stage – and the off-stage characters can be just as elusive as those who are on-stage, even if their elusiveness is played out in different ways. Shakespeare, off-stage, was exactly this kind of elusive self. Despite the hundreds of books written about his life, we know very little for certain about Shakespeare the man. That doesn't stop writers from asserting that he was any and every possible thing – from the culpable pliant tool of the Tudor state to a Catholic old believer secretly conniving against Henry Tudor's mercurial Protestant dynasty. This only means that the biographies written about him are filled to brimming with what 'might have', 'could have', and 'would have' been – which means that his biographers can say more or less whatever they want about him. The results are happy fictions. You can enjoy them – without believing them. They are speculations about a *possible* life.

One of the more interesting of these speculations is that Shakespeare came from a recusant Catholic family. Recusants were Catholics who refused to attend the services of the Church of England. If this is true, it means he grew up in a household that carried on religious rites banned by the English Protestant state. The evidence for this is that (possibly) Shakespeare's mother, Mary, was a distant relation of the prominent Warwickshire Catholic family, the Arden family – and that (possibly) Shakespeare's father, John, lost his mayoral office because of religious non-conformity. Like most of Shakespeare's biography, all of this lies in the realm of 'may be' rather than plain fact. Yet if it is true, it does explain a lot about Shakespeare's drama. Conversely, if it is not true – and it may very well *not* be true – it still, in a manner, if only in an apocryphal manner, *remains* true. For something akin to the paradox of being, seeing or growing up 'Catholic in a Protestant world' shaped the mental world of Shakespeare. If he did not experience this antinomy exactly, he perforce was exposed to something very much like it.

What are important are not the specifics but the structure of the formative experience of a dramaturgical society and a performative self. Being, seeing or growing up 'Catholic in a Protestant world' is as good a metaphor as any to illustrate the kind of bifurcated structural experience that gives rise to a dramaturgical world. Shakespeare was not a recusant Catholic. But he either came from a recusant household or (if not) he had neighbours and teachers who were recusant Catholics. Warwickshire and Stratford-upon-Avon were Catholic strongholds in an officially Protestant world. Whether this divide was experienced firsthand or else observed second-hand in childhood – or even a bit of both – such bifurcation is an exemplary formative experience for the 'actor self'. It sets up a sharp dramatic tension between the social 'me' and the existential 'I' – to put it in George Herbert Mead's terms. The recusant Catholic lives a double life – not unlike the convert in a disbelieving world. The recusant must adhere to official beliefs in public and confess unofficial beliefs in private. This self is necessarily divided – Catholic in private and Protestant in public. The recusant lives two lives at once. The recusant appears in public in disguise, wearing a mask.

Observing that and mimicking that is great training for an actor – or for the 'actor self', the *personality*, who impersonates his own self or her own self, and presents that feigned self in public. Recusants double the meaning of everything they say and do. In a parallel manner, they impersonate their own person. The accomplished 'actor self' in turn learns to *impersonate the impersonator*. In doing so, the actor learns to do by volition what, for another person, is a matter of necessity. The actor thus turns nature into art. The actor does ironically, wittily, comically, and mimetically what others do by way of sufferance. Neither party can do otherwise.

The 'actor' self, the master of the 'presentation of self' in public, acquires in this manner an unusual sensitivity to the dual track of meaning. On this dual track, what makes sense is also a kind of nonsense – or rather nonsense is the bridge between two contrary senses. Wit and comedy function as the hyphen between dramatic polarities – the rapid-fire switch between 'I am' and 'I am'. The gifted child immersed in a divided world, where the double meaning of everything has been magnified and is highly charged, acquires a reflex-like capacity to produce paradoxical thoughts and contrasting concepts with astonishing speed. At the top of the scale, one ends up like Shakespeare, who learns to dramatize all worldviews and all concepts. This does not mean that there is a procession of cut-out 'Catholic' or 'Protestant', 'Puritan' or 'Pagan' characters in his plays – like some medieval pageant. On the contrary, what he creates are *individuals* composed of the delicate cross-cutting and allusive interweaving of meanings – characters who are in some measure not ever what they are. These are characters possessed of unutterable depth – adroit blends of incongruous universals become immortal and immaculate particulars.

The process of impersonation of the impersonator – and the underlying drive toward the impersonal that this represents – has one further interesting effect that is worth noting. Let us call this the 'feedback effect on the self'. The 'actor self' impersonates. The 'actor self' plays roles. As these roles multiply, the 'original self' or person of the actor shrinks. The 'original self' or person – the first 'who I am' – becomes a minimal self. The minimal self is a peg on which roles are hung. The smaller the 'original self' becomes, the larger are the number of roles which can be performed – and the greater is the repertoire of impersonation. The smaller the 'original self', the less there exists a self in the traditional biographical sense. The 'impersonating self' does things that are recorded. Shakespeare wrote 38 plays. He had a highly productive artistic life. But in proportion to the expansion of the feigned self of the artist who imagines or performs an astonishing array of characters, the biographical self diminishes. In a biographer's sense, 'William Shakespeare husband of Anne Hathaway' hardly exists. His life was not filled with high drama. He is not a very interesting biographical subject – in spite of the number of biographies written about him. The reason for this is that his real self was a thin self. This is true of great artists who, as their admirers often glumly report, are disappointing to meet in the flesh.

As persons, they are not interesting. For what they are interested in is *work*, the act of creation, and into that goes their personality. In the same vein, it is often remarked that it is virtually impossible to figure out what Shakespeare thought about politics or religion – or any of the other big-ticket items that make for interesting life stories. In contrast, what we mainly remember about Christopher Marlowe are not his plays but his life – that he was knifed and murdered by an associate in the Elizabethan secret service. What we remember – indeed what *posterity* chose to remember, or cared to remember – about Shakespeare are the characters and lines he created. What resonates is his work, not his life.

The 'Catholic in a Protestant world' kept his cards very close to his chest, as anyone who is a conservative and who works in today's liberal university must do. Puritans – then and now – are unforgiving. But that is to the benefit of art. For the most interesting artists – like the most interesting personalities in life – communicate indirectly. They listen patiently to the prattle of their peers – and then say or do, act or react, dramaturgically, adopting masks and speaking ironically. They communicate indirectly through characters and roles. The kinds of speculations that get the contemporary heart racing – that Shakespeare was bisexual and so on – miss the point. If his work is androgynous – if he writes male and female, high and low, comic and tragic parts equally well – it is not because he had a racy life but because he did not. He was the consummate dramaturge because he learnt to disguise his own self. He learnt to be what he was not – to blank his original self or minimize it.

Pick your sexual metaphor – androgynous, hermaphrodite, or bisexual. What is being described is simply the double life of the human self. Shakespeare in another life might have turned to the excitements of the secret service to play out this double life, but in the life he had, he didn't. We catch glimpses of his original self in his work. He doesn't like lawyers – that is pretty obvious.[10] But then who does? This is a rare glimpse of his first self, a glimmer that shines through his enormous capacity to be what he is not. 'To be not to be' – the inverse of the 'I am that I am' – is the genius of dramaturgy. It is the ability to become expert in appearances and disguises, to excel as the ambidextrous soul, the one who plays the role of daughter and son equally well – master of double coding, mistress of metaphor and analogy, servant of contrast and handmaiden of simile, king of playacting and queen of role making, the one who never speaks directly, but who only ever speaks through parts, characters, figures, and masks: Plato and Kierkegaard in one.

The Collective Imagination

Shakespeare, Plato and Kierkegaard each personify great societies, or rather great periods in which those societies shine. The Elizabethans, the Greeks in the fourth century BC, and the Europeans in the 1830s and 1840s – each represent a pinnacle of creation. The peaks do not last long. This was especially true of the European peak. By 1870, the European moment was over. As Nietzsche complained, the 'isms' took over – nationalism, romanticism, socialism, anti-Semitism, feminism, progressivism, environmentalism, vegetarianism. All manner of crank and cranky ideologies swept over the Europe of Hegel, Tocqueville and Coleridge. By 1870, the zenith of European science and technology had been reached. Everything that followed, even the crackling era of Einstein and Bohr, was down-hill by comparison. The Franco-Prussian War of 1870–71 was the first of a series of disastrous wars that crippled the spirit of Europe. After the First World War, the Second World War and the Cold War, and a hundred years of absurd ideologies, Europe intellectually was a spent force. It was not always that way, though.

Why is it then that some societies impress themselves durably, even indelibly, on history? They become after a manner immortal, ever-after influencing the ways in which we think about 'who we are' and 'what we do'. In contrast to this there

10 Most memorably of all, the rabble-rousing line from Dick, the crony of Jack Cade: 'The first thing we do, let's kill all the lawyers' (*2 Henry VI*, 4.II).

are hundreds of thousands of other recorded societies that enter and exit history, each with distinctive beliefs and technologies, morals and stories that leave little or no enduring impression behind them. The answer to this question begins with mythology. Mythology is ripe with a double-edged quality. Take for example Niobe's Rock on Mount Sipylus. It is a weeping rock. Rainwater runs through the porous limestone. But it is also the rock that cries. The woman who dared taunt the gods was petrified by them. She weeps for her children. A is not-A. The intuition that A is not-A marks the step from the animal (strictly speaking) to the human being. Intuition is the bed-rock of Art, Philosophy, and Science along with Friendship, Love and Justice. Intuition makes the act of imagination possible. Imagination is the ability to think A as not-A. This same doubling makes civilization possible. This is why Hegel is correct when he says that artworks combine the particular and the universal, the seer and what is seen. Art is material and spiritual at the same time. The spirit is what appears in its disappearing. It is what goes inwards as it moves outwards. It is what pretends realism. Thus what it cancels, it retains. Societies in crisis and civilizations in retrenchment lose this ability to double.

The capacity to double, to be a double, and to think intuitively is built up over a long period of time. The capacity expands and shrinks across time. Intuition is the means that we have for comprehending the unity of contradictions. It is the condition of 'being-at-one-with', which is to be both 'two' and 'one' at the same time, different and same, 'one' (singular) and 'with' (coupled), united and separate. In the act of intuition, union and separation *coalesce*. The first intense social flowering of this occurs with the ancient Greeks. This was a collective phenomenon. It yielded works of Art, Philosophy, and Science. It reverberated in acts of Friendship and Justice. Love, *agape*, arrived later – too late for the Greeks. Even so, this does not mean that the Greeks were not devoted to their children. It does not mean that Niobe did not feel tenderness for her children. All parents of children from the dawn of anthropomorphic time have affection for their off-spring. But such affection is not 'Love' in the sense of the 'Idea of Love' that appears with Christianity, and which is pivoted on the story of Jesus, the paradoxical 'god who dies', the divine figure borne to the human being, the uncanny consubstantial oneness who is simultaneously 'in' and 'with' and 'outside' God. Only after the story of Jesus is it possible to conceive of love as *being-at-one-with-another*. In light of this, not only the love of God, but everyday human love becomes 'romanticized'. It acquires the double-edged quality that is routinely noted by everyone who experiences it. Its joys are sorrowful, its sorrows are ecstatic, and its satisfactions are borne of sacrifices.

How is such a thing possible? By analogy this is also the question of: how and why the Greeks? How and why the Romans? How and why the Elizabethans? How and why the Americans? Each one of these constellations contributes something that is both unique and indispensable to the development of the collective imagination. So how and why did the movement that Jesus inspired end up as a socio-cultural powerhouse? It was hardly prepossessing. As Orlando Patterson wryly notes (1991: 293), it began as an apocalyptic sect on the distant periphery of the Roman Empire, and yet managed to grow, first, into a cult in the urban centres of the Hellenistic semi-periphery of the empire and then to finally mature into a Church in the Roman metropolitan centre. This Church, afterwards, spread across the face of the earth – reinventing itself endlessly, not least through self-division, over most of the globe through the course of two millennia. Even in the age of secular modernity, Christianity remains influential in the most enduringly powerful modern society, the United States. It played a central role in the creation of European capitalism. It plays today a key role in the growth of East Asian capitalism.[11]

How then does one explain Christianity's appearance in the world? From where and whence did such a thing come? There are many possible answers of course. Some are purely religious. We can point to the phenomena of mystery, eschatology, salvation, prophecy, sacrifice, and martyrdom. These religious phenomena all preceded Christianity. They echoed through the worlds of Hellenism and Hebraism and developed in the religious well-spring of the Middle East and the Eastern Mediterranean. We know from the way the angry gods of Middle East still wage interminable war on each other, that this is fertile religious ground. Yet Christianity was different from anything that preceded it. Prissy accounts stress Christianity's debt to the Hebraism of the Golden Rule – 'as you wish that man would do to you, do so to them'. But given that this is the most ignored injunction in human history, it seems most improbable that it explains the emergence of Christianity. No matter whether it is the Talmudic version ('What is hateful to you, do not do to your fellowman. This is the entire Law; all the rest is commentary') or the Christian one ('do unto others') or the modern Kantian version, I think we are safe in saying that such happy clapping universalism was never the source of Christianity or its appeal. Rather, and more importantly, there is another characteristic kind of Jesus phrase that is of an entirely different order. For example: 'Love your enemies', 'Pray for those who persecute you', 'To him who strikes you on the cheek, offer also the other'. Now first a caveat: very few people do love their enemies, including very few Christians, though quite a few people manage not to hate their enemies. Still, not hating your enemy is a mental disposition that Stoicism had made its own long before Christianity. But the fact that few people love their enemies does little to diminish the importance of the Jesus maxim. For the point of the maxim has little to do with its explicit content but rather with its form. It is a paradox.[12]

It is in this that the answer to the question lies: why Christianity, and in turn why a handful of great societies or great socio-cultural periods, from the Greeks

11 A matter explored further in Murphy 2010b.

12 The centrality of paradox not only distinguishes Christianity from its predecessors but also from what comes later. As Chesterton observed, where the Christian Trinitarian God is a contradiction in terms, the God of Islam is free of contradictions. And quite possibly for that reason Christianity made wine a sacrament, while Islam banned it as a poison.

and Romans to the Americans? The answer lies in their enigmatic core of paradox. They are all founded on, in and through paradox. They are lived through and by contradictions, antinomies and antitheses that, despite everything, make sense. Socio-cultural constellations must make sense. Most societies, though, are limited in the scope of their sense making. They must both produce meaning and be meaningful. They are limited for the most part to their own time and space. Some societies, however, escape that limit. This does not mean that they escape all limits, but merely the boundaries of local time and space. These societies, or rather their cultural core, are universal. As Patterson says of Christianity, they are de-nationalized and de-historicized (300). Correspondingly, Christianity belongs to no one people and no one time in particular.

Christian universality is evident in the uncanny existential quality of Jesus.[13] This quality is closely connected to the conception of a religion without law. Jesus distanced himself from the orthodox legalistic Jewish attitudes, such as the concern with purity. He ate what his fellow Jews regarded as unclean food and enjoyed 'drinking wine to a degree that was offensive to any rabbi'. He associated with prostitutes, publicans and imperial tax collectors. His favourite, Mary Magdelene, was a woman. Neither legislative piety nor social purity entered into this constellation. Jesus' Christianity posed the question of how it is that a spirited, lively, free society can exist – one that is not dependent on cloying piety, deadening law or the obsession with purity. The answer to this question lies in the nature of paradox. So much of the teaching of Jesus is paradoxical. While Christianity was a religion of freedom, the Christian is depicted by Jesus as the worthless slave of God. The Christianity of Jesus offers no commandments in the Old Testament mould, only God's love and the love for God. Yet the Christian love for God was commanded by God. Only the master of a slave commands love, and that is no love at all. Love that is commanded, as in 'love me', is a paradox. Christianity abounds in mysteries: Christ who is born of a virgin and who dies on the cross rises from the dead; Christ's death on the cross is the death of death; the death of death gives the mortal believer faith in an eternal life. All are impossible possibilities, which is what a paradox is. Their power resides in their paradoxical nature.

Paradoxes, though they seem to be simple contradictions, in fact are nothing of the kind. The Christian slave to God finds freedom through that enslavement. Patterson puts it this way (303): 'We surrender totally to God, as a perfect slave does to his master. (Yet) in our surrender we are relieved of our slave like spiritual impotence'. It is the paradoxical nature of this slavery that Nietzsche did not understand. The master of the mobile armies of metaphors misunderstood the most powerful and the most enigmatic source of those metaphors – paradox. Take the bible as an example. It epitomizes scriptural religion – the religion of the book. Yet Christians ushered in a religion that made the messenger not the message the object

---

13 This character is beautifully conveyed by John Carroll in *The Existential Jesus*. See also Patterson 1991: 298–301.

of their devotion. No wonder the unorthodox Catholic Marshall McLuhan thought that the medium was the message. To wit, *God save us from messages!*[14] But note one odd thing: the Romans at their best were not moralists either. Stoicism, for example, was an ethic of indifference. Like and unlike Stoicism, the attraction of Christianity was two-fold. Like Stoicism, it distanced itself from the suffocating law of the moralists. But, in the same breath, it envisaged a God with the capacity for love and for gift giving. Another paradox! The Christian God *is impassive* and yet the Christian God *is not impassive*. The same God that loves you and gives you freedom, Patterson notes (314), also places the burden of salvation on you as an individual. 'Each man will have to bear his own load,' as Saint Paul put it in his *Letter to the Corinthians*. The freedom given to us by God is a burden. Freedom weighs us down with responsibility. The freer I am, the heavier is my weight, and thus the less free I am. Christian freedom is a paradox. Freedom issues from the Christian's enslavement to God and is realized in burdensome self-discipline. We like to help those who help themselves.

The paradox of a loving but impassive God is matched by a series of other, ever-deepening paradoxes – of which the 'death of death' is possibly the most profound. Jesus' death, his crucifixion, that very Roman way of nailing up trouble-makers, was a death that was the negation of death. One can understand this in a way that fewer and fewer human beings now do – that is, the death of death as a symbol of an after-life. I am not sure that even many Christians believe that anymore. Yet I am also not sure that belief is the point. You would be hard-pressed to find anyone today who believes in resurrection either. Yet resurrection remains a very powerful story. The requirement of a story, though, is not to believe it but to suspend one's disbelief in it. The power of a story lies in its enigma, and paradox fuels enigma. Afterlife and resurrection are symbols of paradox. It is the paradox of the death of death that makes them interesting. Paradoxes are interesting because they are impossible and yet they are meaningful. They are contradictions that make sense.

A 'nonsense that is meaningful' is the limit case of human sociation. It is what lies at the root of human creation. From paradoxes arise the most durable and most impressive socio-cultural forms.[15] A society or a social movement that is constructed on such a base has immense cultural power. Most societies lack such

14 Not least the messages of newspaper columnists and magazine writers who want to thrust their piety and unimpeachable moral purity down our throats. One of the most abiding irritants of modern life is the way that scriptural or creedal religion morphed into tiresome, secular forms – producing people who are sincere in the view that they have the word that will improve us or save us, and make us better, whether we want to be made better or not. It is a pity that the old-fashioned concept of hell has disappeared. If it had not then we would be able to happily assign all those infernal journalists and pundits to the Seventh Circle of Hell.

15 Chesterton (1902/2008: 16) remarked that existence was a contradiction in terms and that an element of paradox runs through the whole of existence. Thus, for example, physically it is impossible to imagine a space that is infinite, and yet equally impossible to imagine a space that is finite.

cultural power. They rise, whither, and die on the vine, and are forgotten with the passing of time. Creation is the discovery of similarity between two things that are different, even immeasurably different. Paradox is the most exemplary case of creation at work. 'Love thine enemies' unites opposites – it finds a most unlikely commonality between what is utterly different, the one who I love and the one who is my enemy. Chesterton pointed out just how paradoxical Christianity was. It imagines an omnipotent God who is incomplete, a God-forsaken God, a desolate God. It imagines liberty as the liberty to bind oneself and a determinate lawful nature that is punctuated with moments of freedom (miracles). Kierkegaard (1859/2009, 1841/1985) made essentially the same point, only with different examples. Namely that Christianity supposes that eternal truth comes into existence in time, that doubt evokes faith and faith brings doubt into the world – in short it assumes a comic absurdity that is deeply serious.

Paradox in such radical cases has very uneasy connotations. Take for instance the matter of slavery. The Christian paradox of freedom is deeply indebted to the social paradox of enslavement. The slave is the one who experiences social death. The slave society regards those who it enslaves as un-persons. They are legally dead and treated by society as if they had no kin. When Aristotle described the slave as a speaking tool, he put his finger on the paradox of the slave's social condition. The image of the speaking tool echoes the still deeper paradox of the slave who is the living being who is dead to society. The Christian idea of freedom is only conceivable against this background. Indeed, as Orlando Patterson suggests, the idea of freedom may only be conceivable because of the condition of slavery in the slave societies of ancient Greece and Rome. Something similar may also apply to the United States in the modern world. I'd suggest that this is so because slavery is an extraordinary contradiction in terms. Arguably, what Christianity does is to invert the extraordinary contradictory condition of a living death in order to imagine another extraordinary contradictory condition, that of freedom.

To do this, or rather in the course of doing this, Christianity envisages – in place of the living death of the slave – a death that negates death. In Saint Paul's words, then, 'the last enemy to be destroyed is death'.[16] From this springs forth life, breath, spirit and thus freedom. In a mirror of the slaves' condition, the Christian promise of the death of death makes of death and life the same thing. In the Christian constellation, death is killed off in order to generate the life, breath, and spirit that constitute freedom. The breath or spirit, or what the Greeks called *pneuma*, is the death of death. Agnes Heller (1982, 1985) taught that there are two irreducible values – freedom and life. In the death of death, they appear as one value.

Patterson observes that, in Jesus' Christianity, the opposite of freedom is the death of the pneumatic breath. Freedom is crushed and slavery begins with the deadening of the spirit (323–31). The equating of slavery with the enslavement of the spirit is interesting. Subtle overtones of Stoicism filter through this idea.

16 1 *Corinthians* 15:26.

Correspondingly, it is not the ownership of persons then that Christianity rises up against, but rather the law. It is true that Christians became important opponents of chattel slavery – but only as late as the eighteenth century. The freedmen, who made up the bulk of the early Pauline Church, were uninterested in emancipating others still enslaved. To understand why this is so, we need to understand that emancipation from bondage is a Hebraic trope, not a Christian one. Jesus offered no model of exodus – no promise of liberation from foreign rule (301). There is no precedent in the Jesus story for national revolution and national resistance. To understand why Jesus offered no liberation theology, we need to understand what it is that enslaves. One answer is sin. But that answer only begs the question 'what is sin?' Sin is not the ridiculous caricature of it – sex. So perhaps sin after all is the enslaving of persons? That is what the abolitionist Hebraic Christianity of the eighteenth and nineteenth centuries concluded. Yet such Christianity is difficult to square with the Christianity of Jesus that conceived of God as a lord and master, albeit a very paradoxical one.

In fact, for Jesus, the enslaver is not the master, the one with the power of life and death over others. Rather the enslaver is the law – the very law which is so often held up by liberation movements as the antithesis of slavery. In Saint Paul's words, 'Christ redeemed us from the curse of the law'.[17] One has to say, among many other things, that this is a stunning indictment of normative sociology. It also suggests that the Pauline Church was different from the Roman Church that later on came to adore the law. Early Christianity looked on law not as an emancipating force but as an enslaving force. Law's emancipation in other words ended in enslavement. The followers of Jesus conceived of slavery as spiritual death. The overcoming of slavery was encapsulated not in an act of emancipation but rather through the death of spiritual death.

The spiritual slave is the one who is powerless under the law, while freedom lies in the contrary state of grace. Law might be Roman law, Hebraic law, the laws of the tribe, the law of purity, the laws of states, natural law, human rights law, welfare state law, and so forth. As Paul put it, it is through the law that we come to know sin.[18] It is by law or commandment that we come to die spiritually. The commandments that promise life, Paul remarks, prove to be death to me.[19] The antithesis of enslaving law is the state of grace. In short, then, behind the law lies spiritual death. Anyone who occupies a place in the bureaucratic machine of the modern university knows that this is true. Life, spirit, the Stoic breath, *pneuma*, is squeezed by the law until it expires. A society without life, without breathing space, is enslaved. It is un-free. But what then is freedom?

Freedom is a gift. It is bestowed. Those who enslave themselves to God receive freedom as a gift. Freedom is not earned. A Christian society is not a Parsonian achievement society. Freedom is not a reward for effort. Rather to be free from

17 *Galatians* 3:13.

18 *Romans* 7:7.

19 *Romans* 7:10.

sin is to be free from the knowledge of the law. If God gives this freedom as a gift, it is because God is a slave master – but a very paradoxical one. God is a slave master who does not only free the slaves but who *frees the slaves who are already free*. If God was simply an emancipator, he would be another Moses. But in fact the God of which Jesus speaks gives freedom to those who are free in virtue of being freely enslaved to God. Thus, like the good Stoic slave master – or even the ordinary Roman slave owner interested in motivating his slaves with the promise of manumission – God bestows freedom on the slaves. Yet, in this case, God does so only by bestowing freedom on those who are already free, or even more strangely, on slaves who are already free.

This paradox of *freedom for the free* may seem like all paradoxes at first glance to be nonsense. But after a while the sense becomes clearer. The paradox, though it was complex, would have been very clear to the freedmen in Roman times. It is a paradox that they were well positioned to understand. Ex-slaves showed no particular interest in their fellows who were un-free, but it would seem that they showed a lot of interest in the paradox of a freedom that could only be obtained by those who were already free. Theirs was freedom in the sense of freedom from the slavery of the law. Was this then a revolt against Roman society and its law fixation? It is difficult to escape that conclusion. But this law fixation was itself, likely, for all of the greatness of the Romans, to have been a symptom of the faltering of Roman society, the beginning of the end of its cultural power based on its own paradoxes of freedom. By the time of Jesus the accountants and the lawyers were in ascendancy in Rome. The Janus-like condition, captured in the image of Romulus and Remus, and later in the paradoxes of Stoicism, whose cultural force had turned the tiny peninsula state of the Latins into a world state of staggering magnitude, was losing its grip on Roman society, even if that world state was still to grow larger before its decline set in irreversibly.[20] The world of Janus of course would remain forever in social memory – an enduring enigmatic source for the imagination. But another enigma, one filled with its own paradoxes, the enigma of the Christian freedman, would take its place. It would now emerge the leading and shaping force of society in history. It would function as this for a very long time to come.

20 This is discussed further in Murphy 2001.

Chapter 4
Metaphor

> The greatest thing by far is to be a master of metaphor; it is the one thing that cannot be learnt from others; and it is also a sign of genius, since a good metaphor implies intuitive perception of the similarity in the dissimilar.
>
> Aristotle, *Poetics*

Creation

By no means are all acts of creation equally difficult to explain. It is straightforward enough for example to describe the interaction of sperm and ovum that creates a child. But the creation of the universe is a more difficult matter to explain.[1] For nothing comes 'before' this moment. Because time is created along with the universe, the concept of 'what precedes it' cannot even be applied to the 'big bang'. If that is not perplexing enough, the idea of 'nothing' poses a further problem. For how can we have a knowledge of nothing, that is of something that does not exist? How can we explain how it functions when it does not exist? How can we who in virtue of existence belong to the realm of 'Being' talk meaningfully of something that is, or else emerges out of, 'un-Being'? If we can do such things, then it is because the human creature is a paradox. It is a creature that is not only dying at every moment of its life, but for much of its existence is conscious of this reality. From ashes to ashes, dust to dust, so it goes. The human being lives in the on-going awareness of its expiration. This is not a morbid fact, but rather, more simply, a pointer to the paradoxical character of human knowledge. Thus it is the case that that which is interesting, and much about the world is not very interesting, is what is experienced, understood and perceived on a knife edge. The imagination is that knife edge. It is the sharp thin border between opposites including between what-is and what-is-not. This is the realm where that which-is and that which-is-not are indistinguishable and for all intents and purposes are identical. This is the uncanny dominion of the non-identical identity.

1 'The endless cycle of creation and destruction of the big bang theory (a singularity would be the result of a collapsing universe) is probably the best explanation of our Universe. If other Universes existed and matter somehow leaked into this domain, well fine. It doesn't change the question of how it all began. I just can't get my head around the creation of something from nothing. How can energy exist without a source? Just try and light a fire in your fireplace without a log or some old newspapers. And don't say furniture'. AcePilot101 post comment on John Gribbin, 'Are we living in a designer universe?', *Daily Telegraph*, 31 August, 2010. http://www.telegraph.co.uk/science/space/7972538/Are-we-living-in-a-designer-universe.html.

This is the interesting time and place where time is place and place is time, and where what is discontinuous is continuous, and art is science, and singularities are dualities, and no law of the excluded middle applies.

Cornelius Castoriadis pointed out that the problem of how it is that something is created out of nothing haunts the explanation of how it is that societies come into being. If you had been born around 400 AD somewhere in Europe, you would have lived in a period of flagging social energies. The great social formation of Rome had existed for 1,100 years. It was on its last legs. In 476, the last Emperor of the Western Roman Empire, Romulus Augustus, abdicated. He surrendered his power to the Germanic general Odoacer. One can point to Roman and Latin influences on the social history of what followed. There were superficial continuities and yet at the same time deep ruptures. Monasticism, the manorial system, serfdom, decentralized kingships, the shift from the dominance of the city to the dominance of the countryside, even the expansion of Islamic power across the Middle East and Mediterranean – all pointed to social and political institutions that were not only adaptations of Roman forms, but were also radically 'new'.

The re-creation of the world started modestly enough. Lawmakers in the rural parts of the late Roman Empire restricted occupational and residential mobility because of labour shortages. That was already a tacit re-imagining of Roman life. The free farmer had been the symbolic *sine qua non* of Rome. Yes the Romans had slave estates, but nevertheless slavery coexisted with freedom in Rome. A Roman slave could aspire to become free, and the freedom of the soil defined what freedom was along with the free mobility of Romans across the vast territory of Rome. Romans had free soil and the freedom of the road long before the Americans. The post-Roman idea of serfdom changed that. It turned free farmers into un-free peasants, *villeins*, tied to the soil. To be tied in such a way meant a radical decrease in mobility. Life thereby was re-defined, re-imagined, and re-conceived. The core metaphors of existence changed. There were medieval notions of freedom but they differed from those of the Roman age. The free will of the medieval Christian imagination overshadowed the free soil and the free roads of the antique Roman imagination. The country eclipsed the city. Protection was sought in place of citizenship. Servility mattered now more than civility. So it came to be that so many of those who tilled the soil, which was the principal medieval occupation, had to ask their lord for permission to marry. Estimates vary, but anywhere between 30 percent and 60 percent of peasant households in England in the thirteenth century were un-free. As in the days of the Romans, the purchase of freedom remained possible. Yet the *villein* placed more value on land acquisition than manumission. This was an effect of the shift of the collective imagination. So was the paradoxical effort of the medieval personality to live in another world in this world, and the resulting fascination with mysticism, miracles, asceticism, and monasticism.

Castoriadis pointed out that the emergence of a new social constellation like that of the medieval world poses an explanatory problem. The problem lies with the nature of explanation itself. For how can reason possibly explain creation? Castoriadis' answer to the problem he posed was that it was not reason but the collective social imagination that posited 'new' social forms. Hegel said that reason unfolded in world history. Castoriadis bracketed the operation of 'reason in history' in favour of the mechanism of the anonymous social imagination. This was based on a valid supposition. For whether it is expressed in history or else in speech, reason supposes that 'B' can be deduced or inferred from 'A'. But what about the origin of 'A' itself? From what is 'A' deduced or inferred? To reason is to derive one assertion from another assertion, one principle from a greater, higher, and presumably more reliable foundation, source, or principle. Reason paradoxically is always invoking authority even if that authority is only 'the evidence of my own eyes'. Reason, at the same time, routinely refutes authority. There is thus an inherent limit to reason. Whatever ultimate reason a person may invoke, this can always be answered with a counter principle or alternate ground of reason. Whatever it is that brings such principles or grounds into being cannot be reason itself. 'B' may be generated by 'A', but 'A' comes into being differently, not by virtue of reason but as a gift of the imagination.

Imagination is not discursive. It does not operate via a train or chain of reasons, each derived one from the other. The media of the imagination are metaphor, synonym, antonym, and antinomy. Each human being has imagination, to greater and lesser extent. But so also does each society. Some societies have a greater flair for antithesis, irony and analogy; others less so. Rome imagined itself as a Janus society – balanced between the senatorial class and the people. Like all double acts, this one eventually exhausted itself. It was replaced by another double act. The most enduring image of the medieval world was provided by Saint Augustine. Augustine was the last Roman and the first medieval personality. His preoccupation with his inner life in his *Confessions* revealed a double self, a self wherein 'I have become a question for myself' (*mihi quaestio factus sum*).[2] The interior of that double self expressed itself in many ways, not least in the divide between the carnal self and the spiritual self. The exterior of this dual self was likewise twinned. It was summed up luminously in the metaphor of two cities, the City of God and the City of Man – coexistent, overlapping, and super-positional.[3]

The early medieval world of monasteries and manor houses evoke, express and encapsulate this doubling. Those who lived in the world did so by retreating from it. In late antiquity the twilight of Rome hinted at the dawn of a new age. Christianized elite Roman families begged off having children. Sexual asceticism allowed human affection to be sublimated into the love of God. The dissipation of Rome echoed in this. Augustine's late fourth and early fifth century vision would in time have many expressions, not all of them so defeatist. One of them was the high medieval cathedral and market town. The chaos of the medieval town and the clarity of its centre dominated by the cathedral and its surrounding market

2 Augustine, *Confessions*, 10.33.50.

3 Augustine, *De Civitate Dei*.

place replicate the subtle and simultaneous antithesis-synthesis (the *parathesis*) of the harmonious City of God and the fractious City of Man. So visibly successful was this constellation, once the depravations of the Dark Ages were thrown off, that the cathedral town is attractive even to modern eyes. Yet moderns cannot re-invent the medieval world, though not for want of trying. From William Morris to Lewis Mumford, the medieval town captivated the modern mind while remaining teasingly beyond its reach. Just as Romans were not Greeks, the inhabitants of medieval towns from Ely to Exeter, Canterbury to Salisbury were not Romans, so then the modern denizens of London or Birmingham are not medieval in their make-up, even those who adore the works of the Arts and Crafts Movement. Some things pass irretrievably – and yet what separates modern and medieval is not absolute. For what makes each of them in their different ways spell-binding is, at its core, the same. This is the double act. The best of modernity like the best of the medieval world doubles.

One of the many ways in which the modern world doubles is for the twenty-first century employee to live in a commuter village that echoes the sixteenth or eighteenth century. In the same way, the nineteenth century industrial city was filled with replicas of Renaissance palaces, gothic cathedrals and Hellenistic temples. Sometimes nostalgia plays its part in this, but on the whole it is a function of the imagination's impulse to conceive one thing as if another. Thus some of the best urban blocks in the world were built in London in the eighteenth and nineteenth centuries around garden squares, a practice that had the effect of pastoralizing the urban and urbanizing the pastoral. The most interesting skyscrapers likewise are metaphorical. Frank Gehry's 2011 Spruce Street NY structure looks like a billowing curtain, Philip Johnson's 1986 Lipstick Building mimics a tube of lipstick, and his 1984 AT&T building replicates a column, while William Van Alen's 1928 Chrysler Building's terraced crown echoes both the burst of the sun and the automotive wheel. What was the first skyscraper is open to contention. Nonetheless Louis Sullivan's 10-storey Wainwright Building constructed in St. Louis, Missouri in 1891, has good claim to being the first. In any case, it is certainly memorable replicating as it does the base-shaft-attic structure of the classic column. Like the most interesting personalities, and the most compelling architecture, the most successful societies double. Thus when they create, they do so not as single entity or single time. Industrial society was never just industrial society. It always also interpolated aspects and symbols of the Pastoral, the Classical, the Renaissance and the Romantic.

We lose nothing because we double everything. We urban pastoralists, we industrial agrarians constantly posit an 'alter' for every 'ego', a Rome for every Greece, and a Jerusalem for every Athens. In every act of creation is an imitation, and in every imitation is an act of creation. This is true not just of social creation but of cosmic creation as well. I am not a physicist but I would hazard that the best explanation of the creation of the universe is an infinite, endless cycle of creation and destruction. In this cycle, without start or conclusion, every beginning is an end and every end is a beginning. The infinite cosmic cycle produces finiteness.

This limitless nature mutates its way through an incessant series of limits. Every warm universe it creates shall expire in cold and shall be reborn with another fiery bang. Einstein briefly flirted with the idea of an oscillating universe. In the last two decades the physicists and mathematicians Randell Mills, Paul Steinhardt and Neil Turok (2007), Roger Penrose (2010), and Paul Frampton have proposed interesting models of a cyclical universe.[4] It is not that creation is born out of nothing – *pace* Castoriadis of the 1970s.[5] Nor it is that creation out of nothing leans on something – *pace* the older, and perhaps wiser, Castoriadis of the 1990s.[6] Rather what the cyclical idea supposes is that 'nothing is something' in the same sense that 'I am a question for myself'. I am not suggesting that societies end with a big crunch any more than they begin with a big bang. But they do lose energy and they also regain it, and these things happen, expiry and renaissance, simultaneously. In the 400s, the last Romans coexisted with the first feudal personalities. They may not have necessarily recognized that in each other – or even more potently in their own selves.

I am reminded in this respect of Ridley Scott's early movie *The Duellists*, made in 1977 and based on a Joseph Conrad short story called *The Duel*. The story is about two French officers during the era of the Napoleonic Wars and the Bourbon Restoration. Over some trivial point of honour the pair engages in a duel – the set-piece of aristocratic society that Napoleon's wars will help erase across Europe. As the years pass, the two of them rise in rank and each time they encounter each other, they duel even though military rules prohibit the practice.[7] That is the first of a number of historical ironies that begin to mount once Napoleon falls from power. One of the pair, d'Hubert, marries into the restored Bourbon aristocracy while the other one, Féraud, becomes a fanatical Bonapartist and a fulminating member of the anti-monarchist party. The historical sequence is that Napoleon abdicated power in 1814, was exiled to Elba, returned to the throne briefly in 1815, and was defeated at the Battle of Waterloo after which he was exiled for good to Saint Helena. Féraud joins Napoleon on his brief return to power; d'Hubert does not. When Napoleon is ousted finally, Féraud is exiled to a village to live under supervision. The ultimate irony is that the Bonapartist, the supposed modernist in the story, cannot give up his obsession with the aristocratic duel, while d'Hubert, happily married into the restored aristocracy, not only lets it go but intercedes behind the scenes to save Féraud from being executed by the Bourbon regime. The obsessed Féraud tracks down d'Hubert and challenges him to a duel. The duel ensues. d'Hubert overpowers Féraud and spares his life on condition that he stops the duelling nonsense. The film ends with the

4 For a journalist's account of the Steinhardt-Turok theory, see Ben Harder (2002).

5 E.g. Castoriadis, 1984 [1978], 323.

6 E.g. Castoriadis, 1997b, 321, 333.

7 'Napoleon I., whose career had the quality of a duel against the whole of Europe, disliked duelling between the officers of his army. The great military emperor was not a swashbuckler, and had little respect for tradition'. So begins the story by Conrad.

Napoleonic modernist frustrated that his querulous life-ambition of pursuing the feudal duel will now never be fulfilled. The aristocrat has put an end to feudalism. The Bonapartist, the herald of supposedly emancipated Europe, sulks on into a bigoted old age, bemoaning the frustration of his honour in a world that no longer has codes of honour or at least ones that you could legitimately strike up a duel over. The character of Féraud points to a militant extremist modernity that is ultra-reactionary to its core and that will become all too familiar in the two centuries that separate us from Féraud himself.

The moral of the story is simply this: irony rules history. It does so because it is upon irony that the turning points of history pivot. Those turning-points are, I think, really a lot like what physicists speculate happens when the big crunch of the oscillating universe turns into another big bang, when the ultra-cold of a practically dead universe reverses into the ultra-heat of a new universe. In a septillionth (or less) of a second – just before all is gone, torn apart into a nothing that really is nothing, a non-state of absolute un-Being in which all finiteness has been shredded into an unqualified in-finiteness or more accurately an unconditional a-finiteness – just in the smallest possible sliver of time before this eventuates, in the very 'nick of time', everything is back. In that septillionth of a moment, the universe will expand at an ever-increasing rate but the size of the universe will continually shrink; the distance to the edge of the universe, which will move away at the speed of light from any point, will move ever closer into the ultra compactness of a singularity where space and time, as we understand it, do not exist. Only paradox can explain the relation between the big crunch and the big bang. The latter cannot emerge casually in time from the former. Neither can the former, which is a-spatial, stand spatially in a relation of contiguity to the latter. The relation of nothing and something is a-causal and discontinuous; in short, it is incongruous. Thus an unfathomable hiatus exists between these two entities that nevertheless and quite obviously have a profound relationship. One might say then that the creation of the universe is akin to a cosmic joke – and one that is good enough to be repeated ad infinitum, the best joke of all.

I shall leave the physicists to argue the pros and cons of the theory of an oscillating cosmos. You and I cannot participate in those debates, alas – fascinating as they are. We can only be interested bystanders. Yet what I can say at least is that both history and the imagination revolve around that which appears to be a little bit like the swing shift of the oscillating cosmos. History, politics and social creation all have their septillionth moments. That is what makes them surprising. What permits us to recognize such moments when they happen or (more often than not) after they happen, and what provides us with the capacity of describing them vividly, is the human imagination. Whether the imagination that you and I possess creates those moments is another more difficult question to answer. You and I, as existential souls, individually, cannot possibly create a Rome, an Athens, or a Jerusalem. But anonymously, collectively, incognito, somehow society does that work. Féraud and d'Hubert were bit actors on the Napoleonic and Bourbon stages, on which even Napoleon and the Bourbon monarchs were bit actors.

We are all bit actors. The best we can do is to avoid the fate of Féraud who has a completely un-ironical relationship to his own and to history's ironies.

Three Systems of Communication

The swing-shifts from one world conception to another are engendered by acts of collective imagination. Each socio-historical constellation is sui generis and yet they all share the same media of creation. They are all brought into being by the successful union of contradictions. The imagination, both individual and collective, is a force of connection. More exactly, it is a force of unlikely connection. The greater the power of the imagination, the more unlikely the connection made. If we think about it, why should we connect freedom with the soil or alternatively with the will? It is only once such connections have been made and become the sediment of social life that we come to think that the connection made is obvious. By that point in time, the connection has become a cliché of life. Imagination acts alongside reason and objectivation in the creation of the world. Each plays a part. Imagination provides the animating metaphors of existence. Reason extends those metaphors rationally. What is imagined spiritually is objectivated materially in the external world. Or as Augustine put it, the imagination imagines within and yet imagines things that are from without.[8] The imagination 'pictures' or intuits shapes and forms and relationships that have never existed. Some of those images are eventually produced. They are given material embodiment, whether as a shoe, a house, or a book. Reason is the middle term between imagination and objectivation. It facilitates and mediates between both, but it cannot replace either.

In the very early medieval world for example, monasticism and manor houses were the material embodiment (the objectivation) of the imagination of a society that collectively thought of itself as parsed between this-world and another-world. The monastery and the manor house were both of 'this-world' and yet were (in their different ways) isolated from it. Authority underscored this arrangement, and the authority of reason played its part in this. Appeals to divine principles, to extra-social grounds, were common. Theistic and hierarchical power prevailed. The period of the High Middle Ages exhibited greater freedom of reason. As urbanism, art, learning, and commerce revived, reason tended to be more often mobilized against reason, and authority against authority. Yet irrespective of whether or not reason is free, or whether authority encapsulates reason or not, it is not reason but rather the imagination that provides an answer to the questions of the how and why of creation. Saint Thomas Aquinas put it firmly. Reason is necessarily complemented by faith. Reason cannot stand by itself. Conversely, we would all go mad if we existed in a ceaseless state of imagining. A thin line separates imagination and delirium, wit and frenzy. Crossing that line is a treacherous matter.

8 Augustine, *Confessions*, V.8.

This is because the human being, the symbolic creature, needs to be adventurous and yet it must also husband its capacities. It relies on both imagination and reason. Imagination or wit permits human beings to both see something as itself *and* as something else, at the same time. A double register lies at the core of the imagination. Figuratively speaking, we 'look' at something. We 'see' more than one thing in the single thing that we 'look' at. We then 'bridge' between bi-focal things and, in doing so, we 'discover' what it is that they have 'in common'. In that lies the act of creation. Having created the 'bridge' and discovered the unlikely resemblance between radically disparate objects, having leapt from the thought of one thing to the thought of another thing entirely, and having fused those 'leaping' thoughts into a single enigmatic image, and having thereby exhausted ourselves in the act of mental gymnastics, we acrobats stop and reason.

An example may help to explain this. One of the great dangers to early modern oceanic shipping was the risk of crashing onto rocks close to shore in the darkness. Thus it became an urgent matter to build light houses to warn ships. But this required structures that could be built on rocky outcrops in the seas and that could withstand ferocious sea gales. How to do this was successfully solved by the great English civil engineer John Smeaton (1724–92). Smeaton designed a light house, located on Eddystone Rocks, 22.5 kilometres south of Plymouth. He did so on the analogy of an oak tree. The structure was fashioned out of dovetailed blocks of granite and modelled on the shape of the oak tree with a large heavy base and low centre of gravity. The analogical equation of stone and tree was highly practical. Science and technology habitually proceed through such models and metaphors. The imagination, thus whilst it is not reason, is not by virtue of that fact irrational. Rather the imagination is ironical. What is more ironic than stone mimicking oak? It is this that separates intellect from reason. Intellect is paradoxical. It equates X and Y, X and not-X, as the English physicist James Prescott Joule did when he demonstrated the equivalence of electrical, mechanical and heat energy.[9] Intellect in this way gives us the premises upon which we reason. Those are not just the premises of science. The intellect also furnishes us with the ends of existence for which we then have to find the means. Such ends and such premises are posited by the imagination. Reason in the sense of rationality is the unfolding or working-through of logical inferences that are drawn from or based on the ends and grounds of the imagination. Imagination allows human beings to make the leap

9 Under certain conditions, i.e. in matters of imagination rather than reason, the law of the excluded middle does not apply. Thus it is not the case that a thing is either something or not that thing, either A or not-A, and that there is no third option. Similarly in regard to acts of imagination though not of reason, the law of non-contradiction also is not true. Consequently, under some conditions, a thing can be both true and not true in the same instant, i.e. both A and not-A at the same time. Hegel's 1812 *Science of Logic* provides the first real challenge to the either/or of Aristotelian logic, though arguably rather than the 'science of logic' the framing of this kind of inquiry as the 'art of imagination' may have been more useful.

from the observation of the bird to the thought of mechanical winged flight. The imagination is the faculty that compounds bird and machine. Reason is the royal road of inference that leads us from imaginative intuition to practical artefact. It is a long and winding road, in part because along that road further analogies always suggest themselves. The thrust of the jet engine is analogous to the thrust of the bird's tail feathers, and so on.

While we readily distinguish between reason and imagination, like most distinctions and oppositions what on first sight appears to be separate may on reflection exhibit clear similarities in nature. It does not stretch things too far to say that the imagination has a rational core, while reason is the hand-maiden of the imagination. The indissoluble link between reason and imagination is important to understand. Madness should not be confused with imagination. Ravings are neither reasonable nor are they imaginative. Likewise prophecies and fantasies, no matter how unusual they may be, are not acts of imagination. The imagination is a practical faculty. It is not a font of unrealistic or impractical ideas. Many of the greatest artists, Shakespeare, Eliot, and Stravinsky amongst them, were very astute in business matters. Similarly the imagination is not the source of infernal, diabolical, extreme, wicked, cruel, hell-bent, heinous, nefarious, or fiendish thoughts and deeds. I am not saying that one cannot have a gothic or abject imagination. The bird-man is as much a product of human imagination as the bird-machine is. The dreadful, the awful, and the atrocious are as much the proper province of art as the picturesque, the pastoral or the polite are. But the source, the genesis, of terrible acts is not the imagination. Such acts arise rather from a lack of imagination. Cruelty and evil are a function of the imagination's failure, its faltering, or its sheer absence.

Bird-man and bird-machine are metaphors. The imagination is metaphorical. Society's medium of re-invention is metaphor. There are more powerful and less powerful metaphors. Some metaphors undermine the act of metaphor. For example the notion that society is information, or that history is reason, have both been very popular ideas at times. But both are also self-defeating metaphors. Both steal away the metaphorical essence of metaphor. The cybernetic image of society and the rational or scientific image of society both fall easily into war with the imagination. This is because both information and reason, which are essential to humanity's functioning, rely for their own functioning on the imagination. Self-referential information and self-referential science are dearth-like.

Information, reason, and imagination lie at the core of our species being. We relate to the world and to our selves through these, each of which can be thought of as a systemic medium of communication. The first and the most primary system of communication – *viz.*, information – is analytic in nature.[10] It relies on the drawing of distinctions and the parsing of differences between objects in the world. This relates to a deeper ontological characteristic of the human being. The human being

10 For further on the three fundamental systems of communication: information, explanation and discovery, see Murphy 2011.

is an objectivating creature. We produce objects. We make things. We create beds, shoes, swords, roads, gardens, houses, cities. We are inveterate makers. To be able to do so, we have to be able to identify the shape and character of objects. The analytic faculty of the mind allows us to identify objects in the world and attribute characteristics to them. In doing so, we separate out the elements of the world, and we isolate and define their specific features. Such analytic distinctions are very powerful. Yet they are also limited. Their strength, which is their capacity to delineate objects and attributes, is also their weakness. They are, by their very nature, limited in their connective force. For what distinguishes does not connect. The connective power of analysis is weak. In analytic forms of communication, we are essentially limited to connecting object and attribute, name and quality. That, more or less, is as far as it goes. The proposition is a simple form of connection that is always limited by the analytic vivisection from which it arises.

The second system of communication connects the propositions we make about the heterogeneous elements of the world. This system of communication takes the names and descriptions, the analytic reports and statements that we make, and weaves them together. The second system of communication is commensurate with 'knowledge' in the full sense of the word. Knowledge as a system of communication involves more than information. This is true no matter how sophisticated the analytic distinctions we draw may be. Knowledge proper requires communicative operations such as inference, argument, criticism, explanation and narration. Knowledge is discursive. It involves the moving from one act of cognition to another in a systemic 'chain' or 'train'. It involves our capacity to reason. However, just as information has its limits, so does reason. Whether we explain, argue, or narrate things, all discourse reaches a point of diminishing returns.

Discourse and reason knit observations, reports, analytic definitions, data and statements into lucid structures whose 'chains' persuade us, but only ever up to a point. All kinds of discursive knowledge, including scientific, technological, legal, political, social, and aesthetic knowledge, reach a limit wherein they cease to satisfy us. We are left feeling that the explanation or narration is not adequate, however elaborate it may be. This is the point at which arguments run out and proofs appear to be un-provable. At this juncture, knowledge stagnates. How then, when faced with such conditions, is knowledge advanced, developed or kick-started? The invigoration of knowledge happens because of acts of imagination. Imagination is synthetic, not analytic. It relies on intuition, analogy, and the ability of creating resemblances between things rather than drawing distinctions. Analogical-synthetic acts of imagination allow us to overcome the periodic stagnation of discursive systems of communication. This is because imagination plays the central role in audacious kinds of problem solving, visualization, projection, anticipation, and creative thought.

We all begin life in a blur. The most important thing that a child learns is to distinguish objects (things, words, events, deeds). The child learns how to differentiate 'mother', 'father', 'food', 'toy', 'flower', and 'car' from the primordial smear into which we are all born. Our first communicative acts are also our first way of systematizing the world for ourselves. These acts are principally acts of *distinction*. We use them to carve up the world, to differentiate and distinguish one object from another. With the passage of time individual acts of distinction grow more sophisticated. The same occurs also on the social level. Immanuel Kant, in the *Critique of Pure Reason*, made the point that acts of distinction tacitly rely on what is a more fundamental cognitive unity.[11] Every object that is differentiated out from the experiential smudge of sensibility has its own implicit spatial and temporal unity. Kant attributed that unity to the working of the human mind. The mind's synthesizing function gives every distinguishable thing its 'object-ness'. Consequently and paradoxically, analysis relies upon a prior synthesis. Conversely without the analytic capacity to differentiate, the world would appear to us as a blur of impressions, each swamping the other. To distinguish one impression from another, the mind differentiates impressions. Each impression or bundle of impressions has its own temporal and spatial unity. Thus each coheres as an object.

In growing up, a child learns to recognize distinct spatiotemporal objects, to name them and characterize them. The child comes to recognize, name and describe an innumerable number of such objects. Thus in order to make sense of the world, the child first has to make distinctions. Parents point to and name objects. Then those objects are given attributes. 'The flower is red'. The world in this way is broken up into discrete entities. Flowers are distinguished from cars, and cars from people. Qualities and characteristics of objects likewise are separable. Colour is distinguishable from shape. The child learns terms for the solidity, extension, motion, number, and figure of objects along with the names for their colour, taste, smell, and sound. Such learning is of inestimable value for the production of objects. Description is accompanied by the manipulation and manufacture of objects. Thus starts the child's long journey through the world of information. Names become ever more sophisticated, and attributes ever more abstract. The flower is broken down into stigma, style, stamen, filament, and petal; qualities are specified as beauty, symmetry, dynamism, and so on. The most sophisticated societies have specialized institutions that coin names and attribute qualities. Finer and finer distinctions are created. More and more terms, both arcane and popular, are generated. This coinage happens in laboratories and astronomical observatories, in newspapers and learned societies, and spontaneously in everyday conversations and discussions. Life is an endless process of naming and characterizing. What occurs in and through this process is human judgement. When we name and describe things, we judge them. We judge their everyday significance, their moral import, their aesthetic nature, their utility, their hedonistic quality, and so on. In doing so, we identify the parts and qualities of the world that are important to us. We also become ever-more capable of operating on, designing and producing objects.

11 Kant, *Critique of Pure Reason*, A108–109.

The most sophisticated descriptions assume that some part, element or quality of the world affects and changes some other part, element or quality. In some cases, this means that part, element or quality A *causes* part, element or quality B. The event 'photosynthesis' for example causes the tree (object) to grow (quality). Most descriptions of this type though are not strictly causal. Rather they suppose some transformative correlation between A and B. In some degree, A affects B. A is an agent that changes in some respect, though not necessarily always, the qualities of patient B. A thus determines, influences, shapes, governs, establishes, disturbs, moves or otherwise has an effect on, either regularly or intermittently, B. We name B, we characterize A. Having drawn such distinctions, the instinct of reason is to bring together what has been set apart. Thus while the world is apprehended as a massive array of distinct names and features, the human mind seeks to establish patterns of connection between the parts, elements and qualities that it has teased apart.

The child that absorbs information, and learns to make judgements, is also the child who asks questions. The most important of all questions is 'why?' Human beings not only name and describe the qualities of the world; they also search for explanations as to why the world is in the state that it is. 'The tree has grown,' the parent observes. 'Why?' asks the child. Answers to 'why' questions suppose that statements ('A *is* B' or 'A *affects* B') can be woven together. We arrange statements into explanatory discourses. We give reasons for our statements. We do this when we reason, argue, and recount. We deploy logic, rhetoric or narration, depending on the circumstance. Discourses, whether in the arts and sciences or in everyday life, are shortcuts. If we assert that 'all persons are mortal' and that 'John is a person', then we conclude that 'John is mortal' thereby avoiding the tiresome bother of considering every person individually and deciding on whether each one is mortal or immortal. But such short-circuits, helpful as they are, have first to come into being. There was a time when the statement 'all persons are mortal' did not exist. For it to exist, human beings had to be able to imagine themselves as human beings. The statement 'all persons are mortal' tacitly assumes that we can imagine a species. It supposes that we are not just part of a tribe (a genus) distinguishable from another tribe (a genus). Similarly it assumes that we are able to separate the species of human beings clearly from other animals and from the gods. This has not always been the case. To reach that point we had to doubly equate our being both with other human beings and with mortality. We are the creature who dies and yet who does not die. We share mortality with animals but possess a 'soul' that is immortal. While the term 'soul' is not commonly used today, the conception of 'being human' invariably conveys a sense of human works and acts (objects) that outlive their creators.[12] The point here is not to debate the nature of the human being or whether there is a common humanity.

12 Acts outlive their creators not only in virtue of memories and stories, as Hannah Arendt observed, but also because of the consequences of actions. While most acts are ephemeral or inconsequential, nonetheless a handful of acts have lasting consequences.

Rather it is simply to indicate that even seemingly commonplace principles of reasoning that allow us to draw rapid-fire conclusions from information to hand have their origins neither in reason nor description but in the imagination. The principles upon which reasoning 'rests' interpolate complex equations and metaphors that neither descriptions nor explanations can provide in their own right.

Descriptions and explanations of the world are very useful. We rely on them enormously. For many or most purposes, they work for us. But descriptions and explanations also fail us. It is then that we turn to that rarer cognitive faculty, the imagination. To understand the imagination, let us compare this faculty with the faculties of analysis and reason. The word 'comparison' itself is telling. It points to the instinct of cognition to compare A and B. At the level of description, comparison serves the function of distinction. It lifts each of us out of the primal blur. The 'cat' is distinguished from the 'mat' when the parent says to the child 'the cat is on the mat'. In this manner, the child is taught how to relate things together by distinguishing or separating them. Like many of the operations of the human mind, this is paradoxical. When the parent says to the child, 'the cat has destroyed the mat', a causal connection of a certain kind is made. The child learns that agents (a cat in this case) affect, influence or determine various patients in the world (a mat in this case). When the child hears this from the parent, it may very likely ask 'why did the cat do this?' This will elicit all kinds of realistic and fanciful explanations from the harassed parent. We ascend from curt explanations to expansive rationales and elaborations. Stories, parables, justifications, defences, arguments and debates emerge from the explanatory impulse. With sophistication come formal characteristics and structures of explanation. Logic, rhetoric, and narration all have forms both strict and flexible. But the world is more complex than can be comprehended either by descriptions or explanations. A child growing up in a hypothetical world of pure description/explanation would be intellectually impoverished. Take for instance the case of emotional education. If the child has taken to bullying the cat, the parent steps in and says 'stop treating the cat like a mat'. In that kind of simple statement we can observe the origin of the arts and sciences, and the via media of the imagination. The parent intervenes to stop the child's cruelty by telling the child that it is treating the cat '*as if*' it was a mat. The child (in effect) is walking all over the cat, figuratively and literally.

The imagination detects unlikely resemblances and paradoxical entities. It envisages 'horseless carriages' just as Aristotle envisaged a machine that moved itself. Of this was borne the 'auto-mobile'. The faculty for observing 'as if' is very powerful. We hear, see, taste, and feel 'as if' A was B. In analysis, we separate in order then to connect, for example, the colour red and the shape of the automobile. In the most sophisticated descriptions, we observe that one thing analytically distinguished (A) changes another thing so distinguished (B). The ignition of fuel sets the automobile in motion. In contrast, the primary function of the imagination is not to distinguish A and B. Rather it is to connect and fuse A and B. The most potent acts of imagination occur where the distinction between A and B is ordinarily thought to forbid a connection between the two. Most imaginings fall short of this though. Take the case of the 'red automobile'. The colour red in many cultures is a signifier of aggression. To 'see red' is a metaphor for anger. This probably has a part physiological basis. In the psychology of colour, red is a 'hot' colour that 'advances' toward us, rather than a 'cool' colour that 'retreats' from us. The string of metaphors, as distinct from the chain of reasoning, brings us to connect the vehicle that moves forward fast with the colour red. Even if there have been millions of red cars in existence, there was once the first red car. That paint job was imaginative, though only mildly so. The connection of red with speed, thrust, dash, momentum, and so on, has a long history, so that such a metaphor was hardly startling. The greatest metaphors, though, *are* startling. In and through them, the imagination draws together that which seems to be very far apart and yet somehow makes the connection plausible. Things that are thought unlikely to be connected (notably opposites) come, via the imagination, to have a probable or perceivable bond. Often this occurs in defiance of reason in the ordinary sense. It usually involves a tacit but nonetheless far-reaching re-description of the world.

The most powerful descriptions of the world are metaphors. Conversely, every description or re-description of the world is also, potentially, a practical intervention in the world. Description and action share two things in common. One is susceptibility to reason; the second is susceptibility to metaphor. Susceptibility is not the same as actuality. That means that reason and metaphor can transform what we say and do, but do not automatically do so. Reason and imagination are acts performed on propositions and deeds. Thus when we devise or decide our deeds, we are able to use practical reasoning to appraise what we are about to do. We do not always do this, but we sometimes do it. In operational decision making, we reason 'if, then'. If we do A, organize B, and follow step C, then we can achieve X or Y. Underpinning this are tacit syllogisms about the world. Yet what we plan rationally does not always happen in reality. When it doesn't, we can refine the inferential calculus of both our plans and our syllogisms. Notwithstanding that, all reasoning has a limit. We can go so far and no further when we reason practically. This is not just because the world is more complicated than we can comprehend in either our plans or our deductions, though that is partially true. It is also because operational 'if, then' reasoning depends tacitly on syllogisms whose major ('all birds have feathers') and minor premises ('penguins are birds') are also descriptions of the world and these descriptions can fail us. They can fail us in a variety of ways. Sometimes they cannot pass the test of induction. That all birds can fly is not true, nor is it true that all flying animals are birds. The ostrich and the penguin cannot fly. Bats are flying mammals.

But the human world is not only empirical; it is also metaphorical and symbolic. Thus we act and intervene and organize not only on the basis that A *is* B but also that A *is like* B. In such cases, B is not simply a description of A. Rather B resembles A. Such resemblances are paradoxical. They are most compelling not where A is most similar to B but where subject A and predicate B are most dissimilar and yet are still undeniably like each other. Thus, in this manner, human beings can have avian characteristics. From the Penguin character in the *Batman* cartoon to the Crow people, the American Indian Nation, to various basketball, skateboard and football players, to the participants in competitions for home-made gliders and human-powered air-craft, bird-men abound. This is not an exception nor is it unusual. The capacity for distinct entities to be both similar and antithetical lies at the core of human culture. It is the protean basis of mythology. Innumerable kinds of angel-horse, ape-man, human-demon, human-horse, dog-bird, bird-mammal, human-lizard, crocodile-fish, dog-wolf, fairy-dog hybrid creatures exist in mythologies under-pinned by elementary syn-antonymic thinking. Comparable thought structures are found in philosophy, literature and science. The syn-antonymic structure is the latent structure of imaginative thought and is a common thread in all acts of human creation. It is a durable structure that insinuates a specific kind of change at its heart, the *switch*, as for example between human and demon.[13] Imagination synthesizes antinomies.

Table 4.1 Three systems of communication

	Objectivation	**Reason**	**Imagination**
Communication System	Information	Explanation	Discovery
Communication Style	Analytic	Elaborative	Antonymic
Communication Media	Proposition	Argument	Analogy
Communication Method	Observation	Reason	Intuition
Communication Outcome	Differentiation	Inference	Resemblance
Communication Form	Report	Discourse	Wit
Communication Function	Distinction	Knowledge	Creation

Practical Reason: From 'If, Then' to 'As If'

Our most powerful descriptions thus do not simply characterize something but rather they indicate that one thing shares in the characteristics of another thing. It is not only that she smiles but that in addition her smile is like sunshine. The further apart and more dissimilar two things are, such as smiling and sunshine, the more evocative and compelling is the metaphor that draws attention to the way in which those two distant things resemble each other. The most interesting metaphors and symbols are those that make similar what is dissimilar. Edison, the greatest inventor of the nineteenth century, developed his idea for the telegraph on an analogy with a water system, of all things (Hughes 2004/1989: 77). In 1971, Bill Bowerman, the designer behind the Nike shoe, imagined three unrelated

13 The role of the switch in the literary imagination, specifically in the Shakespearean imagination, is discussed by Murphy (2009) and Davis (2007).

objects as one – the sole of a shoe, the waffle, and the tire, the basis of the waffle sole and a very successful business.

Like everything else in the world, attempts at metaphors and symbols can go awry or prove inadequate – just as our deductions, inductions, and plans do. All play a part in practical reason and each can fail. Warfare is a good example of the limits of practical reason. While in hindsight there was evidence that it was coming, no government predicted the Japanese attack on Pearl Harbor in December 1941. Even the preternaturally foresighted Winston Churchill told his Defence Committee as late as October 12 of that year that he 'did not believe that the Japanese would go to war with the United States …'. This was a rational assessment. It was based on the rational maxim that *if* Japan went to war with the United States, *then* Japan would be defeated. That maxim proved in deed to be true. The problem with rational maxims in war, though, is that an enemy may not be rational or else may not observe the same rational maxim as its opponent. In the case of Pearl Harbor, as one historian of the Second World War has put it, the views of the British and American governments in their assessments of Japan's war plans were 'distorted by logic'.[14] Both governments:

> possessed strong intelligence of an impending Japanese assault. Yet it remained hard to believe that the Tokyo regime would start a war with the United States that it could not rationally hope to win … (Hastings: 205).

Logic is very serviceable in practical matters. But it has its limits, all the same. It is at the limits of logic that the imagination comes into play. Imagination allows us to see that in a logical game an opponent may behave illogically.

Churchill was an exceptional war leader precisely because he could, and frequently did, qualify logic with acts of imagination. He possessed a remarkable imagination evident in his inexhaustible wit and literary facility.[15] Churchill was a master of the syn-antonymous political phrase. Endless numbers of these pepper the fifteen million words he composed in his lifetime. These voice everything from existential irony ('The glory of light cannot exist without its shadows') to military realism ('To try to be safe everywhere is to be strong nowhere') to historical

14 In a different context, Churchill himself remarked: 'We must beware of needless innovation, especially when guided by logic.' House of Commons, December 1942.

15 His close friend, the Oxford physicist, Professor Frederick Lindemann (Viscount Cherwell), observed of Churchill: 'All the qualities … of the scientist are manifested in him. The readiness to face realities, even though they contradict a favourite hypothesis; the recognition that theories are made to fit facts not facts to fit theories; the interest in phenomena and the desire to explore them; and above all the underlying conviction that the world is not just a jumble of events but there must be some higher unity, that the facts fit together. He has pre-eminently the synthetic mind which makes every new piece of knowledge fall into place and interlock with previous knowledge; where the ordinary brain is content to add each new experience to the scrap-heap, he insists on fitting it into the structure of the cantilever jutting out from the abyss of ignorance' (Jones 1993: 432).

paradox ('The longer you look back, the further you can look forward').[16] In so many things, including his profound grasp of the equipollent opposite, Churchill was a man out of his time. When the European tide turned to tyranny, he rallied the English language and its reservoirs of wit, irony and paradox against that tyranny. In the 1930s, he was thought to be all washed up. He was a curious fossil in the 'mass age'. Yet for all the self-adoration of that age, it proved itself less than imaginative. Almost all of the more self-consciously 'up-to-date' political figures of Churchill's time are today forgotten or else their names are associated much like stains with disastrous policies. Those of his peers who remarked on Churchill's language painted him as a brilliant archaism. He was known for his 'Elizabethan' phrases and his 'Augustan' rhetoric. His contemporaries were not wrong. Yet they misunderstood the significance of this. For syn-antonymous language communicates imagination.

Some of those who worked with Churchill at high levels in the hot-house of war-time government complained in their private diaries of Churchill's flights of fancy. Yet precisely fancy, Churchill's 'jets and gusts of image and association' (Nicholson 1940), accounts for why he became possibly the greatest political leader of the modern age. He is certainly in a tiny class of remarkable leaders of enduring importance such that though he roused and led a nation, his example is universal.[17] While he was at the helm of Britain at war, he acted on the stage of world history and ultimately became a model that transcended both his own nationality and his own era. As a war-time leader, Churchill was always careful to balance and check his fancy with the rationality of government. He had pet projects, but he made no major strategic decision during the war without the approval of his generals. Yet he did wear out his subordinates with an endless stream of ideas, which accounts for much of their grumbling. That in itself is striking. It suggests that compared with more prosaic reason, imagination has a greater wear and tear on the mind. Its aerial 'leaps', to use the common metaphor, have a gut-turning quality that seems as much as anything to elicit irritation in those contemplating the raw output of the imagination. In its tidy version, wrapped up as the history of great ideas, it is domesticated and safe. The historian places the imagination at a comfortable distance. Up close and personal, it is much more intimidating and confronting.

Imagination comes into its own when reason fails. Reason most often falters in times of emergency. By all of the dictates of reason and logic, Britain should have been defeated by Germany before the United States entered the war in late 1941. Britain's land armies were inferior to those of Germany. Its air force was smaller. British production of war materials lagged behind Germany's industrial powerhouse. Yet Britain was not defeated. This was because of Churchill's mystical

16 1. Churchill 1932: 8; 2. Churchill to Australian Prime Minister John Curtin, 19 January, 1942; 3. Address to the Royal College of Physicians, London, 2 March 1944.

17 Standard contemporary studies of Churchill include Jenkins (2001), Rose (2009), Johnson (2009), Keegan (2002), and Gilbert (1991).

faith in the destiny of his island nation. Such faith was not irrational, but neither was it just another species of rationality. Churchill was not a visibly religious person. Puritans and dogmatists irritated him. All the same, his writings are filled with a subtle kind of deist imagery. The appeal he made in one of his great speeches in 1940 to the 'sunlit uplands' is typical of this.[18] The image is domestic and majestic at the same time. Churchill's strategy to resist invasion successfully until America could be induced to enter the war was rational. But the faith he embodied, his faith in the fortitude of a people to resist and survive, trumped the even more daunting logical reality that Britain could not withstand invasion by a more powerful enemy. Churchill in 1940 told the British public that faith 'is given to help us and comfort us when we stand in awe before the unfurling scroll of human destiny' (2004: 234). In the abyssal years, from 1940 to 1942, faith defied what reason supposed – that defeat or surrender was in the offing. It is not the case that the Battle of Britain, the struggle for supremacy in British air space, was won by faith and not reason.[19] Rather it was won by a collective imagination that united faith and reason. Churchill, the personification of that imagination, paid scrupulous attention to the most practical and intimate details of war planning. He was a gifted organizer of systems, and was able to shake recalcitrant government ministries into action. Before the First World War as First Lord of the Admiralty, he gave the British navy a general staff planning capacity for the first time in its history. As Minister of Munitions in the First World War he radically overhauled the production logistics for provisioning the allied armies. He pioneered the idea of an air force and agitated for the development of the tank. All these efforts, like his later war prime ministership, relied on a mastery of operational logic. Yet they equally required imagination.

The invention of the tank neatly illustrates the relation between 'if, then' (logic) and 'as if' (imagination). As the nineteenth century advanced it became clearer that *if* science could be applied to the battlefield *then* warfare could be industrialized. That logical-operational frame was easy enough to state. Bringing it into reality, however, required imagination. Where logic is sequential or methodical in nature, imagination is syn-antonymic. Accordingly the tank was conceived as an 'armoured tractor'. It combined or hybridized the agricultural machine and the military function. Various conceptual and production prototypes of the tank appeared in the nineteenth and early twentieth centuries. James Cowen proposed the idea of a 'steam tractor with cannon' at the time of the Crimean War. The British government rejected it as impractical. The British engineer

---

18 'Hitler knows that he will have to break us in this Island or lose the war. If we can stand up to him, all Europe may be free and the life of the world may move forward into broad, sunlit uplands. But if we fail, then the whole world, including the United States, including all that we have known and cared for, will sink into the abyss of a new Dark Age made more sinister, and perhaps more protracted, by the lights of perverted science' (Churchill 2004: 229).

19 The Battle of Britain took place in the summer and autumn of 1940.

David Roberts in 1904 through 1909 developed various prototypes for the British army of a 'tractor on caterpillar track' though he never included artillery with it. The Austrian engineer Gunther Burnstyn took Roberts' idea a step further and in 1911 designed an 'armoured tracked vehicle'. The Austrian government declined to offer him a contract to put the machine into production. The Australian Lancelot De Mole proposed a 'chain rail vehicle' to the British War Office repeatedly through 1912–17. The French Colonel Jean-Baptiste Eugène Estienne in 1914 advocated for the 'armoured car' idea, the militarization of the automobile, which proved unsuitable for rough terrain. In 1914 Major Ernest Swinton, Britain's official war correspondent, argued an idea for an 'armoured tractor' first suggested to him by his friend the South African engineer Hugh Merriot. Swinton's proposal for the armed tracked vehicle was made to Lieutenant-Colonel Maurice Hankey, Secretary to Britain's War Council. Failing to interest the Army in it, Hankey sent a memorandum to the Committee of Imperial Defence, on which he also served as Secretary, where it caught the attention of the First Lord of the Admiralty, Winston Churchill.

Churchill, who spent a life-time ignoring departmental boundaries, convinced the Prime Minister of the day, H.H. Asquith, of the merits of the idea. In the face of the continuing disinterest of the Army, Churchill created a 'Landships Committee' in his own department that set the practical development of the tank in motion. Churchill's coinage, the 'landship', was yet another classic antonymic-cum-analogical step on the road to the practical invention of the tank. Churchill's proposal to Asquith contained the core conceptual elements of the tank as a working artefact: an industrial tractor using the caterpillar system and incorporating an armoured bullet proof shelter and guns (Gilbert 1991: 293). In February 1915 Churchill commissioned the Director of Naval Construction, Eustace D'Eyncourt, to design a land-ship, dubbed for secrecy purposes a 'water-closet' and then a 'water-tank'. While Churchill was not responsible for the genesis of the tank-idea, he was responsible for its final development. After the war, the Royal Commission on War Inventions concluded that 'it was primarily due to the receptivity, courage and driving force' of Churchill that the idea of using the tank as an instrument of war 'was converted into a practical shape' (299). Churchill's receptivity and drive were a function of his imagination. He had no difficulty in the slightest picturing the combination of military weaponry and industrialized agricultural machinery, or in imagining the usefulness of such a machine in crossing rough terrain and trenches. In a memorandum to the British Cabinet late in 1916, while he was serving as an officer on the Western Front, Churchill wrote memorably (with allusions to Homer) of a 'collective metal shield' pushed along on a caterpillar capable of traversing obstacles, ditches and trenches. That same period, keen to discover any way he could of shortening the war, found him also speculating about 'torpedoes fired from seaplanes' (336).

The Syn-antonymous Imagination

The imagination at its peak is syn-antonymous. It interpolates opposites. It forges connections and analogies, bonds and metaphors between things that seem on face value so far apart. If one looks at the great period of twentieth-century science, dating from 1900 to 1930, it is one of the notable characteristics of the period that the syn-antonymous imagination is given free reign. This reminds us of the similarly syn-antonymous era of the High Renaissance, even though its twentieth-century counterpart was much shorter lived. European science between 1900 and 1930 is filled with marvellous ideas about space-time (Einstein), matter-energy (Einstein), position-momentum (Heisenberg), and wave-particle (Bohr). This distantly mirrors the flood of paradoxical imagery that courses through Shakespeare's writings. Whether it is reflecting on the 'heavenly comforts of despair' or observing that 'in poison there is physic', Shakespeare repeatedly, doggedly, and seemingly effortlessly, draws on the quantum nature of the imagination.[20] Particular historical epochs encourage such thinking. Shakespeare lived in a time of fierce imaginative contrariety. Donne, Montaigne, Paracelsus, Pico, Bacon, Castiglione and many others approached the world in a similar manner. To assert that by human deeds 'sweetest things turn sourest' was natural.[21] In such locutions we reach the limits of language. We communicate what is beyond communication. In doing so, we arrive at the ultimate vocation of communication.

Understandably what is ultimate in communication is rare. Certainly it is rare for communicative contrariety to become a pervasive feature in art and science. This is what makes the late Renaissance so creative. We see a short burst of the same in the early twentieth century. Then it peters out. The syn-antonymous imagination retreats after 1930. The tyrannies of the 1930s signal this retreat rather sharply. It is striking that the final entry in Alan Lightman's collection of outstanding twentieth-century science documents dates from 1972. Even allowing for a certain passage of time before great ideas are broadly recognized, the record of the latter two-thirds of the twentieth century is thin. Lightman's collection includes 25 papers.[22] Four are from the first decade of the century, four from the second decade, and five from the 1920s. Then the numbers decline: three from the 1930s, one from the 1940s, two from the 1950s, five from the 1960s, one from the 1970s, and none after that.[23] We have reaped the harvest of the seeds that we have sewn. Despite its omnipresence, information technology failed to match the depth of innovation on

20 *Measure for Measure*, IV.iii, 109–11; *2 Henry IV*, I.i, 137.

21 Shakespeare, Sonnet 94.

22 One of the visible losses occasioned by the age of the dictators was the decline of German-language science. In Lightman's 2006 collection of leading science papers, there are 25 papers in total including seven originally published in German. All but one of the German language papers dates from the period 1900 to 1927 (xv).

23 Further evidence of the long-term decline of the arts and sciences after 1930 is discussed in Murphy, Marginson, Peters: 87–138.

the Promethean scale of electricity or the automobile (Cowen 2011; Murphy 2010a, 2010b). The period between 1990 and 2010, the era of the knowledge economy, was dismal. In real terms the returns on each research investment dollar shrank. Telecommunications, pharmaceuticals, advanced materials, alternate energy and bio-technology all failed to fulfill their 1990s promises.[24] Without the impetus of antonymous discovery, team-based big science suffered as much as individualistic fine art did in the dismal post-modern era.

The economist Tyler Cowen (2011) suggests that this declining rate of return is of an even longer historical nature. He argues that

> … it was easier for the average person to produce an important innovation in the nineteenth century than in the twentieth century … Meaningful innovation has become harder, and so we must spend more money to accomplish real innovations, which means a lower and declining rate of return on technology.

---

24 'Think back to 1998, the early days of the dot-com bubble. At the time, the news was filled with reports of startling breakthroughs in science and medicine, from new cancer treatments and gene therapies that promised to cure intractable diseases to high-speed satellite Internet, cars powered by fuel cells, micromachines on chips, and even cloning. These technologies seemed to be commercializing at "Internet speed", creating companies and drawing in enormous investments from profit-seeking venture capitalists – and ordinarily cautious corporate giants. Federal Reserve Chairman Alan Greenspan summed it up in a 2000 speech: "We appear to be in the midst of a period of rapid innovation that is bringing with it substantial and lasting benefits to our economy." … With the hindsight of a decade, one thing is abundantly clear: The commercial impact of most of those breakthroughs fell far short of expectations – not just in the US but around the world. No gene therapy has yet been approved for sale in the US. Rural dwellers can get satellite Internet, but it's far slower, with longer lag times, than the ambitious satellite services that were being developed a decade ago. The economics of alternative energy haven't changed much. And while the biotech industry has continued to grow and produce important drugs – such as Avastin and Gleevec, which are used to fight cancer – the gains in health as a whole have been disappointing, given the enormous sums invested in research … There's no government-constructed "innovation index" that would allow us to conclude unambiguously that we've been experiencing an innovation shortfall. Still, plenty of clues point in that direction … [The] stock index that tracks the pharmaceutical, biotech, and life sciences companies in the Standard & Poor's 500-stock index dropped 32% from the end of 1998 to the end of 2007, after adjusting for inflation. The information technology index fell 29%. To pick out two major companies: The stock price of Merck declined 35% between the end of 1998 and the end of 2007, after adjusting for inflation, while the stock price of Cisco Systems was down 9%. Consider another indicator of commercially important innovation: the trade balance in advanced technology products. The Census Bureau tracks imports and exports of goods in 10 high-tech areas, including life sciences, biotech, advanced materials, and aerospace. In 1998 the US had a $30 billion trade surplus in these advanced technology products; by 2007 that had flipped to a $53 billion deficit. Surprisingly, the US was running a trade deficit in life sciences, an area where it is supposed to be a leader' (Mandel 2009).

This is consistent with the observation in Murphy 2010a and 2010b that the peak of European science and technology (and also the arts and humanities) is 1870, a point made separately for science and technology by Cowen. Cowen is correct when he observes that major technology gains were made in the nineteenth century principally by amateurs while increasingly smaller gains are made today by institutionalized experts. Even then, Cowen notes that we have exhausted the mid-range gains made by expanding the education systems that produced the first generations of highly-qualified scientists and technologists. Underlying this is the more basic fact elucidated by Cowen that most contemporary innovations bring only slight additional benefits to the majority of the population quite in contrast to the waves of innovations from the 1880s to the 1940s such as electricity, electric lights, automobiles, aeroplanes, pharmaceuticals, mass production, the phonograph, tape recorder and radio. It might be concluded from this that after the creative peak of 1870 a series of applications and elaborations of creative science occurred through to the 1940s. Beyond that point the long-term effects of a declining collective imagination begin to become clearer to the observer. Both the rationalism and the irrationalism of the twentieth century play a part in the drying up of innovation. The innovation lobby also plays its part, because it believes it can detach innovation from basic discovery. Once creation falters innovation declines or else it becomes directed to frivolous ends. Once this happens, income and wealth creation, which is dependent on ever-more inventive waves of industrialization, begins in a relative sense to shrink.

The title of the most famous twentieth-century work on the method of science, Karl Popper's *Logic of Scientific Discovery*, signifies part of what went wrong. It was first published in 1934 as the *Logik der Forschung* at the very turning point when the short period of titanic twentieth-century science ebbed. This book, along with the rest of Popper's works, is a brilliant statement of the power of discursive rationality set against the tacit background of tyranny. However, discovery is not discourse. It does not matter whether discourse is conceived as refutation or as justification. Either way, discovery cannot be explained in terms of explanation. A discovery precedes logic. It comes before argument. It is an artefact of intuition or insight. It is not communicated through explanatory forms, irrespective of whether those forms either serve to defend the truth of propositions or criticize their fallibility. The propositions of discovery are ingenious contradictions more than anything. They are true and false, positive and negative, affirmative and critical in the same instance. They are, as Neils Bohr put it, 'complementary', or, as Bohr's sometime assistant Heisenberg conceived it, 'uncertain'. In a word, they are syn-antonymous.

The crises of the early 1930s and the rise of the European dictators were part of a larger crisis of the collective imagination. The tyrannies caused a fierce effacing of imagination. But once their paroxysm was expended, other more prosaic sanitizations occurred. Reason recovered its faculties after the totalitarian era but less so did the imagination. The embarrassing epistemologies of the post-modern decades (1970–2000) signalled both a widespread unease that reason was not enough and a simultaneous failure to specify the other of reason in other than irrational terms. The net consequence of this was an over reliance on pedestrian reason. This proved perfectly proficient for many purposes excepting when insights of imagination were required. This begs the question, though – why is it that reason is not enough? The answer, simply put, is that reason supports or refutes conjectures but it does not produce them. If profound conjectures that touch on the ambidexterity of reality are not generated, then, although science will continue to rationally extrapolate from known premises, the production of new constructive axioms and thus new rich prolific fields of inquiry will elude it.

There is a second reason that reason is not enough. This second consideration points to reason's self-contradictory propensity to undermine itself. The voice of reason is normally accompanied by an implicit claim of universal validity.[25] In practice, though, there is almost always a second and dissenting voice of reason in any discursive situation that in response says 'Not me, I disagree'. The philosophical character of reason has great difficulty reconciling the fact that whatever courts assent encounters dissent and whatever begins in dissent invariably makes statements that demand assent. The demand for assent has many overtones. Some of those overtones are distinctly domineering. However it is articulated, reason always makes a truth claim upon others, and, as a claim, it bears the unmistakable character of an 'ought, should or must'. It is difficult to ignore even the most courteous claim to truth. A claim demands something of others. Even the politest request to assent is a type of pressure. Often the insistence on 'what is reasonable' can be overbearing.[26] Conversely, though, the dissenter who dissents

---

25 This is a point elaborated by an epistemological tradition that runs from Kant's *Critique of Judgement* to Habermas' *Theory of Communicative Action*.

26 A classic example of this is the post-modern kitsch science of 'global warming' and its supercilious claim, made in the face of many well-informed and serious critics, that it was a 'settled science' underpinned by an unimpeachable 'consensus' of views. Such rhetorical tactics neatly illustrate the way in which reason readily becomes haughty. The flip side of imperious reason is a kind of reason that is credulous. One of the results of stupid reason is moral panics. This is what the millennial-era frenzy over global warming proved to be. As William Happer, the Cyrus Fogg Brackett Professor of Physics at Princeton University, observed (2011), climate politics became a climate crusade, which had '… much in common with the medieval crusades … with true believers, opportunists, cynics, money-hungry governments, manipulators of various types, and even children's crusades …'.

'Let me summarize how the key issues appear to me, a working scientist with a better background than most in the physics of climate. CO_2 really is a greenhouse gas and, other things being equal, adding CO_2 to the atmosphere by burning coal, oil, and natural gas will modestly increase the surface temperature of the earth. Other things being equal, doubling the CO_2 concentration, from our current 390 ppm to 780 ppm will directly cause about one degree Celsius warming. At the current rate of CO_2 increase in the atmosphere 'about 2 ppm per year' it would take about 195 years to achieve this doubling. The combination of a slightly warmer earth and more CO_2 will greatly increase the production of food, wood,

against imperious pressures to assent in the name of some kind of standpoint outside of universal reason (usually some kind of irrationalism, however it may be dressed up) simply inverts the game of pressure without eliminating it. The voice of what is 'not universal' either presumes the assent of others or else dismisses such assent as irrelevant: either way this is an arrogation that is the first step on the royal road to dictatorship. Under these conditions, criticism and critique can end up generating the most despicable kinds of punitive orthodoxies.

The philosophical character of the imagination in contrast to that of reason assumes an ironic standpoint. Imagination treats assent and dissent as equipollent. Conceived from the always incongruous standpoint of the imagination, dissent generates assent and assent creates dissent. From a certain perspective, these opposites are identical. The imagination is syn-antonymous. It makes a side-step around the often suffocating pressures of reason, irrespective of whether reason is confirmatory or critical. The imagination conjectures. It does so by conjecturing a paradoxical union of opposites. This might take the form of mythological bird-men, technological land-ships or the time-space and position-momentum of the physicist. At the point when the cognitive capacity to make opposites identical dries up, the sciences, as much as the arts, begin to falter. That is what in retrospect we see happens in the latter two-thirds of the twentieth century. The tyrannical era of the 1930s in Europe is a visible turning point. The restoration of reason after the defeat of the tyrannies though proves to be no augury of the imagination. The slackening of imagination becomes apparent by 1970. The post-modern era lasting from 1970 to 2000 was lacklustre in both the arts and the sciences.

---

fibre, and other products by green plants, so the increased CO_2 will be good for the planet, and will easily outweigh any negative effects. Supposed calamities like the accelerated rise of sea level, ocean acidification, more extreme climate, tropical diseases near the poles, etc. are greatly exaggerated'. …

What happened in the period of climate alarmism was 'the co-option of climate science by politics, ambition, greed, and what seems to be a hereditary human need for a righteous cause'. …

'What better cause than saving the planet, especially if one can get ample, secure funding at the same time? Huge amounts of money are available from governments and wealthy foundations for climate institutes and for climate-related research. Funding for climate studies is second only to funding for biological sciences. Large academic empires, prizes, elections to honorary societies, fellowships, consulting fees and other perquisites go to those researchers whose results may help "save the planet." Every day we read about some real or contrived environmental or ecological effect "proved" to arise from global warming. The total of such claimed effects now runs in the hundreds, all the alleged result of an unexceptional century-long warming of less than one degree Celsius. Government subsidies, loan guarantees, and captive customers go to green companies. Carbon-tax revenues flow to governments. As the great Russian poet Pushkin said in his novella *Dubrovsky*, "If there happens to be a trough, there will be pigs". Any doubt about apocalyptic climate scenarios could remove many troughs'.

A small resurgence of intellectual energy took place in the 1980s (Murphy 2010a, 2010b). But this exhausted itself quickly by the end of the decade. One comical sign of this exhaustion was the subsequent rise of national research management schemes in many countries. These schemes were an unconscious response to falling real levels of discovery. It is as if the bureaucratic auditing of research performance became a satirical substitution for audacious research and a palliative for latent national anxieties that high-level discovery in the arts and sciences was faltering. The audits contrived various measures of quality and quantity of current research produced in near-contemporaneous five or seven year spans. This was a meaningless exercise as long as the current output was not compared with historic output. The drill functioned simultaneously as amnesia about the past and a lightning rod of national anxiety that the overall quality of inquiry of the present, and the per capita quantity of that inquiry, was worse than that of the past. A sober look in the long rear view mirror suggests that indeed it was.

In the sciences the last truly remarkable leap in the twentieth century was the discovery of the significance of DNA. The story of this discovery begins in 1944 at the Rockefeller Institute for Medical Research when Oswald Avery with Colin MacLeod and Maclyn McCarty drew the connection between Deoxyribonucleic acid (DNA) and genes. The researchers asked and answered the question – what was the chemical means of inducing 'changes' in organisms that could be transmitted as 'hereditary characters'. The key presupposition was the following: 'Biologists have long attempted by chemical means to induce in higher organisms predictable and specific changes which thereafter could be transmitted in a series as hereditary characters' (Avery, MacLeod, McCarty: 137). What this encapsulated was the syn-antonymic idea that in *constancy* (hereditary transmission) lay *change* (variable traits). The constancy-change antinomy was later flattened out in various ways. Notably it was over-determined by the then-popular mid-twentieth century metaphors of language and grammar. The Columbia University biochemist Erwin Chargaff much later recalled that, when he read Avery's experimental results, he concluded that these were 'the beginning of the grammar of biology'. This was 'the first text of a new language' (Chargaff: 639). A language can be decoded and thus understood if one knows its structural characteristics such as its grammar.

The structural form of the chemical media for transmitting inherited characteristics was deciphered in 1953 when Francis Crick and James Watson working in the Cavendish Laboratory at Cambridge isolated the double helix structure of DNA.[27] The key insight was to think of DNA as a structure, 'as if' chemistry was a kind of architecture and the chemist was a three-dimensional model builder (Watson 2007: 87–109). The forte of Crick and Watson was to apply, with inspired truculence, the methods of physics and chemistry to biology, violating discipline boundaries for the sake of a much more productive intellectual duplexity

27 'We wish to suggest a structure …' are the opening words and thematic focus of Watson and Crick's historic article 'A Structure for Deoxyribose Nucleic Acid' (1953).

(188). Maurice Wilkins, at King's College London, using X-ray crystallography, proposed that DNA had a regular, periodic (crystalline) structure and that this structure was organized as helices, curves in three-dimensional space. The helical assemblies were either two or three intertwined chains bonded to each other (87, 99). Crick and Watson completed this structural approach, by concluding the exact shape of DNA. Linus Pauling and Max Delbrück had proposed that copying of genetic molecules would involve structures of complementary shapes. Rosalind Franklin had considered, and then dismissed, a model involving molecular symmetry. Crick and Watson's acceptance of the symmetrical model idea led them to build a three-dimensional stereo-chemical model of complementary, symmetrical, pairs of hydrogen atoms organized in curving, spiralling chains that run in opposite directions – the double helix.

The elements of this structure – periodicity, helices, oppositions, symmetry and complementarity – were all common-place in the architectonic structures of nature. The structural model of Crick and Watson was later part-replaced by what subsequently became known as 'decoding' the genetic information 'encoded' in DNA. What caused the emergence of this 'life is like information' metaphor is difficult to say with any precision. The key role that message decoding (cryptography) played in the Second World War may have created a tacit frame of mind for such an equation. The popularity of language as a mid-century model for philosophy may have played a background role also. Interestingly though, the metaphor of the semiotic code does not appear in Avery's or Crick and Watson's original papers.[28] The analogy with code-cracking is a later addition. Rather at the heart of the two pioneering papers is a much more interesting intellectual contrariety. This is the paradox of bio-chemical changes that transmit structure (characteristics) and conversely a bio-chemical (helix) structure that causes alterations.

Beware of metaphors. They mislead as much as they lead. Avery and Crick and Watson's paradox of structure-alteration is profound. It plumbed the mystery of life. Less can be said for the equation of life with an information code. The twentieth century was addicted to linguistic analogies. The idea of the 'information society' became wildly popular at the close of the century. But in truth these semiotic-information metaphors were rather lame. They betrayed the diminished aspirations of a less than fertile age. That age was more often prosaic than creative. Creation is ineffable. While its metaphors are of necessity an artefact of language, they are also of necessity an artefact that points *beyond* language. In symbols or words they must paradoxically hint at what cannot be said. Thus if effective they are not metaphors of information or discourse at all. On the contrary they intimate what cannot be stated, whether in description, analysis or rational elaboration. In many ways an act of intellectual creation will always be elusive. This is not because it is irrational but rather because it happens so swiftly, in a flash.

28 The Coldspring reprint of the original Crick and Watson *Nature* paper has much later annotations that introduce the terms information and code. See: http://www.exploratorium.edu/origins/coldspring/ideas/printit.html.

It is never explained. Often it is barely stated. The imagination lies on the border between the discursive and the non-discursive regions of human understanding. Some understandings we state. Some we elaborate. The deepest understanding is the most difficult to put into words or symbols. Not everyone is a Churchill or a Heisenberg. They are rarities. Nonetheless the imagination and its means of communication are not rare. Wit, irony and paradox are the common possession of the species. They are not late arriving. What makes human beings 'human' is their capacity to think ambidextrously through an endless series of couplets that compound reality and fiction, experience and anticipation, and so on. Because of the capacity for contrary cognition, for thought that productively interpolates contradiction, incongruity, and irony, human beings can reflect, dissemble, satirize, strategize, and parody, in short, they are able to imagine. In and through this lies the path to invention and discovery.

PART II
Collective Creation

Chapter 5
Art

Historians have noticed, all down the centuries, one peculiarity in the English people which has cost them dear. We have always thrown away after a victory the greater part of the advantages we gained in the struggle. The worst difficulties from which we suffer do not come from without. They come from within. They do not come from the cottages of the wage-earners. They come from a peculiar type of brainy people always found in our country, who, if they add something to its culture, take much from its strength. Our difficulties come from the mood of unwarrantable self-abasement, into which we have been cast by a powerful section of our intellectuals. They come from the acceptance of defeatist doctrines by a large proportion of our politicians. But what do they offer but a vague internationalism, a squalid materialism, and the promise of Utopias?

Winston Churchill, 'England', Speech to the Royal Society of St. George, London, 24 April 1933

Museum Cultures

In 1971 George Steiner declared America a museum culture.[1] He might as well have pronounced it dead. America, he judged, collected the intellectual treasures of other societies, put them on display and stored them away. Whilst it adapted and extended the great works of culture it was not ultimately responsible for the acts of creation that set them in motion in the first place. This was the European kettle calling the American pot black. Truth told, by the time Steiner wrote his essay, Europe and America had both become museum cultures. The definitive turning point was the 1930s. The period 1900–1930 was an era of some major work in the arts and sciences. It fell below the peaks of the eighteenth and nineteenth centuries and far below the epoch of the European Renaissance. Nonetheless, the contributions of Bohr and Braque and their ilk remain impressive. There were echoes of this greatness in the 1950s and 1960s. Crick and Watson, Pollock and Rothko, Hayek and Derrida had their merits. Yet they still fall short compared with Einstein and Faraday, Kant and Hegel, Turner and Cézanne. Or perhaps

1 'Creation of absolutely the first rank – in philosophy, in music, in much of literature, in mathematics – continues to occur outside the American milieu. It is at once taken up and intelligently exploited, but the 'motion of the spirit' has taken place elsewhere, amid the enervation of Europe, in the oppressive climate of Russia. There is, in a good deal of American intellectual, artistic production (recent painting may be a challenging exception) a characteristic near-greatness, a strength just below the best. Could it be that the United States is destined to be the "museum culture"?' (Steiner 1971: 111).

more precisely they are the end, not the beginning of something. The view of contemporaries at the time was that 1968 was the harbinger of an intellectual renaissance. But in retrospect the 1968 revolt flooded the engine of creation rather than re-ignited it. By 1970, what was in train was the post-modern age of the museum.

The post-modern era (1970–2000) did not invent the museum. Nor was it even the first age in which the museum subsumed the functions of church and temple. Rather this was an era of larger, more pretentious, more enveloping museums in which the mountainous accumulation of insignificance replaced the arduous making of meaning. By the end of the period, the world was awash with museums. From art to ethnography, terror to photography, agriculture to aquatics, they spawned. This was a world in which the mechanics of cultural creation was overawed by the machinations of the cultural industries. Museums, galleries and universities produced a new class of place-hunting, status-obsessed culture bureaucrats whose job was to collect, archive, arrange, catalogue, promote and transmit minutiae.[2] From the sense-making whole, culture was transformed into a kind of glorified bric-a-brac. Some of this was populist; some of it was inscrutable. All of it was superficial. Important works and objects bobbed around indiscriminately in a sea of trivia and finer points.

Just as in the universities of the period endless minor disciplines, sub-disciplines, and sub-sub-disciplines proliferated, with short shelf-lives, devoted to marginal often pointless studies, the world of museums produced ever-more arcane variants. Of these, none perhaps was stranger than the atomic museums. These museums memorialize the age of nuclear weapons (Gerster 2009). Yet like most of their ilk they raise as many questions about the nature of memorials as they settle. The atomic museums shared two general problems of post-modern culture. They confused trivia with significance and trauma with culture. In the American version of the atomic museum, curators are coy about the human consequence of the atom bomb. They direct attention to the details of atomic technology instead. In Japan, the reverse is true. Atomic museums there are preoccupied with the human suffering caused by the destruction of Hiroshima and Nagasaki. All of that is perfectly understandable. Yet the approach in both cases creates lack-lustre museums. Even when human suffering is displayed relentlessly, audiences do not necessarily engage with it in a way that would leave its mark on the human soul. The latter effect – *viz.*, the transformation of the human soul – is a rare one. Its medium is art. The aesthetic dimension is what gives meaning to human experience. It shapes experience in such a way that allows human beings to make sense of the grievous, joyous and momentous events in their lives. All human beings respond to the aesthetic dimension. It is a part of their species-being, the anthropology of humankind. We are an aesthetic species. Human artefacts,

2 Daniel Bell called them the *culturati*, 'the distribution sector of cultural production, for whom the shock of the old has become the chic of the new' (*The Cultural Contradictions of Capitalism*, 1976/1996).

societies and institutions are shaped aesthetically. That shaping imparts meaning. It enables human beings to make sense of their world.

All seasoned visitors to museums, not least of all those who visit art museums, will recognize how many of them lack this aesthetic dimension to a surprising degree. The museums that grew up in response to the age of sublime destruction are no exception. While they are sobering, they are also, for the most part, artless. The museums of war, atrocity, atomic weaponry, and holocaust all tell stories – stories of suffering, evil, heroism, and hell. But it is not so evident that those stories, despite their dramatic provenance, actually engage deeply or in prolonged ways with the human imagination. To create an aesthetic effect, museums often try and overwhelm us. An institution which does that seeks to subject us to the artistic sublime. It invites us to look upon the over-awing power of technology or human suffering or something else that is terrible or mighty. Yet often such strategies do not work. Visitors come and go, and are not that moved. Blockbuster exhibitions in art museums are a case in point. They promise to overwhelm but they often leave audiences feeling under-whelmed or cheated. This is so not least because, after more than two centuries of wide exposure to it, everyone is immune to the shock-and-awe tactics of the aesthetic sublime. From aesthetic modernism to movie special effects, we have learnt to be jaded by impressive spectacles.

Often when sublime effects fail, administrators turn to the conceit of storytelling. Museums tacitly rely on models of literature, history and the chronicle as organizing principles for exhibitions. They justify this in the name of something called 'the education of the public'. Yet such story telling rarely succeeds when it has to deal with blistering, lacerating historical experience. How do you tell the story of Germans and Jews – or Poles and Jews, Americans and Japanese, Japanese and Koreans, Serbs and Croats – such that it resonates with each party simultaneously? How do you tell a universal story? In fact, in practice, universal stories are not told. Instead, most museum stories are kitsch. They either are official kitsch, nationalist kitsch, moralizing kitsch, or post-modern kitsch. Official kitsch demands that difficult subjects are side-stepped, nationalist kitsch is risibly one-eyed, moralizing kitsch incites finger-pointing about 'goodies' and 'baddies' whilst post-modern kitsch simply inverts the order of those 'goodies' and 'baddies'. There are a large number of kinds of kitsch, but they all share a common trait. They are all artless. Consequently, they fail to generate meaning or, more precisely, they generate pseudo-meaning. So Americans visiting Hiroshima feel an instant but equally short-lived penitence in the face of relentlessly explicit depictions of Japanese suffering – while Japanese visitors feel irritation at the relentless expectations that they identify (eyes downcast) with the unveiled representation of untold morbidity. All exhibitions of the sublime powers and megalithic horrors of modernity run into a common problem. Audiences switch off. They switch off because the exhibits they view cannot generate sustainable meanings, no matter what air of significance they may be couched in. No amount of self-important patina or earnest signposting can create meaning.

Only serious art can do this. This is art that colludes with religion, philosophy and science, and that is fortified with metaphysics.

Art fortified with metaphysics is art that is not kitsch. Serious art does two things that kitsch fails to do. It is always double-coded and it is always inexplicit. The difference between art proper and kitsch is like the difference between erotic imagery and pornography. Erotic images play endlessly on the simultaneous doubling of dressed and undressed, coy and frank, passive and active. Pornographic images in contrast are explicit. They leave nothing to the imagination in the specific sense that the imagination, which is fundamental to art, is uncanny. The imagination constantly conjugates what we ordinarily think of as separate and distinct – whether it is clothing and nakedness, or sadness and happiness. Nineteenth-century critical opinion, later helped along by the popular sensation caused by the theft of the painting from the Louvre Museum in 1911, elevated Leonardo da Vinci's *Mona Lisa* to its current standing as the world's 'greatest work of art'. Doubtless there will come a day when it will lose this cult status – a status which is a kind of kitsch, a reflex of the infantile 'must have', 'must see'. Notwithstanding that, the regard for the painting is warranted in the simple sense that da Vinci's painting engages, as any decent work of art does, in an act of doubling. It communicates an enigma. Mona Lisa's smile is happy and sad at the same time. That is what art does. It conveys mysteries that produce meanings. The mystery element is the conjugations of opposites. The artistic and imaginative capacity of humankind fuses together what ordinarily is set asunder. In that fusion, or out of that fusion, arises meaning.

Art does what the artless museum fails to do. It is able to combine the imagery of victory and defeat, armed might and civilian causality, virtuoso combat and impersonal warfare in the same conjugation. This is difficult to do. This is why serious artworks, like serious cultural institutions, are rare. Even in great museums, only a handful of the works on display merit sustained attention. We constantly cite Greek tragic drama and Shakespearian historical drama for good reason – they deal with unbearable divisions without resorting to artless caricature. Tasteless triumphalism, stage villainy, moralizing self-abasement, disingenuous exculpation, sanctimonious anti-heroism, self-flagellating abjection, and national rage – all are to be avoided. For this reason, drama might be a better metaphor for the aesthetics of a great museum rather than literature or sublime effects. This is because drama interpolates competing forces. A dramatic character cannot be plausible without a formidable opponent or antagonist – even if in practice most drama fails on that score, as most attempts at art fail to command the doubling that lies at the heart of creation.

Living in a Kitsch World

Doubling mirrors something that is fundamental in the nature of the human species. In her philosophical anthropology, Agnes Heller (2005) pointed out that all human beings without exception, in being born into the world, confront a dual inheritance that is part genetic and part socio-cultural. For each human being, the experience of the genetic and social aprioris is both unique and universal. Every human being confronts this dual inheritance, but each one of them does so in their own way. The human experience is thus filled with double meanings. Each human being must cope with the gap between society and nature, and genes and culture, and also the gap between their own self and others, and ultimately between I and me, the self's own doubling as it negotiates between nature and culture, and itself and other selves. As Heller observes, human beings cope with the gap between society and nature by laughing and crying. Laughter and tears release momentarily the tension that is felt in virtue of being caught between the two aprioris, the two conditions of being human.

There are many forms of laughter and crying. Laughter can be kind or cruel, conformist or subversive, sceptical or twee, scatological or polite. There are tears of rage, sadness, fear, sorrow, melancholy, and depression. In their most elementary forms, laughter and crying are affects. In *A Theory of Feelings*, Heller notes that affects are very distant cousins of animal instincts. They are triggered by external stimuli and have a quasi-compulsory character. Affects include rage, fear, shame, disgust, gaiety, shock, curiosity and sexual attraction. Affects are paralleled by drives that include sex, thirst and hunger. Such drives or appetites, like the impulsions to reduce fatigue and pain, are triggered by internal biological stimuli. Yet human beings also have a very curious relation to this biological impulsion. This is because they stand mid-way between culture and nature. Thus they utilize fantasy to satisfy drives.[3] Ever the contrary species, they will also seek out the very thing that their drives compel them to avoid (Heller 1979: 73). Human beings often live dangerously, and will even voluntarily starve to death in certain

3 Fantasy is not the same as the imagination. The distinction between fantasy and imagination is well made by both Cornelius Castoriadis and Roger Scruton in their respective philosophical theories of the imagination. Scruton points out that, in the case of fantasy, affect-feelings are real but the way of satisfying those feeling or releasing the tensions connected to them is via fantasy objects that are not real. In the case of the imagination in contrast, neither the feelings connected to the imagination nor the objects that satisfy those feelings or abate them are real. Paradoxically, though, the very fact that feelings and satisfactions may be played out entirely in the imagination is very useful for creating real-life scenarios precisely because the feelings that a person imagines are separable from their own drives and affects, and from their own life. In simple terms, the imagination (as against fantasy) is objective. That makes the imagination very powerful in creating new things that have efficacy in the world.

circumstances.[4] This hints at something that becomes increasingly important in the structure of human feelings as they mature. This is their ambidextrous nature. As the cognitive component of these feelings grows, so does the degree and importance of this Janus-like malleability. The fundamental cause of this ontological ambidexterity is the human condition of being located in-between nature and society.

In ontogenetic terms, affects and drives belong to new-born, childish or juvenile feeling states. Feelings dominated by cognition characterize human maturity. None of those states though are actually age-specific, as adult human conduct can be easily dominated by affects and drive-type behaviours. Cognitive feelings stand to drives and affects as love does to sex, taste does to appetite, intuition does to curiosity, sorrow or regret does to sadness, and intellectual joking does to nervous, tittering and embarrassed effusions of laughter by those who have not yet quite grown up. Feelings associated with prudence, judgement, choice, deliberation, guessing, expectation, certainty, doubt, liking and aversion – and so on – play larger and larger roles as individuals mature. There is an ascent in human feeling from drive and affect via cognitive feelings of freedom to the most complex of human feelings, those associated with the imagination. The richest and deepest kinds of human feelings, the emotions, have an uncanny double structure. The well-known saying that there is a thin line between love and hate sums up the pinnacle of human feeling, the sense that however we choose, there is something un-chosen in that choice. Thus feelings of certainty begat doubts, doubts are the basis of feelings of faith, aversions end in liking, choices in compulsions, expectations mutate into providential feelings, and providential feelings reverse into feelings of pure contingency. This happens in the human imagination. This ambidexterity is the most distinctive thing about the human species. The imagination allows human beings, not least in their complex structure of feelings, to connect the unconnected and to reconcile that which is in opposition. What human beings distinguish in freedom, they unite in imagination.

The human species negotiates the gap that lies at the core of its species-being through acts of imagination. The imagination is the root of art and science – and of human creation more generally. One of the most powerful ways that human beings resolve the tension between nature and culture is by acts of creation. That is to say, in creation, we bridge or fuse what normally in experience is set asunder. In creation, we marry what is ontologically divorced. Acts of creation connect the unconnected. Thus when we ask ourselves the question 'what is art?', the answer is that art is one of the forces of the imagination that allow us to meld nature and society, genetics and culture, self and other, I and me, mine and thine into one thing.

As feelings develop through the stages of freedom and imagination, they become individualized. The quasi-instinctual or biological character of affects and drives becomes less significant. Out of this emerges what we call human

4 The philosopher Simone Weil's starving herself to death in London in an act of solidarity with the residents of German-occupied France is a case in point.

personality or idiosyncratic character. Human attractions and antipathies become less stereotyped, more eccentric and less group-defined. For instance, unlike affects, feelings of freedom and imagination are not contagious. They are not set off by external triggers. While groups and even whole societies can be 'affected', for instance by moral panics, the greater the cognitive components of feelings, the more human beings respond selectively and individually to the world around them. Or as the Stoics put it: if it is not in my control, I am not going to get agitated by it. Affective moods in contrast are communicable. This is socially significant, for it is the affects that demagogues and kitsch-meisters manipulate. They target child-like or juvenile feelings of shame, disgust, sadness and embarrassment. Such feelings manifest in up-turned and down-turned mouths, tittering, nervous or childishly-boisterous laughter, foot-stamping rage, down-beat corporeal collapse and up-beat rowdy riotous jumping about.

It is odd that modernity, for all of its manifest sophistication, has witnessed mass explosions of affective feelings – or, more precisely, regressive emotions that are built on affects.[5] Both the nineteenth and twentieth centuries saw the kitschification of the world.[6] The scale of the phenomenon was unprecedented. It was accompanied by the equally unprecedented phenomenon of totalitarianism. Walter Benjamin suggested two reasons why kitsch all of a sudden proliferated in the nineteenth century.[7] One explanation was the explosion of technology. Once industrialism arrived, the number of technological creations far outstripped art's capacity to give them adequate form. Aesthetics was overtaken by engineering. A visit to any computer museum today illustrates the consequence of this. The exhibition invariably is a litany of once-seemingly futuristic designs that now, for the most part, look excruciatingly out of date.[8] The problem lying at the root of all of this is that the aesthetic capacity to create classics has gone missing. It was displaced by fashion. No matter fashion's charms, which are many, its talismanic allure can only cause us to suspend our disbelief for a brief time. That fact itself is a function of just how much of the imagery and design produced in the age of technology is time-bound rather than time-less. Even the second comings of 'retro' fashion cannot obviate this.

Walter Benjamin's second explanation for kitsch pointed to the decline of traditional social authorities that previously regulated human fantasy. Fairy-tales, classical myths and bible stories provided cautionary explanatory schemas for dreams and nightmares. These schemas fell into disuse as industrial modernity rose. The consequence of this was paradoxical. Cognitive feeling-states of all

---

5 On the possibility of building emotions on affects, see Heller 1979: 94.

6 Roger Scruton offers one of the few philosophical accounts of this kitschification of the world in *Modern Culture*, chapters 6 and 8 and *The Aesthetic Understanding*, chapters 10 and 14. For an early study of the kitsch phenomenon, see Robin Boyd, *The Australian Ugliness* (1960).

7 This is beautifully essayed by Winfried Menninghaus (2009: 39–58).

8 They look like much of 1980s record production sounds.

kinds intensified – as the sceptical tenor, freedom, independence and imagination of the modern world expanded. Yet this was accompanied by the amplification of regressive feeling-states, sometimes in a totalitarian guise and sometimes in the guise of kitsch. In the early twenty-first century, we saw plenty of instances of totalitarian theocratic rage. At the opposite end of the spectrum, in democratic societies kitsch was commonly exhibited in politics, education, and art. Film, for instance, was once a very promising art form. By the turn of the twenty-first century, for most intents and purposes, it had become the vehicle for the fantasy-like representation of drives and affects. It infantilized at every turn, leaning either in the direction of the grotesque or the sentimental. Totalitarian rage and infantilized film-making coalesced in the 2001 attack on the Twin Towers in New York City. The terrorists got the idea for the attack from the endless stream of Hollywood fantasy-images of planes crashing into buildings.

Democratic societies in the second half of the twentieth century were sentimentalized. Friedrich Schlegel defined sentimentality as 'shallowly emotional and lachrymose'. He observed that it is 'full of those familiar noble feelings, the consciousness of which makes people of no character feel so unutterably happy and grand' (Menninghaus 2009: 49). Schlegel's definition tells us much about the interior landscape of many of our contemporaries. They are in love with their own noble feelings and infatuated with the dreams of their fathers. This speaks to an infantilized social psychology. Such dream kitsch promises a tensionless world that will be delivered by the vaguest of agencies, viz. that of 'change'. Its political expression, as Walter Benjamin noted, is a weak messianic power (Menninghaus 2009: 48). This power, in the case of democratic societies, pledges a kind of pain-free salvation – a *pharmatopia*. It is symbolized by the mask of cool. Its outward face is that of disengagement. Yet behind the seemingly tensionless mask of equanimity, the rage, anger and foot-stamping of the infant continues unabated. The staging of this power is pure kitsch. It parodies the worst bad taste of a Cecil B. De Mille spectacle. A classic example of it was the Greek temple stage set, built by pop brat Britney Spears' set designer, for Barack Obama's appearance in Denver at the 2008 Democratic Party Convention. Here the Star Trek aesthetic met Attic democracy via the sensibility of the Howard Johnson hotel chain and a *KISS* stage show – making it the ultimate tasteless shrine for the pseudo-messiah of the age of democratic kitsch.

Imagination

What defines kitsch in art is the absence of mystery. Conversely, what characterizes serious art is the presence of enigma. What gives rise to enigma is incongruity. Art, serious art, arises out of incongruity. At the heart of great art is the enigmatic union of incongruous qualities, exemplified by Mona Lisa's smile. Various communicative acts – from wit to paradox to metaphor – make these possible, and what results from them: the strange doubling, and the double meanings, that characterize the absolute spirit – religion, philosophy and art. What kind of species-being finds satisfaction in the absolute spirit? The answer is a species that lives a double life – such that everything in its purview is capable of being symbolic of something else. There is nothing in the human experience of the world that cannot be a symbol, metaphor, analogy, cipher, allusion, intimation, or mask of something else. Communication epitomizes this doubling. All communication, not least artistic communication, *re*-presents the phenomena of one medium in another medium. The fluid body is carved in stone, the lyric is sung, and the three-dimensional figure is painted on a two-dimensional surface.

This doubling is immaculately captured in René Magritte's painting *The Human Condition* (National Gallery of Art, Washington, D.C., 1933). The painting canvas depicts a scene of the external world and a painter's canvas that depicts the external world, and in this case all depictions are (almost) identical, and yet there is a metaphysical gap between them all, signalled by the edge of the canvas both *in* the painting and *of* the painting itself. This further indicates that 'the representation' and 'the world' are alike but different, and that we constantly translate between the media of art and the media of the world. In his 1928 work *Attempting the Impossible*, Magritte imagines the brushstrokes of the painter bringing to life a real person. This reminds us that the imagination constantly does something impossible. That is the nature of serious art, art invested with metaphysics. Metaphysics is the aspiration to the impossible. This is what religion, the sacred, the mystical, and the numinous are. All of them allude to the miraculous passage between media. These include the leaps that human beings regularly make between flesh and spirit, mind and body, canvas and reality, I and me.

Doubling permeates all aspects of being human. Our past self is both separated from and united with our present self. The same applies to our present and future self. This kind of doubling endows human beings with self-reflexivity and self-consciousness. It gives them their peculiar self-transcending and self-alienating self. Human beings, so often, display a conspicuous drive to be someone else. They put on masks, perform roles, and act out double lives. The identity of the human self is non-identical. The 'I' interacts with 'me', and invariably with 'mine' as well. This is even more so in the relation of the self with others, where the most important human relations, such as those of love and friendship, generate complex non-identical identities that meld difference and sameness. 'I' and 'you' and 'us' and 'we', and 'I' and 'me' and 'you' and 'thou' and 'mine' and 'thine' and 'ours' – all mutate and circulate around each one of us, in interesting ways. The happy person falls in love with the melancholic person, the sociable soul with the misanthrope, the confident being with the timid one.

Love unites incongruous pairs. One of the ways that love does this is through the medium of laughter. Agnes Heller's theory of laughter, which points to the gap between the genetic apriori and the social apriori of human beings, and humour's mission to bridge that gap, also points to a larger human sense of 'the division of things' that can only be overcome in uncanny and enigmatic ways. In all such overcoming, there are three moments. Each of these moments is echoed in the three great theories of the joke: the Kantian moment of *incongruous pairing*, the Freudian moment of the *psychological release of tension*, and the Hobbesian moment of *unsentimental power*.[9] Incongruity is an expression of the pervasive doubling of human experience. In release, the tensions between these doubles are reduced and polarities are united. Such integration can only be achieved unsentimentally, because it can only be achieved by uncanny means.

Un-sentimentality is necessary because the condition of ontological tension being released is that it is always, at the same time, maintained. This can only be achieved in the absence of sentimental identification. Thus, a classic bridging of the gap between nature and society is the idea of natural law which supposes that the laws of society are as immutable as nature itself, while a second classic resolution of the same gap is the scientific idea of the laws of nature which supposes that nature is as capable of transformation as society is. If both of these ideas confute each other, so be it – for in each case that is exactly what ideas that are creations of the imagination do. They are at their core self-contradictory, though always in interesting and productive ways. Rather than expressing the law of logical non-contradiction, they embody the law of contradiction. This is to say, they are metaphorical at their heart which means that they interpolate opposites – such that ice is fire, gods are mortal, life is still, grace resists gravity, the inn is a castle, and the meadows laugh. Through the lenses of the imagination, the world is filled with stone roses, the odour of speech, the frozen music of architecture, the spider web of laws, and the trickle-down theories of economists.

The ideas of the imagination, the most important and most fertile ideas that we have, resolve tensions by retaining them. In touching ice, there is the sensation of heat, yet ice is still cold. The imagination 'sees' (metaphorically) connections between what otherwise is unconnected. The core of the imagination connects the unconnected. Everything, from the vantage-point of the imagination, is 'as if', 'as it were', something else, including its own functioning which we also describe metaphorically. The imagination in many respects functions 'like a joke'. It puts together what is incongruous. As in humour, these are conjurations that do not make sense and yet at the same time make perfect sense. As in the joke re-told by Voltaire: 'I heard you love walking alone. So do I. Then we can walk together'. Laughter (here) is the recognition, and also the resolution and the preservation, of the gap between aloneness and togetherness. The imagination is a larger version of the same.

Joking in particular and the imagination in general are unsentimental. Conversely, the fundamental causes of kitsch and of failed art are two-fold: one is explicitness, the other is sentimentality. To imagine something 'as if' is to re-present something allusively. It is to re-present it in terms that are not its own. Allusion is the opposite of explicitness. It relies on distance. It is oblique. It refers to its objects and summons up the other indirectly through metaphor and symbol

9 For Agnes Heller's discussion of archetypal theories of the joke, see Heller 2005: 131–6.

and parable. As with the all-too-explicit, sentimentality is likewise unimaginative. For the sentimentalist, everything is a mirror of that person's sense of their own self. Life is a reflecting pool and the image reflected is the ego's own suffering and salvation. The sentimental ego cannot imagine the other. This is because the sentimental ego is deficient in emotions of the imagination, such as feelings of sympathy. When the sentimentalist sympathizes it is always in effect with himself, not with others. This finds many cultural expressions.

Take the case of the institution of the museum. Contemporary museums, those of the age of the sublime – the museums of holocaust, nuclear war, civil war, genocide, and so on – consciously or unconsciously elicit downcast eyes and a tear on the cheek. They sentimentalize suffering. They make the viewer of the exhibition the emotional centre of the exhibition. When viewing an exhibition that is sentimentalized, the museum visitor responds to what is exhibited by asking 'what if that happened to me or my children?' In the sentimental mode, I project myself in the place of another. How would *I* respond if *I* had been subject to a vicious beating, rape or a death march? How would *I* have felt living in excreta and dirt? These are natural questions for human beings to ask themselves. Yet these same questions are often confused with morality or ethics. Thus much of what passes for moral experience in the present age ends up being a kind of enlarged narcissism. I put myself in the place of another person. I respond with pathos. I cry for myself in the guise of crying for another individual.[10] Projection and identification with others should not be confused with acts of imagination. The former are subject-centred, the latter (the act of the imagination) is objective. In imagination we create worlds. These are totalities that contain a multiplicity of actors and acts, none of which we necessarily *identify* with. We can love the characters *qua* characters in a gangster movie without seeing ourselves as one of them.[11] When projective identification replaces imaginative objectivity, morality turns into moralism. Imaginative sympathy is thereby transformed into narcissistic pseudo-sympathy.

In contrast to narcissistic pseudo-sympathy, imaginative sympathy is unsentimental. Neither my desires nor my aversions are artefacts of my imagination.

---

10 'Sentimental feeling is easy to confuse with the real thing, for, on the surface at least, they have the same object. The sentimental love of Judy and the real love of Judy are both directed towards Judy, and involve tender thoughts of which she is the subject. But this superficial similarity marks a deep difference. The real *focus* of my sentimental love is not Judy but *me*.' Scruton, *Modern Culture* (1998/2007: 64).

11 Imaginative feelings respond to imaginary objects. 'In a sense it is even wrong to say that it is *I* who feel grief over Desdemona's fate. I imagine such a grief, and am drawn into sympathy with the thing that I imagine. We might say that here there is neither real object nor real feeling, but a response in imagination to an imagined scene'. In fantasy in contrast to the imagination, the objects of fantasy are unreal enough, but the feelings are vicarious affections. Or as Scruton puts it, in fantasy in opposition to the imagination, 'there is a real feeling that fixes upon an unreal object, in order to gratify vicariously what cannot be gratified in fact'. Scruton, *Modern Culture* (1998/2007: 59).

If I am an artist, and I imagine the character of a successful lawyer or a millionaire for a story, I do not wish to be that lawyer or that millionaire. *Imagination is not desire or fantasy or wish-fulfilment.* It does not identify with others. Rather the imagination keeps its distance. It relates to others obliquely. When someone fantasizes about the glamour or excitement 'being a writer', that person identifies with writers. The 'I' is drawn to a fantasy image of writers. Actual writers, serious, real writers on the other hand treat writing as work, craft, and hard graft, not as an object of desire. A writer may fantasize about winning awards or selling large volumes of books, but serious writers do not confuse their desires with the acts of their imagination.

The difference between desire and imagination is straightforward. The imagination grasps both desire and the cost of desire at the same time. The imagination is the human faculty for recognizing the ambidextrous nature of creation. With warmth comes cold, with success comes failure, and with all desires comes the price that we pay for the realization of any of our wishes. Be careful what you wish for, because it might come true. Pay attention to the opportunity costs of your desires. In fantasy, in contrast, every object is attainable and without a price. There is no tragedy in fantasy. There is no hard work and no sacrifice, and no resistance from others, and no barrier to what we want, or certainly no obstacle that is not a part of what we want. *The imagination, far from being fantastic, is rooted in reality.* It does leap, it does make unusual connections, it does surprise us with the long bow it can draw between things that we would normally not associate. But it does not suppose that the heat of ice is anything but cold and will give us frost-bite. It does not presume that our allies, lovers or friends are not obdurate.

Tear-jerking

To see others as a replica of oneself, and to see one's self succeeding in life without struggle and pain, is the work of fantasy and the pseudo-imagination of sentimentality. This is kitsch dreaming at work. It is what gives rise to the maudlin morality of Hallmark cards and modern social activism – in equal measure. There is a significant public appetite for this kitsch morality, and most modern cultural institutions are tempted by it. Some cultural entrepreneurs are master tear-jerkers. The doyen of post-1970s museum design, Ralph Applebaum, was once described as having:

> a rare ability to draw emotion from passers-by. He knows, for instance, how to make people cry in public. He is perfectly capable of disarming viewers with displays of poignant beauty and promise, or overpowering them with graphic proof of tragedy and loss.[12]

---

12 Barbara Flanagan, 'Interior Magazine, Designer of the Year', 2000. The portfolio of works of Applebaum's museum design firm, Ralph Appelbaum Associates, is enormous.

When the soprano sings Andrew Lloyd Webber's 'Don't Cry for Me Argentina', the intent of the song is precisely that the audience should cry. That is the essence of kitsch. It doesn't matter whether it is the child dying of cancer, or the fatuous Eva Peron in exile – in crying for them, you are crying for yourself.[13] You have social license to return to a childish state. You may dress this up as morality or tragedy if you like. Cultural institutions may dress it up for you in that way also. But it is still kitsch feeling – the feeling-state of a kitschified world in which grown-up feelings give way to the infantile affections.

In our kitsch world, everything from presidencies to cultural forms to higher learning is dominated by the pull of narcissistic sympathies and the push of brittle personalities who dress up the obsessions with their own self in mawkish and sappy concern for others. Brittle, petulant, and foot-stamping children have come to rule the world and the art of the world. Egotism, conceit and self-importance are their by-words. Much (too much) of the art, and many (too many) of our cultural institutions are overly fascinated with rage, shame, and indignation, and with attempts to bridge the gap between nature and culture with crocodile tears and moralizing slush. The social circus that surrounds this is a carnival of narcissistic vanities and anxious self-flagellating affectations.

The contemporary state of feeling is one in which emotions build on affects. In simple terms, highly reflexive individuals – many of whom are the products of elite universities and art worlds, highly versed in the world of free feelings – spend an inordinate amount of time mobilizing affects. Many of these individuals are fascinated with making an 'impact'. They behave like the minor figures of the era of High Modernism who were obsessed with the puerile 'shock' of 'the new'. The elemental feelings that register shock and impact are affects. Preoccupation with them is always a sign of the failure of the nerve of serious art. There are endless rationales for this failure, and most of them have a pseudo-political and petulantly pietistic air about them. From government policies to art exhibitions, fear, rage, indignation and shame affects are routinely mobilized in the name of doing social good and avoiding social harm. Highly stylized representations of threat, harm, and violation are directed at audiences in order to trigger feeling states of dread, fright, panic, alarm, fury, frenzy, seething, resentment, ire, offence, embarrassment, indignity, ignominy, and dishonour.

So should we then *not* represent suffering? It hardly befits us to pass over – in silence – wicked deeds and terrible acts. Yet, equally, kitsch does not do suffering justice. It fails to *re*-present it, even when it represents it. It fails to

---

It includes the United States Holocaust Memorial Museum, the National World War One Museum, the Civil War Visitor Centre Richmond, The Foundling Museum, the Holocaust Museum Houston, the Jewish Museum, the Japanese American National Museum, and the National Civic Rights Museum. http://www.raany.com/index.html accessed 17 October, 2009.

13 The totalitarian equivalent of this kitsch emotion is pity. Hannah Arendt observed how, from the French Revolution onwards, pity functioned as a totalitarian social emotion.

communicate it, even when it turns the dread of suffering into something that is highly communicable. It fails to double suffering and injustice – to translate it from one idiom to another, from one medium to another, and from one world to another. The most powerful communication of the nature of wickedness and suffering is indirect. It speaks to us through parable and allusion. In making suffering explicit, in setting it out in gross terms, up-front, in forensic detail, with obsessive attention to historical verisimilitude, it in effect sentimentalizes it. Unconsciously or not, it seeks to jerk tears from us. It elicits from us the emotional reaction of child-like crying. These are not tears shed at a Joycean wake. They are maudlin and infantile tears.

That does not mean however that relentless cheerfulness is the appropriate response to suffering either. Pangloss was a pain in the neck, after all. Grown-up penitence, lament, mourning, and sorrow all place us in a proper relationship to pain and loss. Nonetheless something closer to the metier of humour than that of lament is often – in the larger sense – a more fitting response to a painful and cruel world. This is not just a matter of taste. It is principally because the mercurial structure of humour – conceived in its largest sense – is closer to the imagination than sorrow is. Grown-up laughter is the intellectual recognition of the absurdity of existence. When we laugh, in a manner born of scepticism and freedom, we reconcile ourselves to incongruity. This includes, not least of all, the incongruity of civilization and barbarism, and of the civilizations that produce barbarism. This does not mean that the bitter harvest of barbarism can be dismissed with a joke. As a matter of fact, there are some things sometimes about which we should not joke. Nevertheless – in contrast to the sorrowful arts – wryness, dark humour, Stoic comedy, picaresque epics, double-imaging, and surreal philosophical art often capture much better the transcendent meaning of experience. This includes not least of all the meaning of the meaningless suffering of those who are caught in the bestiary.

Experience has a religious connotation. I mean 'experience' here in the sense that religion is not something that we do, but something that is done to us (Tacey 2009). *We meet experience with endurance – that is, with faith*. Godot's waiting in the bleak zone is a stoic comedy and a perfect oblique comment on the eternal return of that which we endure with bleak ironic patience. Kafka's Josef K., waiting figuratively in the antechamber, is similar. Metaphysical humour deals best with suffering in the same sense that the best defence against tyranny is satire. One of the great metaphysical purposes of humour is to rally against the inconsistency and illogic of tyrants with the inconsistency and illogic of what is comical. Charlie Chaplin's *The Great Dictator* (1940) in that sense is an unsurpassed critique of the modern tyrant. Humour possesses remarkable unsentimental power. Likewise the psychological release triggered by humour is fundamental to catharsis and consolation. And without catharsis and consolation, what exactly is the function of institutions that memorialize terrible events?

Ours is kitsch world. Its dominant sentiments are sentimental. The taste of our dictators is kitsch.[14] The pictures on the walls of the houses of Uday and Qusay, the psychopathic sons of Saddam Hussein, would have embarrassed even Hallmark cards. Overweening sentimentality is the obverse of homicidal terror. The former is the pretence that the latter does not exist. Democracies, though they are much less prone to psychopathologies, are dogged by their own kinds of sentimentality. In democracies, kitsch is less a disguise of terror than it is a way of ignoring reality. Kitsch politics in democracies is not new. One looks back in bemusement at the mentality of democracies in the 1930s. Whilst dictatorships were aggressively arming themselves, democracies became infatuated with the kitsch belief in unilateral disarmament. This foolishness was not just political. It betrayed a deeper uncertainty that afflicted the democracies. In contrast with the parliamentary regimes of the nineteenth century, their confidence in themselves had been sapped. They had become self-accusatory, often self-hating. The source of this was an underlying loss of cultural power.

The rise of kitsch was the sign of the decline of cultural power. In itself art is not political. The political views of artists generally speaking are either uninteresting or silly. Art nonetheless is a measure, perhaps *the* measure, of cultural vitality. If art declines, then the larger culture declines. So when the term 'kitsch' first appeared in the Munich art markets in the 1870s, it was a sign of a tectonic shift. That shift was registered by Nietzsche at the same time. Nietzsche's philosophy of the 1870s and 1880s was an unrelenting protest against the 'era of dissolution' that he was living in and that he knew he was living in.[15] His time was a world of late cultures, broken lights and weak men. This world had inherited contrary drives and values. Yet what did it do with this contrariety? The weak man's fundamental desire, Nietzsche observed, is that the war that he is should end. For him, happiness is a sedative. Kitsch is the weak man's art. Pseudo-art, like pseudo-science and pseudo-philosophy, became increasingly common in the decades that followed the turning-point of the 1870s. The weak man prevailed in culture. The *reductio ad absurdum* of this was the trumpeting of creative economies and knowledge societies in the late twentieth century. The louder the chorus of boosters, the more empty the claims proved to be.

The effects of the cultural shift that was first registered in the 1870s have been various. The sum of these effects has been significant. In the first instance,

---

14 'Rock 'n' roll legend has it that, during the Sixties, a record executive was invited to the baroque mansion of singer Ike Turner. Observing the mirrored ceilings, whale-shaped television and waterfall in the living room, he was moved to remark: "Man, so you can spend a million dollars at Woolworths." This came to mind yesterday, looking at pictures of Gaddafi's compound, invaded by rebel forces. Perhaps it was the surreal teapot-and-teacups fairground ride in his garden. Or the zoo, stocked with animals supplied by African dictators. Perhaps it was the murals, or even the huge gold sofa shaped like a mermaid and bearing the face of his daughter Aisha' (Moyes 2011).

15 *Beyond Good and Evil* (1886/1973: Part 5, Section 200).

the decline of cultural power was accompanied by a proliferation of violent dictatorships. It simultaneously saw the spread of democratic incontinence. The best way of understanding democratic incontinence is to consider the example of the welfare state. When the welfare state was introduced in the democracies in the first half of the twentieth century, it was designed as a system of co-contributory insurance. Individuals would co-pay amounts into a state system to insure themselves against unemployment, sickness and old age. The state in various ways subsidized the payments, much as an employer co-contributes to a superannuation scheme. This method of social co-insurance was a sensible arrangement. Yet, later on, it was replaced by a system of entitlement that eliminated individual contribution to the system and individual responsibility for the system. The consequence was a ballooning of the costs of the welfare state and reliance on unsustainable sovereign debt in order to pay for it. Americans, who generally liked the idea of individual responsibility, were told that they made contributions through the tax system throughout their working lives to Social Security and Medicare. But in reality the payments made to claimants were drawn down from annual taxes. So over a life time the total entitlements received by a taxpayer exceeded the total taxation levied on the taxpayer.[16] That was democratic incontinence.

Democratic incontinence is the consequence of kitsch thinking. Kitsch thought is a fantasy in which uncomfortable realities are airbrushed out. In a political fantasy it is possible for a society to receive more in benefits than it raises in taxes.[17] That is a recipe for fiscal disaster that is made worse by another fantasy that permits a state to borrow the gap between income and outgoings without any hope of repaying the borrowings and without any possibility that the productive benefit of such borrowing might match the cost of the borrowing. That was the condition of Europe, America and Japan at the end of the first decade of the twenty-first century. Sentimentality cannot resist the allure of any half-baked scheme that promises to improve human well-being. Ideologists paint moral pictures much like kitsch artists do. The political moralist is the Jeff Koons of the legislature. It is not that we cannot speak of harm or good, but rather when the kitsch ideologist does this, the cloying language that is used strips words of all of their irony and paradox. It reduces them to a state of fatuous self-identity. It strips them of their antitheses. It eliminates their antipodes. The unsentimental is not per se

16 'Myth: The elderly have "earned" their Social Security and Medicare by their lifelong payroll taxes, which were put aside for their retirement. Not so. Both programs are pay-as-you-go. Today's taxes pay today's benefits; little is "saved". Even if all were saved, most retirees receive benefits that far exceed their payroll taxes. Consider a man who turned 65 in 2010 and earned an average wage ($43,100). Over his expected lifetime, he will receive an inflation-adjusted $417,000 in Social Security and Medicare benefits compared to taxes paid of $345,000, estimates an Urban Institute study' Robert Samuelson 2011.

17 A classic case of the incontinent democratic state was Greece. In 2010, its revenues were 39 percent of GDP; its expenditure 49 percent of GDP.

hard-hearted, cold or stingy. Rather it is a union of contraries. The generous act, it knows, is born of economic prudence. To do unto others requires us to do unto ourselves, and vice-versa.

Kitsch thinking comes in waves. For example, following years of hard-bitten realism, the product of the worst kind of warfare, the era after 1945 was flush with all kinds of sentimental ideologies. The mentality of the 1930s instantly returned. The dictatorship of Soviet Union was idolized by the democratic intelligentsia. Socialism was ascendant. If you wander around London today you see the result. Almost any building built between 1950 and 1980 is vile. The sentimental world of English socialism designed buildings that were almost without exception ugly to view, hostile to the casual passer-by, and exceedingly boring and unpleasant to live in. The proof is in the eating of the pudding. The pudding was awful. Nietzsche was wrong about many things, but he was right about this. The sentimental world of the post-modern weak man lacked toughness, endurance and energy. It encouraged cowardice, pettiness and timidity. It was base and importuned human beings to abase themselves. The English intelligentsia in the 1950s and 1960s packaged sentimentality as socialism. But it might as well have been nationalism, feminism, liberalism or environmentalism for the difference it made. At its core, it was kitsch thinking. Modern ideology is kitsch thinking. Kitsch is a function of the age of ideology. As "isms" mount in influence, kitsch emerges.

It was Nietzsche (1878/1994: Section 5, Comment 276) who observed that man makes the best discoveries about culture within himself when he finds two heterogeneous powers governing there. A person may love the plastic arts or music, and still be moved by the spirit of science. If he is not to end the contradiction by destroying the one and completely unleashing the other, then what remains to the man is to make the large edifice of culture out of himself such that both powers can live there, even if at different ends of the edifice. Such a thing is conceivable, Nietzsche went on, if between those two powers are sheltered conciliatory central powers, with the dominating strength to settle, if need be, any quarrels that break out between them. Winston Churchill called that a grand alliance of powers. Churchill spent a life time practicing what Nietzsche recommended without ever having read him. He conciliated between Whig and Tory, conservative and liberal, and was always ready with a witty quip to demolish the kitsch pretensions of the dominant 'ism' of his time, socialism. Socialism created a crass world in which officials looked on humanity through innumerable grills and pigeon-holes and across innumerable counters, and said to them, 'Tickets, please'.[18]

Churchill had enough strength to ridicule political kitsch. This strength was born of contradiction. Great individuals with great imagination are walking contradictions, and the same is true of great societies. Such societies possess a vivid collective imagination. The imagination, Nietzsche observed, is analogous to the edifice of culture made of multiple powers. This edifice in a single individual is

18 Churchill, 'Liberalism and Socialism' 4 May 1908. Kinnaird Hall, Dundee.

similar to the cultural architecture of whole eras (1878/1994: Section 5, Comment 276), and vice-versa. Wherever a great architecture of culture develops, Nietzsche concluded, its task is to force opposing forces into harmony without suppressing or shackling them. Kitsch thinking does the obverse. It lionizes weakness, encourages indulgence, sanctions unrealistic choices, and heralds effete efforts. It is culture's toxin.

Chapter 6
Economy

Debt and Democratic Incontinence

If kitsch is the sign of the prevalence of the weak man in culture, then debt is the sign of the triumph of the weak man's culture over economic behaviour. Debt is not always a bad thing. Invested soundly, it can be productive. But often it is the too-easy option. Individuals choose to borrow rather than save or forego consumption. States borrow rather than tax. When this happens, debt becomes kitsch finance. The first decade of the twenty-first century was a decade of kitsch finance. This was evident in most of the major OECD economies. Personal debt ballooned. So did mortgage debt, student debt and sovereign debt.[1] Individual and collective expenditure exceeded income. There were economic reasons for this, but also cultural ones. It was a function of the prevalence of the weak man in culture. The weak man in culture encouraged not the democratic imagination, but rather democratic fantasies. The promise of fantasy is that anything can be achieved without cost or sacrifice.

Modern democracies promise citizens more and better public goods. Expectations of public health, education, welfare and defence rise in a progressive line. But the capacity to pay for public goods fluctuates cyclically. It rises and it falls. When cyclical decline contradicts progressive expectation, fantasies tend to flourish. One symptom of these fantasies is over-the-top public borrowing. Such borrowing occurs when states spend money without having the actual capacity to do so. Ultimately, whatever a state spends it must generate the same amount in income. A state's primary income is taxation. A state cannot always balance its income and its spending in the short term. During emergencies such as war, expenditure will leap ahead of income. Conversely if an economy does not grow sufficiently, its income will fall behind spending. When a state is short of income, it can reduce spending, raise the level of taxation or it can borrow money. While a recession means less revenue for a state it also paradoxically increases demands on spending. States are obliged to provide income or support for the unemployed. The progressive drive to provide ever-more public goods also generates fantasies that entitlements can be expanded while income is shrinking. So rather than cut spending, states will then raise taxes. This, though, is often impractical. Citizens may reasonably object that the gain from additional spending cannot justify the

1 The recommended debt ceiling for states in the European Union was 60 percent of GDP. Greece's debt-to-GDP ratio reached 115 percent in 2009 triggering a paralysing debt crisis in 2010.

loss represented by the additional tax. This is especially true because taxation impacts growth, the key source of taxes. Beyond a certain threshold, higher taxes discourage business activity. That same activity is the source of tax revenue. Thus exorbitant taxes may shrink rather than grow the state's income. This is counter-productive.

With spending and taxing confounded by decreasing income, states that are short of income are tempted to borrow money. But borrowing creates its own conundrums. Borrowing is a tax deferred, and nothing that is deferred lasts forever. Borrowings have to be repaid with interest. Deferral nonetheless opens the door to another fantasy. This is the fantasy that whatever is put off, will magically not happen. It is in this way that public borrowing readily becomes a kind of kitsch finance. It stands to real money like the most lurid tabloid journalism stands to truth. The relation is distant. To make matters worse, some fantasists also nurture the belief that costless borrowing is possible. They recommend that inflation be allowed to whittle away the value of money borrowed.[2] But in doing so high inflation whittles away the value of a nation's savings. The promise of costless borrowing is a variation on the fantasy that a state can spend money without having to tax its citizens with all that implies, including the important question: are we getting value for the money we spend?

Fantasies have enormous attraction because they promise that ends can be achieved without sacrifices. Even the most sophisticated democratic societies are susceptible to them. The United States is by no means the most egregious example of a kitsch economy. Indeed, far from it. It is the world's most significant economy. It emerged from the military-industrialization of the Second World War as the world's economic leviathan. It successfully re-booted its economy a number of times after that: as blue-collar coke-town industries declined in the late 1970s, as the first generation of computerized industries struggled in the early 1990s, and as the market value of internet industrialization collapsed in 2001. Yet each re-boot was less sure than it appeared to be. This uncertainty was veiled behind borrowing. Individuals, companies, and government borrowed, ferociously. America moved from being a creditor to being a debtor nation. Public income repeatedly fell short of national aspiration.

The story of American gross public debt as a percentage of gross domestic product is an interesting one. For most of its history, accumulated public debt was less than 20 percent of American GDP. Wars were the main exception to this tacit rule. Public debt rose to 40 percent of GDP during the American Revolution. During the War of 1812 it was just under 20 percent. During the Civil War and the First World War it peaked at just under 40 percent, a figure that was repeated during the Great Depression years of the 1930s. Briefly debt reached 120 percent

2 Conversely, states can print money to cover their deficits, but that simply creates inflation, which is a hidden tax. It also is a larceny on those who lend to states. In any case, lenders are not fools and they simply demand higher interest rates to lend to duplicitous states.

of GDP in the Second World War and then steadily declined across three decades from 1949 to 1982 through the Truman, Eisenhower, Kennedy, Johnson, Nixon and Carter administrations to around 35 percent of GDP. Then it escalated for the next 30 years through the Reagan, Bush 1, Clinton, and Bush 2 administrations to over 60 percent of GDP. Then it radically escalated in 2008 with the election of Obama administration to 80 percent and more of GDP.

Why did this happen? War is part of the explanation. The Bush administration funded a trillion dollar war in Iraq by borrowing. Ronald Reagan's administration spent the Soviet Union into submission, thereby winning the Cold War. During the second Clinton term in the more peaceful post-1989 era, American public debt dropped slightly from just over to just under 60 percent of GDP. But the dynamics of war and peace alone cannot explain the escalation of public debt after 1980. America went through the Revolutionary War, the War of 1812, the Civil War, the First World War and the Great Depression with its gross public debt barely rising above 40 percent. It is true that as time passed warfare became more mechanized and technological and thus more expensive. Still, those same technologies also represented greater wealth generating capacity. Or did they? The American economy grew quite robustly in most years between 1980 and 2008. Yet the extent of American borrowing was an unconscious sign that the technological drivers of that growth were not as profound as they seemed to be.

Public finance is a function of income and expenditure. In turn, income is a creature of wealth creation, while expenditure depends on national goals. Each one needs to be in sync with the other. In the 30 years between 1980 and 2010 this synchronicity was lost. National goals are progressive in nature. They escalate in a linear manner. Wealth generation in contrast is cyclical. The years between 1950 and 1980 were part of an upward cycle where wealth in large measure kept in sync with national aspiration. In the great economic cycles or long waves of the nineteenth century, aspiration and wealth creation were closely aligned. In the twentieth century this was less obviously true. In the years between 1980 and 2010 the alignment was under great stress. The loss of alignment was papered over for a long time. Public debt was one way of doing this. Debt was a kind of ideology. It made the economy appear stronger than it was. Hand-in-hand with this went ideologies of creativity. A booster mentality back lit the decades of the 1980s, 1990s and 2000s with a mercurial false light.

No modern era repeated to itself more often that it was 'creative'. Every ounce of scientific, technological and philosophical mediocrity was met with cannonades of applause. No applause was louder and more deafening than that which met Barack Obama as he campaigned in 2008 for the presidency of the United States. He was hailed as the unsurpassable super-smart, super-able candidate. What he really hailed was the triumph of kitsch. His rhetoric gave the game away. Media, corporate and university intellectuals as one pronounced it dazzling, brilliant and transfixing. Yet what was lionized as memorable was instantly forgettable. What was meant to be poetic was glib. What was supposed to soar was a simulacrum of flight. Practically without exception, the intelligentsia adored the candidate. Yet what did Nietzsche say? That theirs is a world of late cultures, broken lights and weak men. Here, then, the weak men cheered a weak man.

It should come as no surprise that weak men when in office do weak things. They borrow rather than tax. They tax rather than energize. They incite consumption rather than production. So it was with Barack Obama. The great moment of American democratic incontinence occurred with his election as President. American public debt rose dramatically from $6.3 trillion in 2008 to $8.2 trillion in 2009. The US federal government spent $1.67 for every dollar it collected in income in 2009. In that year it was projected that public debt would reach more than $20 trillion in 2020 at which point it would cost $900 billion in interest repayments (five times the level of repayments in 2009) and would approach the level of debt that America had coming out of the Second World War.[3] On one estimate by the US Office of Budget and Management, total public debt was projected to equal 200 percent of GDP by 2035. In 2007, American government revenue was $2.568 trillion. In that year the United States spent $2.728 trillion and had a deficit of $160 billion. In 2011, the Congressional Budget Office projected for the year an income of $2.230 trillion, expenditure of $3.629 trillion and a deficit of $1.399 trillion.

A state can reverse indebtedness. It can do this by imposing higher taxes, cutting spending, or by growing the economy which generates greater revenues without requiring higher taxes. If this does not happen, it means a shift in spending from education, health and defence to interest repayments.[4] In 2010, the US federal government spent $30,543 per household, collected taxes of $17,879 per household, and ran a budget deficit of $12,664 per household (Riedl 2010). Of the spending, $1,585 went on interest on the federal debt. Money costs money – now and in the future. One key reason that borrowing fulfils the fantasy of achievement without sacrifice is that it obliges later generations to repay today's borrowing. This is a presumptuous burdening of the future. Once an economy begins to revive, excessive government borrowing also crowds out lending for private investment (Committee on the Fiscal Future 2010: 29–30). The sources of capital are finite.

3 Source: Congressional Budget Office. The annual US federal deficit currently exceeds 10 percent of GDP. To achieve a public debt ratio of 60 percent in 2020 would require annual deficits not greater than 3.5 percent of GDP in the intervening years. See also Marron 2010.

4 Because the US dollar is the international reserve currency, used in international transactions and perceived as a safe haven for investors, the US is able to borrow money at competitive interest rates.

Table 6.1 United States GDP growth rate on an annual basis adjusted for inflation[5]

1999	2000	2001	2002	2003	2004	2005	2006	2007	2008	2009	2010
4.1	5	0.3	2.45	3.1	4.4	3.2	3.2	2	1.1	-2.6	2.8

In 2008–10 the debilitating effects on the economy of the weak man in culture became apparent. The global financial crisis signalled the on-set of a prolonged period of low growth. The chickens of democratic incontinence had come home to roost. The longest and deepest world recession since the 1930s was in train. The downturn in 2008–10 was not as severe as 1929–31 but significantly worse than the contractions in 1945, 1982, 1991, or the flat-lining in 2001. Each downturn marked a significant economic turning-point: the shift from military to civilian industrialization in 1945, the collapse of the classic smokestack industries and the rise of the computer industry, the end of the first generation of computerized industry and the rise of the Internet industry generation, the collapse of the Internet boom and the rise of the sub-prime housing boom. Recessions correct economic dysfunction. The dysfunction that led to the 2008–09 recession and subsequent low-growth quarters had both superficial and deep causes. It began in a banking crisis. The banking crisis was created by bad loans. The bad loans were a function of decisions to loan money to high risk recipients. Those decisions were made because banks had little alternative.[6] Existing industries were mature and fully invested. New industries offering high returns that were secure failed to appear. The last wave of new industrialization occurred in the 1980s with the emergence of the information technology sector. Nothing equivalent emerged in the decade of the 2000s. So bankers and governments convinced themselves of the prudence of property speculation. Mortgages were approved to people who could not possibly repay their loans. High risk loans were packaged with low-risk loans and sold on to other banks. A house of cards was created and it collapsed. The banks were blamed. After all, they did engage in a confidence game. So did the central banks nominally supervising them. But the delusions of the decade were almost obligatory as there was nowhere else for the funds of banks to go.

5 The normal rate of growth of US gross domestic product over the long term is 3 percent per annum.

6 So when commentators like Robert Shapiro (2011), former Under Secretary of Commerce for Economic Affairs in the Clinton Administration, complained about financial institutions amassing trillions of dollars without expanding business lending and holding those trillions in 'wobbly asset-based securities', they miss the point that sound business lending requires sound businesses to lend to, most especially in expanding sectors.

What followed the global financial crisis was the beginning of an extended period of low growth and high unemployment in most OECD economies. Aside from war, the most difficult problems for public policy to deal with are recession and weak growth. To cope with these, governments have limited, mainly pernicious, options. They can reduce public spending while trying to minimize the impact of that on the unemployed and on the unemployment level. They can increase taxation and yet it is difficult to do that in a recession without discouraging business investment. They can borrow money in lieu of tax revenue, yet they must repay the debt with interest from tax revenues or else start an insidious Ponzi-like spiral of borrowing to repay borrowing. At the end of the day, the only real cure for economic recession is economic growth – and in so many ways that is beyond the direct control of the state. This is because the driver of modern capitalist growth is the collective imagination. Successful modern economies periodically re-invent themselves by the creation of new industry sectors. This is partly a function of individual technological and aesthetic creativity. It is equally a function of that handful of modern societies that are capable of eliciting invention because at the core of those societies is a remarkable capacity to master deep-going paradoxes.

It might seem at first glance that there is a great distance between sound financial policy and the imaginative core of a modern society. Yet they both reflect each other. Both set the tone for each other. The state has no place for the weak man of finance, just as the collective imagination has no place for the weak man of culture. Neither sound finance nor audacious imagination is sentimental. The imagination is realistic and not given to fantasy. It deals with what is incongruent not with what is easy. It requires the strength to find similarity in what is dissimilar and commonality in what is different. Karl Marx predicted that capitalism would collapse because of its contradictions. Marx was wrong. If anything, capitalism thrives on contradictions. It does so because contradiction is the life-blood of the imagination. A number of modern capitalist economies have been astonishingly successful. They have created much more wealth in the last 200 years than in the whole of the rest of human history. Economics alone does not explain their success. Underlying the economic factors have been cultural forces. Capitalism is as much a function of culture as it is of commerce. Most particularly it is a function of what we saw Nietzsche call a cultural architecture in which opposing forces are harmonized. That requires toughness. It requires strength to treat contradictions as complementary. It requires hardiness not to be seduced into thinking that a state can borrow or tax an economy back to robust health. It requires firmness to balance income and expenditure. It requires imaginative realism to meld other oppositions not just those of spending and revenue that need to be reconciled in order to grow GDP and income.

The Economy Wars

When the world recession started in 2008, the economy wars flared again with intensity. They had been dormant for a long time. After 30 years of culture wars, their return to centre stage came as a bit of a relief. In one corner, we had the followers of John Maynard Keynes (1883–1946), who were filled with a kind of self-belief that we had not seen since the 1960s. They had a few scores to settle. In another corner were the market-friendly followers of Friedrich Hayek (1899–1992) and Milton Friedman (1912–2006). They were looking a bit bloodied after having dominated public policy for two decades. Looking on sceptically from outside the ring was another cohort, the admirers of Joseph Schumpeter (1883–1950). These were, as usual, less combative than the other pair, and had a quizzical eye trained on both of the pugilists.

Part of the scepticism of the Schumpeter camp was a wariness of public policy tout court. It did not matter whether this was a policy bent on big government or one in love with small government. Schumpeter had been a student of the great Austro-Hungarian Empire Finance Minister, Eugen von Böhm-Bawerk. Schumpeter himself was the first Minister of Finance of the modern Republic of Austria. He seemed to take away from that unusually intimate experience of public policy a strong sense of the need for economists to look beyond the policy cycle, and explore the deeper structures and long-run temporalities of economies. Schumpeter was a great economist who at the same time understood the power of history and society in shaping economies. He also appreciated the power of the imagination. He observed that modern capitalist economies were driven as much by creative impulse and imaginative insight, as they were by the more commonplace behaviours that arose out of greed, interest, need or calculation. It was not that societies could not – or should not – control such behaviours or alternatively encourage them depending on prevailing economic philosophy. It was just that some of the most decisive economic outcomes could not be determined by such policy tools. Somewhere beyond them, in a larger social-historical zone, lay the human drive to innovate and create.

This view is at odds with both Keynesianism and the contending philosophies of Friedrich Hayek and Milton Friedman. It sits at a tangent to both 'liberal' and 'neo-liberal' views of the world. Whether it is the social liberalism of the Keynesian or the classic market liberalism of the anti-Keynesian, each exemplifies the manner in which economists became enthralled by the temporal horizons of public policy and indifferent to the deeper cultural and historical causes of economic and social prosperity. Economic crashes, such as the one that occurred in 2008, trigger a stock set of responses. Keynesians suppose that capitalist economies tend to stagnation and that the motive force of these economies is immoral. Economies accordingly must be stimulated by government spending in order to return an economy to prosperity, and then must be regulated with a sure hand. Thus, contracts for public works are used to sustain businesses. Government bail-outs rescue firms from insolvency. In a recession, with declining revenues, a government can still spend more if the state increases tax levels, borrows from banks, or prints money. All economic policy tools, however, have limited and negative effects. Higher taxation means less consumer spending and less investment. Government borrowing competes with private borrowers, restricting business access to credit and pushing up the price of money. The repayment of high levels of public debt is a long-term drain on the economy. Printing money on the other hand causes rampant inflation and government spending is often wasteful. Neo-liberals are a much more optimistic breed than Keynesians. They assume that capitalism tends to prosperity, politics is a primary cause of recession, competition is effective, and self-interest is not immoral. Market failures are caused by too much regulation, too much taxation, and too much government borrowing. Yet market liberals on the whole show only a muted interest in the roles of management, technology, and industrialization in securing the success of markets. The firm is peripheral to their explanation of economic dynamism.

Schumpeter's understanding of capitalism differed in significant and interesting ways from both Keynes and Hayek. He thought that the capitalism that he observed was dynamic not stagnant, but that its dynamism came not from markets in general but from the power of innovation that had been unleashed by modern industrial capitalism. Schumpeter took a long-term view of economies. Looked at from an historical standpoint, economic crashes were a normal part of the dynamics of modern capitalist economies. Periods of genuine prosperity and long-term increases in wealth and general standards of living are followed, as night follows day, by a sequence of speculative boom, slide, panic, crash, and recovery. Boom-time actors never predict, and cannot predict, the time of the crash. They always think the good times will last forever. In fact though, business cycles trend in waves, up and down. These waves cycle over the short, medium, and long term. Schumpeter was most interested in the long-term dynamics of capitalist economies because these, he observed, had the most important effects of all. Public policy, in contrast, is concerned principally with short-term effects. Public policy instruments have moderately foreseeable impacts that run over periods of 18 months to three years. Very few tax or spending policies have observably sustainable or predictable effects beyond that. However, as Schumpeter outlined in his classic work *The Theory of Economic Development* in 1911, the most powerful drivers of modern capitalism work over periods of 20, 30, 60 years and more. These are the forces of innovation that create new industrial sectors.

The first chapter of *The Theory of Economic Development* set out a model of a static capitalist economy. Its paradigm reflects the tradition of economics from Adam Smith to John Stuart Mill to John Maynard Keynes and what they considered the typical components of a capitalist economy. According to this model, capitalism, like all economies hitherto, had no real endogenous driver of growth. Schumpeter noted that a handful of economies, beginning with Britain in the 1820s and Germany in the 1840s, behaved differently. They had a built-in source of expansion. Schumpeter set out to explain the nature of this in the brilliant second chapter of *The Theory of Economic Development*. 'Development' referred to those changes in economic life that are not forced from without but that arise from within triggered by their own initiative (Schumpeter 1911/2008: 63) In an endogenous growth economy, change does not occur continuously but in fits and starts. This type of economy does tend not toward a homeostatic equilibrium but rather toward a dynamic equilibrium.[7] This form of equilibrium is mildly enigmatic and suggests a kind of balance that is slightly off-balance all the time. Schumpeter explained the discontinuous change, the periodic ruptures, and the disturbances in the economic equilibrium of modern capitalist economies with one word: innovation. Periodically, the most advanced industrial economies go through a phase of intensive innovation. At the heart of these innovation periods are new combinations of economic materials and forces. What follows from these new combinations are new goods, new methods of production, new markets, new sources of supply, and new kinds of organization. They in turn create new leading industrial sectors. The Manchester cotton industry in 1780s, the railroads in the 1830s, Pittsburgh steel in the 1870s, the Detroit car industry in the 1910s, and the Silicon Valley information industries in the 1980s exemplify this phenomenon.

The ICT industries reached maturity around 2000. The pricking of the dot.com stock market boom symbolized this situation. Thirty years from today, ICT companies will probably resemble the car companies of the 1970s – far removed from their glory days. At the point of a serious market recession, a compelling question surfaces: what new leading industrial sector will emerge? Unfortunately, it is very difficult to predict who and what will be the shakers and makers of any next economic boom. Certainly, though, it is never the 'known quantities' that constitute a new sector. If they did, how easy it would be to foretell the future. In reality, it is the 'X factor' – the factor that is not known – that is most important. From the standpoint of the unknowable future, capitalism's next 'new wave', whatever it proves to be, will not be 'green technology', the pop economics obsession of 2008.[8] Versions of that neologism have been commonplace since 1973 when the

---

7 Most of the language of economic equilibrium derives from aesthetics. The case of dynamic equilibrium is no exception. The term was coined by the American artist mathematician, Jay Hambridge (1867–1924). See Hambridge's *The Elements of Dynamic Symmetry* (1926/1967). The paintings by Paul Klee or the architecture of Ludwig Wittgenstein and Frank Lloyd Wright are aesthetic examples of dynamic equilibrium.

8 From 1997 onwards, Spain invested heavily in 'green jobs'. Each job cost the equivalent of $US 800,000 representing the effective loss of 2.2 jobs in other areas of the economy (Alvarez 2009). In the United States, the Obama administration instituted a $38.6 billion loan guarantee program that it promised would create 65,000 jobs. After spending half of the money, the scheme had created 3,545 new jobs. Like other countries, Australia expanded green bureaucracies with resulting wasteful schemes including cash-for-clunkers, green loans, solar panels, and renewable energy research and development. Most green energy technologies exist solely because of state subsidies. The Australian Productivity Commission (2011) estimated that were subsidies to be removed, the comparable costs of electricity generation would be $400 a megawatt hour for solar, $150 to $214 for wind power, $97 for gas and $78 to $91 for coal. Among the worst of the green technologies are

economist E.F. Schumacher (1911–77) published his influential volume of essays *Small is Beautiful* (1973). Schumacher, a young protégé of Keynes, was deeply influenced by Catholic mysticism. While the intuition of the mystic is arguably a better cognitive model than rationalist prediction when dealing with the tricky matter of social creation, Schumacher's insight was original in the 1970s, but not today. Whatever will form the leading economic sector in 2038 is unknown, and it is only now being conceived in obscurity. It is the uncanny conjunctions of the imagination that create the figments of a new economy. Such conjunctions are like the punch lines of truly funny jokes. We do not see them coming. They are not predictable. They are certainly not risible clichéd conjunctions like 'the green automobile'.[9] When personal computers first appeared, the typical reaction was that 'they won't catch on'. Most observers did not say: 'oh let's trade in the mainframe computer for the PC'. IBM certainly did not say that, and it nearly destroyed the company. Similarly when technology becomes a favourite of public policy ('a computer on every school child's desk'), it is already much closer to being a sunset than a sunrise industry.

---

the wind farms. They are visually ugly, noisy, and kill large numbers of birds caught in their blades. Divers report benthic organisms are disappearing in the vicinity of wind turbines, understandably as water is an excellent conductor of sound vibrations.

9 The following, reported by the *South China Morning Post* (Chen 2009), is a classic example of the triumph of green rhetoric over intellectual substance:

'A beaming Tony Blair posed for television cameras holding a sleek, shiny solar panel as smiling officials and film star Jet Li looked on. They announced an ambitious plan to bring modern, clean power to the world's poor. In the next five years, the programme would bring solar-powered street lamps to 1,000 villages in China, India and Africa, where people are so poor they still do not generate any of the greenhouse gases blamed for global warming. The plan was announced at a factory in Guizhou in southwestern China – one of its poorest provinces. However, would Blair, the former British prime minister, and Li have been smiling if they had known a factory must burn more than 40kg of coal to produce the panel – 1 metre by 1.5 metres – they were holding? Forty kilograms might not sound much. Nevertheless, even the country's least efficient coal-fired power plant would generate 130 kilowatt-hours of electricity burning that amount – enough power to keep a 22 watt LED light bulb beaming 12 hours a day for 30 years. A solar panel is designed to last just 20 years. Jian Shuisheng, a professor of optical technology at Beijing Jiaotong University, estimates it takes 10kg of polysilicon to produce a solar panel with a capacity of one kilowatt – just enough to generate the energy to keep a fridge cool for a day. To make that much polysilicon on the mainland would require the burning of more than two tonnes of coal. That amount of coal could generate enough electricity to keep the fridge running for two decades'.

Irrationalities of this kind abound in green schemes. Take for example the banning of plastic shopping bags. Bin liner sales in South Australia doubled when free plastic shopping bags were banned in 2009 (Swallow, *Adelaide Advertiser*, 2011). And because most bin bags are made of thicker plastic than traditional bags, they take longer to break down in the environment.

New industry sectors provide the basis of sustained periods of economic and social prosperity. Orthodox policy instruments such as state taxes or budgets play only a minor role in economic innovation. Cities and regions are much more central to such innovation, a point made very clearly by the urban economist Jane Jacobs (1969, 1986) and, later on, by the urban sociologist, Richard Florida (2002). What will then serve as the next new powerful industry sector? What will supplement, and in part succeed, the quaternary information, education, research, and development (IERD) sector? The most that we can reliably predict, based on past experience, is that cities and city-regions will continue to be the crucible of new sector creation.[10] They are the point of intersection of art, science, production, and distribution. Perhaps, given the speed of state-directed urban creation that we see in China and elsewhere, the template-like 'manufacture of cities' might even emerge as the quinary sector of the future. However, in spite of the fact that we can imagine this possible development, the dynamics of large-scale urban economies remain far from being fully understood because economic factors are invariably overlain with unpredictable aesthetic factors. In urban economies, aesthetic, design, and taste cultures intersect powerfully with housing and infrastructure demand. The discipline of cultural economics that might explain this phenomenon remains undeveloped. In addition, the mutual suspicion of art and economics does not help this state of affairs. Even an economist with bohemian connections like Keynes held the two at arms' length. Keynes's view of economies echoed that of Edwardian elites – namely that capitalism was a failure that proved itself only insofar as it generated wealth for Bloomsbury-style art. That art was intrinsic to modern capitalism was an idea that was inconceivable for elites raised in pre-capitalist cultures, as it is equally for elites steeped in post-1960s anti-capitalist cultures of complaint.[11]

A cultural economics would explain the relationship between the arts and sciences, on the one hand, and economies, on the other hand. The city, historically, has played the key mediating role in this relationship. Cities do several things. First, they are the place where the arts and sciences flourish. Second, they create aesthetically mediated demand. Third, they introduce science into everyday economic and social life through technology. Modern economies grow through aesthetically mediated and technologically mediated demand. Art and science do not create this demand directly. Rather their works are conveyed in a series of steps from artistic and scientific discovery through various institutional media, notably universities, galleries, and laboratories, and then via firms and organizations, into the familiar products, processes, forms, and artefacts of daily social and economic life. The chain of discovery-innovation-firm-organization-product-process-artefact is a long one. It is also one that is not continuous. Entropy commonly happens at all points along this chain. Correspondingly, established markets and firms play

10 On the role of cities in the history of creation, see Hall (1998).

11 On the adversary mind-set of mid and late twentieth-century cultural elites, see the critical assessments of Daniel Bell (1976/1996) and Robert Hughes (1994).

little role in the creation of new industry sectors. Schumpeter observed that it is new firms at the leading edge of new industries that are the core of capitalist innovation. Alternatively, as he quipped, '*add as many mail coaches as you please, you will never get a railroad thereby*' (1911/2008: 64). New firms are created by entrepreneurs, a class of business leaders who are distinct from both the owners and the managers of businesses. The business class of entrepreneurs is perhaps best understood in terms of what the philosopher Hannah Arendt (1958) called 'action'. Action is the human capacity to initiate and lead – to bring things into the world. The business class of entrepreneurs create new firms that create new types of goods, technologies, markets, supply chains, and forms of organization that provide the basis for new industry sectors.

Innovation and Invention

In the wake of *The Theory of Economic Development*, much of the most interesting work of twentieth-century economists was devoted to rethinking the neoclassical formula that land, labour, and capital are the key factors of production. In the nineteenth century, Alfred Marshall already had added 'organization' to the neoclassical list. Information, knowledge, technology, cities, arts, and sciences followed Schumpeter's theory of the role of the entrepreneur. Fritz Machlup (1902–83) and Robert M. Solow (1921–) observed, respectively, that information and technology were as important factors of production as the trinity of land, labour, and capital (Machlup 1962/1973; Solow 1956). Machlup was a friend of Hayek from their days at the University of Vienna; Solow was briefly a student of Schumpeter at Harvard University and later a close associate of the great American Keynesian economist Paul Samuelson, another one of Schumpeter's students. Machlup coined the term 'the information society', and by the end of the twentieth century, Machlup's and Solow's ideas had spawned the popular notion of the knowledge economy, which crystallized for understandable reasons in the wake of the rise of the information technology industries. As California's Silicon Valley grew into an economic powerhouse, the literature on knowledge economies ballooned. One of the central institutions of the knowledge economy was the university. Both Machlup and Solow were cited by Daniel Bell in 1973 when Bell prophesized 'the coming of the post-industrial society'. One of Bell's many canny observations concerned the central role of the research university in post-industrial societies. The research university played an economic and ideological role similar to that of the church in medieval society. The sociologist's prognosis would eventually be echoed by professional economists. Indeed, such was the popularity of this idea that the American liberal political economist Jeffrey Sachs in 2005 even included the funding of universities, laboratories, and research as a key developmental step for nations seeking a way out of poverty (Sachs 2005: 58, 259).

Schumpeter was more cautious. When he wrote his classic work in 1911, he was well aware of the role that the arts and sciences played in modern economies. In fact, the theory of the arts and sciences as an economic driver goes back to eighteenth-century philosophers and political economists like Nicolas de Condorcet (1743–94).[12] They observed the centrality of inventive knowledge ('the advancement of the arts and sciences') to modern capitalism – in the same way that Adam Smith (1976/1970: 483, 502, 506–20) had noted the key part that 'foreign commerce' cities play in dynamic economies. However, Schumpeter also drew a distinction between innovation and invention. Innovation was the function of the entrepreneurial class. Invention was the responsibility of the creative class. There was a division of labour between the two. Schumpeter noted (1911/2008: 88) that it was not part of the role of entrepreneurs to find or create new possibilities. 'These are always present, abundantly accumulated by all sorts of people. Often they are also generally known and being discussed by scientific or literary writers'. The function of the entrepreneur was not to find or create 'the new thing' but rather to lead others to accept or adopt it. However, as Schumpeter also accepted, this was not a strict 'division of labour' between business, on the one hand, and the arts and sciences, on the other. Schumpeter was aware that leadership was just as important in the arts and sciences as it was in business and that the acceptance of significant new ideas is just as difficult in a university as it is in a company, possibly more so. He observed that the history of science is one great confirmation of the fact that individuals find it exceedingly difficult to adopt a new scientific view or method (1911/2008: 86). Thus, by Schumpeter's own hands, his carefully crafted distinction between invention and innovation begins to break down. As in all of the great works of creation, there is instability at the heart of things. Identities generate distinctions, and distinctions generate identities. That is the very nature of the process of creation that Schumpeter was trying to understand.

Interestingly, Schumpeter thought that innovation was more difficult to achieve than invention – because innovation is the enemy of habit. Habits, including the habits of thinking, are very efficient. Rather than having to consciously think through every task that we do, we form habits and act subconsciously on them in a time-efficient manner. One cost of this practice, though, is that when someone wants to implement change, the forces of habit rise up – Schumpeter noted – to bear witness against the embryonic project. An entrepreneur is a person with the will and the drive to wear down the forces of habit and side-line the naysayers who cry out that 'this is the way it has always been done'. Consequently, an entrepreneur must possess a series of distinctive traits: a desire to struggle against well-worn ways, to enjoy getting things done, to seek out difficulties, and engage in ventures (1911/2008: 93–4). In fact, Schumpeter was saying, in effect, that if Andrew Carnegie (1835–1919), who invented the idea of the vertical integration of a company, had not had the ability to impress that idea on his associates and

12 On the role of knowledge as factor in modern developmental philosophies of history, see Heller (1982), chapter 15.

wear down their opposition to it, his idea would have meant little. He would never have reaped a massive fortune from the steel business. While Carnegie's story is exemplary, it is just as true that the inventor must struggle mentally against well-worn ways, enjoy getting things done, seek out difficulties, and engage in new ventures. Thus, in the end, Schumpeter's distinction does break down. Invention and innovation share common characteristics.

Appositional Thinking

Given the number of times words such as 'new', 'change', and 'innovation' occur in his work, it may be a surprise to note that Schumpeter described himself as a conservative. It is certainly surprising insofar as the role of the entrepreneur is to struggle against ingrained habit. One of the definitions of being conservative is to stand for habit against change. However, just as most of the revolutionaries of the modern age created systems of sclerotic reaction, perhaps it is less surprising that Schumpeter, the self-declared conservative, also became the prophet of innovation. The situation resembles the Big Bang, the moment of the creation of the universe when nothing switched into something. If habit is the first economy of the human species, a recipe for the efficient use of energies, then habit turned against inefficiency is a powerful force for change. If that is a paradox, then so is the act of creation that allows economies to defy stasis and grow.

Everything is its opposite. In that idea lies the core conception of creation. Schumpeter once said that he had long planned to write a book on conservatism. If he had written it, it might have begun with a meditation on the idea of value-free science. The phrase 'value-free' tends to be met with bemusement by social scientists today. However, Schumpeter thought of value-freedom in an interesting way. A value-free science was a science that embodied all of the contradictory values of a society – by being one step removed from them. That was conservative in the sense that the conservative is, in a subtle manner, a sharp critic of all forms of ideology. Schumpeter belongs to a class of twentieth-century intellectuals and writers who include G.K. Chesterton, Evelyn Waugh, Marshall McLuhan, Kenneth Burke, Saul Bellow, Daniel Bell, Hannah Arendt, Agnes Heller, Christopher Lasch, Cornelius Castoriadis, Roger Scruton, Robert Nisbet, Christopher Hitchens, John Carroll, and Peter Berger. Each one of this group defies simple ideological classification. Some began, but none ended their intellectual careers as socialists or liberals ordinarily understood. Some were not camp followers even to begin with. Often they are best identified not by any kind of 'ism' at all but rather by a tone that either is wry, ironic, comic, or sceptical. Tone replaces ideology. It is notable that many among this group either wrote humorous works or else wrote books or essays about comedy.[13] Arthur Koestler, in his illuminating treatise on

13 Waugh, *Scoop: A Novel about Journalists* (2000); Bellow, *The Adventures of Augie March* (2001); Burke, *On Symbols and Society* (1989), 261–7; Heller, *Immortal Comedy*

the creative act, *The Act of Creation* (1964), observed at great length the structural parallel between comedy and creativity.

A person can be a conservative of the left as well as of the right. That is not incongruous, for the very nature of the conservative is to deal in incongruities. Wry tone rises above the bellows of modern politics. Chesterton put it well: 'The whole modern world has divided itself into Conservatives and Progressives. The business of Progressives is to go on making mistakes. The business of the Conservatives is to prevent the mistakes from being corrected'.[14] The aspiration to

(2005); Hitchens, 'Scoop' and 'The Adventures of Augie March' in *Love, Poverty, and War* (2004); Berger, *Redeeming Laughter* (1997). G.K. Chesterton's body of work in both fiction and non-fiction is peppered with the comic structure of paradox. Marshall McLuhan was inspired to write by his early encounter with Chesterton. McLuhan published an article on him ('G.K. Chesterton: A Practical Mystic') in the *Dalhousie Review* 15(4), 1936. McLuhan's student, Hugh Kenner, contributed an excellent introduction to Chesterton, *Paradox in Chesterton* (1947). McLuhan built his understanding of communication on brilliant paradoxes like 'the medium is the message', 'the typographical essay', 'knowing is making', 'the mechanical bride', and the 'global village'. He also observed that the good humour needed to enter into fun and games is the mark of sanity and reason. McLuhan was the classic joker intellectual. A conservative Catholic, he was sceptical of moralists and moralism. He combined a love of satire with a joker's intellectual tool kit. He explored paradox by rummaging through mysticism, Pythagoreanism, hermeticism, modernism, cynicism, stoicism, new criticism, and the heterodox orthodoxy of Gilbert Chesterton's Catholicism (Theall 2006). McLuhan had a deeply satirical and paradoxical cast of mind. In his view, good communication was a kind of appositional poetics. This was a view shared by many of McLuhan's peers – ranging from the New Critics William Wimsatt and Cleanth Brooks through to Kenneth Burke. This was a tradition of thought enchanted by what McLuhan's Cambridge teacher William Empson once – delightfully – described as 'knotted duality'. It is a state, Empson explained, 'where those who have been wedded in the argument are bedded together in the phrase'. This is a state that, long ago, was recognized by the ancient Stoics. It is the state of antilogy, and its model is the *dissoi logi* or the double argument of the speaker who combines two opposing arguments into a single argument. McLuhan reduced such arguments to brilliant catchphrases. In a larger sense, McLuhan and his kindred spirits exemplify the flourishing of a strand of culture in North America that has its roots in the Renaissance and the Elizabethan world picture. Kenneth Burke (1989) called this cultural current *the comic corrective*. It is fascinated by phrases or scenes that have an agonistic logic. These phrases and scenes anchor sense in the non-sense of self-contradictory mottos.

14 'The whole modern world has divided itself into Conservatives and Progressives. The business of Progressives is to go on making mistakes. The business of Conservatives is to prevent mistakes from being corrected. Even when the revolutionist might himself repent of his revolution, the traditionalist is already defending it as part of his tradition. Thus we have two great types – the advanced person who rushes us into ruin, and the retrospective person who admires the ruins. He admires them especially by moonlight, not to say moonshine. Each new blunder of the progressive or prig becomes instantly a legend of immemorial antiquity for the snob. This is called the balance, or mutual check, in our Constitution'. G.K. Chesterton, 'Column', *Illustrated London News*, 19 April 1924.

be free of the hum-bug of ideology, including the hum-bug of conservatism, might be another way of understanding Schumpeter's sense of himself as a conservative. He promised for a long time to write a book on conservatism, but did not, which might be the best kind of book on the topic. The attitude of the conservative is one of dry humour. It is marked by a gleeful insistence in deviating from any right direction in thinking. It is executed in witty observations that deliver unexpected twists and turns or in the screwed-up face that signifies impatience, disgust, or discomfort with human folly. The conservative and the humourist deal in ways of marrying incongruities. This might appear to be a useless talent excepting that the most successful societies in human history have been riddled with the most amazing contradictions and yet managed them with grace. Here we see explained the conservative prophet of innovation. What Schumpeter shared with other conservatives was an unusual sensitivity to appositions. Appositions conversely are what drive dynamic economies.

It is difficult to tie down who or what a conservative is because of this appositional streak. A good example is the American conservative sociologist Robert Nisbet. Nisbet (1970) thought of the sociological tradition and society itself as being pivoted on a series of central 'unit ideas'. These 'unit ideas' were composed of affinities and oppositions. Conservatism, to the extent that it was an ideology, identified with the concepts of community, authority, status, the sacred and (in a negative sense) alienation. But the conservative, and Nisbet was an outstanding example of the type, understood that such concepts were inextricably linked to antitheses and conceptual opposites. Thus the modern world was a function of community with society, authority with power, status with class, the sacred with the profane, and alienation with progress. It was not that one could be strictly unravelled from the other. Thus many of Nisbet's intellectual heroes, as he himself noted, were liberals like Tocqueville and Weber whose conclusions were conservative. Their tacit conservative carriage was one of concept and symbol, as well as one of tacit attitude (1970: 17). In the works of Durkheim and Simmel he observed the values of political liberalism and of cultural conservatism at the same time. In the same manner, in Schumpeter we can see the fascination with dynamism linked profoundly to the conceptual opposite of the eternal return of capitalism's cycles and waves, or as he famously observed, capitalism's creative destruction.

Schumpeter's sense of his own self as a conservative was intimately bound up with his view of modern capitalist economies. He observed that what kept those economies growing were bursts of innovation. Yet those bursts, though not precisely predictable, came in periodic and repetitious waves – long, medium and short waves. Fundamental to the spectacular cloud bursts of ineffable creativity was the ability of entrepreneurs to think in new ways about products, markets, and organizations. Yet there was always something curiously repetitive at least in an historical sense about these 'new' moments. The new repeated itself time and again. The new was naturally old. It invariably replicated the same classic structure of creation. New ways are always combinations or conjunctions of concepts that people think of as different, separate, and hitherto unrelated.

To achieve such combinations, the mind cannot be too partisan or too fixated on one side, one thing, or one approach. Ideology in contrast means fixation on one value or set of values in a world that is subject to multiple and irreducible value currents and antitheses.

Schumpeter wrote generously about Marx and Keynes and Marshall, and many other economists of many different outlooks because he understood that great ideas come out of an uncanny confluence of contradictory precepts. The conservative stance is to take a sceptical view of all of these in order to see what can be done with each of them. The underlying impulse is to conserve them all in order to overcome them by marrying them together. Overcoming is not an act of abolition but an act of conjuration that takes opposing qualities and, through uncanny tactics, forges new ideas from old precepts. Andrew Carnegie took the lateral-horizontal-procedural (what today is often called the 'network') idea of a market economy and fused it with the vertical-hierarchical-personalized forms of the medieval and pre-capitalist imagination that the Social Darwinists, whom Carnegie admired, loathed. This scenario may have been very contrary – but it was also, so far as the act of creation was concerned, entirely consistent. Carnegie laid the template, or part thereof, of modern organizations. In the same spirit, it may have been paradoxical that the conservative Schumpeter was the great modern prophet of innovation, but this was for a very good reason. The kind of sceptical conservatism typified by Schumpeter illuminates the dynamism of modern capitalism because it grasps the kind of appositions that make it possible. It is difficult to over-estimate how peculiar these appositions are.

Appositional thinking is helpful to explain the dynamic mutating forms of successful modern societies and economies, without falling into the trap of idolizing pyrrhic fashions. The cult of the new is conspicuously mindless. Ironically, it requires a conservative instinct to explain innovation. What matters in acts of creation is not so much what is new, which often is uninteresting, but rather the surprising takes on what is old.[15] That in a nutshell is the problem of the creative economies. They exist, but what drives them is difficult to identify, let alone to subject to public policy prescriptions. The simplistic equation of 'the new' and 'the creative' can be very misleading. Schumpeter was the first to distinguish between creative industries and mature industries. Creative industries appear dramatically as if out of nowhere. They capture appositions, unlikely combinations of ideas that are seized upon by mercurial entrepreneurs. Eventually with the passage of time, creative industries slow down, as invention idles and innovation turns into convention, and the profits of innovation decline. However, at their peak, these industries race ahead on the back of startling ideas. They prove

15 As Scruton (1998/2007: 45, 82–3) notes, so many of the great modernist artists of the twentieth century (Stravinksy, Moore, Matisse, and so on) were traditionalists. What makes something original, he suggests, is not defiance of the past or a rude assault on settled expectations, but the element of surprise that a given work invests the forms and the repertoire of tradition.

themselves to be much more dynamic than other industry sectors. There is always an element of 'the new' in this. However, one should also be wary of overstating the significance of the new.

As Schumpeter often observed, creation comes through the unlikely combinations of what exists. The word 'unlikely' is important. The unlikely character of protean combinations requires exceptional insight. The act of conjuration underlying them is very unusual. Terms like progress, contemporary, modern, up-to-date, and so on are not always very helpful in understanding these conjurations. Words like these point to the temporal dynamic of creation, but what they screen out is the appositional structures of innovation and invention. It is not time that explains creation but rather the finding of similarities in what is dissimilar. Creation connects the unconnected. This process is much closer in nature to poetic analogy than it is to social progress. The assembly line radically changed the methods of industrial production. Henry Ford's car assembly technique had a significant impact on the organization of labour in the twentieth century. Someone at some time along the way looked at the dis-assembly techniques used in the Chicago slaughter houses and meat packing plants of the late nineteenth century. Not every person's way of looking at things is the same. Someone looked at the dis-assembly line and imagined it in reverse where the parts of the animal were not pulled apart but were put together, this time as an automobile. Later in the 1960s, Andy Warhol, who grew up in then industrial Pittsburgh, reworked this idea into 'the Factory', a multi-medium, output-driven art loft studio in New York City. This in turn was echoed in the early twenty-first-century business model of the 'art firm'. From the slaughter house to the aesthetic company, we see the analogical power of the mind at work. The analogy drawn is not a literary one per se, but it is no less powerful for that.

Creative Achievement in Real Terms

One of the great laboratories for understanding the 'breath of capitalism' – the diaphragm-like growth-and-recession pattern of modern capitalist economics – is the 1980s. That period illustrates a number of very Schumpeter-type issues – the role of ideas-production in economic life, and the very interesting matter of where those ideas come from. The 1980s saw the start of what became known as 'post-industrialism'. Post-industrialism is an imperfect term. It implies that the driving forces, the catalysts, of this era were fundamentally different from the industrial age, whereas in fact it was only the symptoms of what those catalytic forces produced that was different. New information and communication technologies saw the rise of new industrial sectors. That was spectacular in its way, but it was not different in ultimate type from what had created a previous series of leading industrial sectors and that had driven capitalist economies since the latter part of the eighteenth century. In every case, the driver was the application of ideas to production, or perhaps more precisely the new ways of conceiving goods, markets, and organizations. 'New' in this case always meant contradictory or uncanny ideas – like the idea of a soft industry or an item of software as opposed to the older notion of hard ware, or the imagining of a computer as something personal rather than institutional.

This is the point where we see Schumpeter exceed all of his students. The best of them grasped that knowledge, information, and technology – all of those iconic words that defined the tail end of the twentieth century – were metaphors for the act of creation. Schumpeter, however, saw that creation was an act of metaphor. He saw that words like soft or hard, industrial or service were not just metaphors for economies, but that the engines of economies were metaphors. He was not suggesting that economics was a kind of literature, but rather that the serious entrepreneur and the serious artist, both rare birds, were comparable in nature. Science, technology, the social sciences, and so on, are important to economies not just because they invent useful, expedient, and efficient ways of doing things, but because they are capable of harnessing the act of thinking which, at its core, where it is most powerful, is metaphoric. A metaphor is a combination, and as Schumpeter repeatedly observed, innovations come out of combinations. When innovations are in the phase of discovery, they emerge out of metaphors. Even the most utilitarian innovation is poetic in its origins.

The year 1980 was very depressing in the United States. Inflation was running at 13 percent, and the unemployment rate was 7.8 percent. The economy was in deep recession. The old powerhouse industries of the American Mid-West had become rust-belt industries. Once the epitome of industrial power, dynamism, and innovation, they were now mature or over-mature industries struggling to avoid bankruptcy. America elected Ronald Reagan as President (1981–89). The 1980s saw America return to economic prosperity. In 1989, inflation was 4.0 percent and unemployment 5.4 percent. The official policy prescriptions of the Reagan era were neo-liberal, small-government policies inspired by the theories of Friedrich Hayek, Milton Friedman, and Arthur Lafter. In fact, though, government spending per capita continued to rise throughout the Reagan years as did government deficits and government debt. Spending to win the Cold War drove this, as did the fact that the conservative Reagan had a large streak of liberalism in his soul. He was a man of interesting contradictions. He had begun political life as a Democrat before switching to the Republican Party. Personal income tax fell dramatically in the Reagan years, but social security taxes rose. Reagan was a man with a grasp of the economics of laughter. He promised that as taxes went down, tax revenues would rise. Liberal economists guffawed. However, in truth, economic policies often have quantum effects of this kind.

What really made the Reagan years an economic success story was the beginning of the rise of the new information and communication (ICT) industries that would transform the face of the American economy. The genius of the Reagan Administration was to do nothing to throttle this new industry sector in its crucial early phase of growth. The ICT industry followed a classic Schumpeter script. It emerged from the heat of recession. It was pioneered by entrepreneurial figures

(Bill Gates, Michael Dell, Steve Jobs, and others). It generated super-profits. It developed separately from existing industries and firms. Nevertheless, its technologies and methods of organization spread to existing industries and firms, transforming them. Then gradually it ran out of creative energy. Its pioneering figures lost interest in innovation. They took their profits and turned to social activism and philanthropy. Gates became the Carnegie of his time. As Schumpeter might have observed, it is a pattern; it has been done before. As the ICT industry took off, sociologists began to talk about 'post-industrialization'. In fact, looking backwards, the emergence of the digital communications sector was part of the normal process of industrial capitalism at work. What happened in the 1980s was one of the periodic re-energizing phases of modern capitalism as a new and unpredicted industry sector took off. American GNP per capita, in Year 2000 dollars, rose from $22,346 in 1982 to $27,514 in 1988.[16] In 1974, 1975, 1980, and 1982 US real GDP per capita had actually fallen. It rose steadily thereafter through to 2008 with the exception of 2001. In 2008 it stood at $38,262 in Year 2000 dollars.

Universities played a part in the ICT-fuelled resurgence in the 1980s. However, as in the case of all invention, the number of university actors was tiny. Discovery in a measurable sense is overwhelmingly the preserve of a small number of research universities, and a small number of professors and graduate students from those institutions. The decisive fact about research, as about culture creation generally, is that it concentrates. The rise of the ICT industry illustrates this dynamic perfectly. The principal technology building blocks of ICT were devised by a small cohort of professors and PhDs from the universities of California, MIT, Harvard, Brown, Stanford, Illinois, Duke, Washington, and Oxford, along with contributions from the IBM, RAND, and BBN corporations, the Swiss CERN lab, and the US Defense Department's Advanced Research Projects Agency.[17]

---

16 http://www.measuringworth.org/usgdp/index.php.

17 The key figures were Paul Baran (UCLA master's in engineering graduate and RAND corporation employee), J.C.R. Licklider (MIT Professor and Head of the Information Processing Techniques Office at ARPA), Douglas Engelbart (University of California PhD graduate and Stanford University), Theodore (Ted) Nelson (Master's in Sociology, Harvard University), Wes Clark and Larry Roberts (MIT PhD in Electrical Engineering [Clark and Roberts] and chief scientist in the ARPA Information Processing Techniques Office [Clark]), Ray Tomlinson (MIT Master of Science graduate and employee of the technology company of Bolt Beranek and Newman), Vinton Cerf and Robert Kahn (Stanford University mathematics graduate [Cerf] and ARPANET administrator and MIT graduate (Kahn), Bill Gates and Paul Allen (Harvard University drop outs), Randy Suess and Ward Christensen (Chicago computer hobbyists; IBM employee [Christensen]), Tom Truscott and Jim Ellis (Duke University graduate students), Tim Berners-Lee (Oxford University graduate and CERN, Switzerland, employee), Marc Andreessen and Eric Bina (University of Illinois undergraduate [Andreessen] and programmer [Bina]), Brian Pinkerton (University of Washington graduate student, later PhD in Computer Science), Larry Page and Sergey Brin Stanford University Master of Science [Page] and PhD [Brin]).

This high level of concentration is characteristic of invention generally across the arts and sciences. As Daniel Bell noted (1973/1999: 245) in 1973, 100 of the 2,500 accredited colleges and universities in the United States – or 4 percent of the total – carried out more than 93 percent of higher education sector research. Moreover, 1 percent of the total – 21 universities – carried out 54 percent of the total of the sector's research output, and 10 universities were responsible for 38 percent of the total research output. Today there are 2,618 accredited four-year colleges and universities in the United States.[18] In 2009, The Carnegie Foundation for the Advancement of Teaching classified 96 universities as 'research universities with very high research activity', essentially the same as Bell's 1973 figure.[19] If we look at the top 20 research universities in the world today, defined by output and citation, we find that not only are they all American universities, but that they are concentrated in specific geographical locations, principally on the Eastern and Western Seaboards of the United States and around the Great Lakes, and in the orbit of major nodal city-regions, some border-hopping.[20] New York City and Boston together with the strips and arcs connecting Los Angeles–San Diego, San Francisco–San Jose, Madison–Chicago–Detroit–Toronto, Portland–Seattle–Vancouver, and Baltimore–Washington, D.C.–Durham–Atlanta are especially prominent. The Houston–Austin–Dallas–Tampa–Miami arc might one day be competitive with the others.

Research and culture creation typically not only concentrate in space but also in time. The rise of the ICT industries was a notable phenomenon in the second half of the twentieth century. However, this was neither the most measurably creative period in American history nor was it time-unlimited. Per capita rates of copyright and patent registrations are a good indicator of national innovation. In the case of the US, the peak year for patents registered per capita in the United States was 1916.[21] The rate trended downward till 1985 where it stood at 50 percent of the 1916 peak. It rose again, as would be expected, in step with the information technology boom from 1985 to the present day. However, even at its renewed highest level in 2005, it was still only 95 percent of the 1916 per

18 The Association of American Colleges and Universities.

19 http://www.carnegiefoundation.org/ The difference between an American research university with very high research activity (A) and a regular doctoral-granting university that carries out research (B) is indicated by the following 2009 Carnegie figures based on 2002–04 data. The mean number of humanities doctorates for A is 45, the mean number of social science doctorates in 38. In comparison, the mean number of humanities doctorates for B is 9 and the mean number of social science doctorates is 10.

20 MIT, California, Stanford, Harvard, California Institute of Technology, Chicago, Washington, Yale, Johns Hopkins, Columbia, Duke, Michigan, North Carolina, Northwestern, New York University, Boston, University of Pennsylvania, Washington University St. Louis, Emory, Vanderbilt. This list is based on data from the 2008 Leiden University index of world research universities

21 The figures cited are drawn from Jonathan Huebner (2005: 984–5) and John Smart (2005).

capita figure. Nationally American registrations of copyrights per capita slightly increased between 1900 and today but only because the number of categories of copyrightable objects increased markedly in the same period – meaning that copyright registration per capita in real terms actually fell. The 1890s appears to be the peak time for copyright creation in the United States once we take into account the increase in copyrightable objects during the twentieth century.[22] In 1871, 12,688 copyrights were registered in the United States, which then had a population of 50 million.[23] That is the equivalent of 0.03 registrations per 100 Americans. In 1900 that figure had risen to 0.13. In 1925, it was 0.15, 1950, 0.14, 1978, 0.15. After this plateau, it rises in 1988 to 0.23, and then falls away again to 0.20 in 1994, then 0.18 in 2000 and 2007. Not only had the nominal figure per capita risen only marginally in a hundred years, but in the period since 1900 many new categories had been added to the schedule of protected works.[24] In spite of all the additional copyrightable works that this represents, copyright productivity per capita expanded negligibly in a century. In real terms, in effect copyright activity shrank. As with patents, the peak of copyright registrations in nominal terms (i.e. not accounting for additional copyrightable objects) occurred at the turn of the century, around 1907, with a nominal rate of 0.14 registrations per 100 Americans.[25]

'Creativity' became a buzz-word in the later part of the twentieth century. The rise of the ICT industries encouraged this development. Policy makers rushed to embrace labels like the knowledge economy, the information society, and the clever country. Universities hopped on the bandwagon. Even so, there is little evidence that the late twentieth century was especially creative. In retrospect, the rise of a new industry sector is not something extraordinary. It is rather the norm of modern capitalism. That is how industrial capitalism functions, as Schumpeter reiterated ad nauseam. Without such invention, we are all dead. Why should we regard it as special? The evidence from copyright and patent registrations is that there was no explosive moment of innovation in the late twentieth century, even if ICT did manage to recover a badly faltering technology momentum that had reached a bleak bottom during the 1970s.

22 Copyright registrations today cover a remarkable spectrum of creative works including non-dramatic literary works, works of the performing arts, musical works, dramatic works, choreography and pantomimes, motion pictures and filmstrips, works of the visual arts, including two-dimensional works of fine and graphic art, sculptural works, technical drawings and models, photographs, cartographic works, commercial prints and labels, works of applied arts, and sound recordings.

23 The figures cited are from the US Copyright Office and the US Census Bureau, Current Population Reports. See also M. Boldrin and D.K. Levine (2008: 100).

24 Categories added to the US schedule of copyright protected works: Motion pictures (1912), Recording and performance of non-dramatic literary works (1953), Computer programmes (1980), Semi-conductor chips (1984), Architectural works (1990), Vessel hulls (1998).

25 Boldrin and Levine (2008), chapter 5.

Achievements in fundamental discovery are even less impressive when we step back and look at them in historical perspective (Murray 2003: 309–30). Per capita measures of fundamental discovery in Europe and North America strongly suggest that the golden age of the visual arts was between the mid-1400s and mid-1500s with a second peak in the mid-1600s. Music creation peaks in the early 1700s and sustains a moderate high through to the middle of the 1800s. Western literature peaks in the early 1600s and again in the middle of the 1800s. Scientific creativity peaks in the later 1600s and then again for a remarkable period from the mid-1700s to the late 1800s. Huebner calculated that high-level technology discovery world-wide peaked in 1873.[26] Similarly, after 1870, the rate of major achievement – that is, the number of outstanding figures, works and events per capita, in the United States and Europe – in mathematics, visual arts, and literature also declines (Murray: 312–20). There were some countervailing trends: an upswing in the number of significant figures (though not works and events) in literature, science, and visual art from 1900 to 1920 and an upswing in technology advances in the period from 1920 to 1950. The film arts flourished in the 1940s and 1950s, as did recorded music from the mid-1960s to the mid-1970s. However, overall since 1870 there has been a long-term downturn in creativity.

The Economics of Laughter

The dynamic of creativity in the last 140 years has trended down with punctuated up-swings. In the United States, the turn-of-the-century, the late 1920s and the late 1980s were relative high spots. The presidential eras of Theodore Roosevelt (1901–09), Calvin Coolidge (1923–29), and Ronald Reagan (1981–89) were the most creative in the American twentieth century.[27] This pattern of punctuation, though, poses an interesting conundrum. In the last 50 years the overwhelming majority of academics in American research universities have identified with the liberal wing of the Democratic Party.[28] However, the peak of American creation

26 Huebner (2005). Silverberg and Bart Verspagen (2003) offer a somewhat different medium-term picture but the same long-term conclusion. Their quadratic analysis show a higher level of innovation during 1850 and 1900 that levels off around 1930, or in the case of patents, 1920. Silverberg and Verspagen's general assessment is that the rate of basic innovation slowed down in the twentieth century after a period of relatively rapid increase in the latter half of the nineteenth century. The authors' caution about this analysis stemmed from the fact that the data they analysed extended only to the end of the 1970s.

27 The history of US copyright registration is graphically represented in the statistical chart in Boldrin and Levine (2008: 100). For US patent registration, see Figure 3 in Jonathan Huebner (2005: 895). For graphic depictions of comparable trends across both the United States and Europe, as it affects major works and inventions, see the charts in Charles Murray (2003: 428, 437, 441).

28 Ladd and Lipset (1975); Carnegie Foundation for the Advancement of Teaching (1989); Shepherd and Shepherd (1994); Hamilton and Hargens (1993); Tierney (2004);

in the last 100 years occurred during Republican presidencies.[29] Few American researchers or cultural figures today would identify with Teddy Roosevelt, Calvin Coolidge, or Ronald Reagan. Most would blanch at the very thought of that. However, such a thought may help us better understand one of the primary social conditions for creativity. Dean Keith Simonton posed the interesting question: what social factor most strongly correlates with periods of peak creation in societies generally? The answer that he drew from extensive historico-metrical data was, in a nutshell, political decentralization – the division of an overarching political world into autonomous states (1984: 143–6). Correlated with this phenomenon is what Philip Tetlock and his colleagues dubbed 'integrative complexity' – the ability to tolerate ideological polarities and synthesize them.[30] High-functioning enigmatic political regimes – i.e. ones that internalize high levels of opposing views and yet at the same time exhibit high levels of integration of those competing perspectives – are crucibles of peak creation (Murphy 2010). A society that can cope with opposition at the same time as it can function in an integrated manner is a society that is able to meld incongruous values into a rich uncanny culture. On paper such a culture might be expected not to work. In practice, such cultures can and do work – wonderfully.

The ancient and Renaissance city states are classic examples (Simonton 1984: 144; Murphy 2001: 15–92, 123–92). The federal-state forms and distinctive city-regions of the United States resemble them in a structural sense (Murphy 2001: 255–314; Murphy 2006). However structural patterns, no matter how powerful, do not in themselves explain the conundrum of why it is that creative peaks in the United States correlate with Republican presidencies. This historical pattern contradicts the common assumption that liberal culture best supports research. Tetlock's conclusion that moderate liberalism best aligns with cognitive complexity is widely cited, though the underlying studies do have their critics.[31]

Rothman, Lichter and Nevitte (2005); Klein and Stern (2005).

29 What about the case of the liberal *bête noire*, the George W. Bush administration? Patent registrations grew dramatically during the Bush years. Compared to the rate of 0.07 registrations per capita in 1994 and 0.09 in 1998, the rate in 2002 was 0.12 and in 2007 had risen to 0.15. The record in copyright registrations was less impressive, with a steady 0.18 registrations per 100 in the same years, compared with 0.20 and 0.21 in 1994 and 1998. Notably the latter figures lag well behind the rates of copyright registration achieved during the Reagan and George H.W. Bush years.

30 Suedfeld and Tetlock (1977: 169–84); Suedfeld, Tetlock and Streufert (1992); Tetlock (1998: 639–52). The toleration supposed by integrative complexity is more closely aligned with creativity than measures of social toleration that Richard Florida uses in constructing his indexes of creative cities. Interesting as the latter are, they are not epiphenomena of the act of creation in the same way that the capacity to integrate conflicting cognitive perspectives is.

31 Tetlock (1984); Tetlock (1986); Tetlock, Bernzweig and Gallant (1985). Critics include Gruenfeld (1995). Gruenfeld's key point is that high-low integrative complexity on the US Supreme Court aligns not with the liberal-conservative divide but with whether

Sometimes in these kinds of matters, especially where the interpretation of data is contested, it is worth going back to basics. About one matter at least there seems to be consensus. A defining characteristic of the imagination is that it comprehends concepts simultaneously in multiple dimensions. The imagination is ambidextrous – and integrative complexity, like value freedom, is an expression of that. However, the very condition of multi-dimensionality begs serious questions about the equation of liberalism and complexity. The psychologist Jonathan Haidt conducted a number of survey studies. From these he concluded that liberals are politically responsive on the dimensions of protection/care and fairness/reciprocity – a commonsensical conclusion.[32] He observed that the same principle applies to conservatives but that conservatives are also responsive to three further dimensions: in-group/loyalty, authority/respect, and purity/sanctity. If the integration of dimensions is a key indicator of imaginative thinking, which very likely it is, then the conservative curiously has an edge over the liberal. It might be countered that the values of order or authority (for example) are not valid values but, if so, that then defines complexity out of the equation of integrative complexity. The imagination *stretches* to integrate contrary dimensions. Can a high-functioning contemporary society be 'Millian' without being 'Durkheimian' at the same time? Can such a society function without an ironic, even comic, relation to what to the great American sociologist Talcott Parsons (1970) called the AGIL dimensionality of modern society – the adaptive (economic), goal-orientated (political), integrative (normative), and latent pattern maintenance (cultural) aspects of these societies?

Ambidextrousness and paradox are characteristics of strong cultures, and strong cultures in their turn are the principal drivers of knowledge (Murphy 2010). Comedy and tragedy are iconic forms of strong culture. They meld the antithetical and incongruous. Shakespeare imagined history in this way (Murphy 2009). Shakespeare could be cutting toward rebels yet damning of tyrants in the same breath. The vocation of science that Max Weber appealed to is similar in nature. Its key tenet, value-freedom, is double-edged in the same way that history and tragedy and comedy are. The double-edge of creation exhibits itself in paradoxes – in which nothing is something, division and integration are identical, reduced taxes mean greater tax revenues, cats are simultaneously alive and dead in the thought

---

the opinion writer is writing for a Court majority (higher complexity) or a Court minority (lower complexity).

32 Graham, Haidt and Nosek (2009). In the article 'What makes people vote republican?' (2008), Haidt reports that: 'In several large internet surveys, my collaborators Jesse Graham, Brian Nosek and I have found that people who call themselves strongly liberal endorse statements related to the harm/care and fairness/reciprocity foundations, and they largely reject statements related to ingroup/loyalty, authority/respect, and purity/sanctity. People who call themselves strongly conservative, in contrast, endorse statements related to all five foundations more or less equally'. See also Haidt (2009a) and Haidt and Graham (2009b).

experiments of science, and warfare economics coexists with welfare economics. Without Eisenhower's Advanced Research Projects Agency and the Cold War, the Internet – the research medium par excellence – would not exist. The military-industrial economy stands to the welfare economy as Spencer Dryden's bed-rock martial drum-beat does to Grace Slick's possessed singing on Jefferson Airplane's 1967 classic hippie-psychedelic masterpiece *White Rabbit*.[33] As Californian Governor, Ronald Reagan had many testy battles with the 1968 generation of students and faculty at the University of California. Confronted on one occasion by protestors carrying banners saying 'Make love, not war', he quipped that they probably didn't know how to do either. However, for of all Reagan's impatience with the baby-boom generation, it was his successor – the ascetic Democrat Jerry Brown – who slashed university budgets and made professors teach longer hours, while Reagan's America saw a jump in R&D spending as a share of GDP from 2.1 percent in 1979 to 2.7 percent in 1984. It has remained around that level ever since (Carlsson, Acs, Audretsch and Braunerhjelm 2007).

The lesson learned is that, sometimes, one's worst political enemy is in fact one's best friend. Lessons in irony, in principle, should find a ready audience among researchers. After all, in matters of the mind nothing is more profound than the economics of laughter. What most becomes the human imagination is wit, and the brevity of wit is the mind at its sharpest. However, while much is said in theory in the defence of irony, wit, and paradox, in practice, earnestness and complaint are often allowed to brush them aside. The dangers of acting that way are not political. The ideology of researchers has a miniscule impact on politics. Researcher bias is like media bias. It has inconsequential effects on the political system. Journalists might be a very liberal cohort, but elections are not decided by their political preferences. As Paul Lazarsfeld (1901–76) concluded in the 1950s, the media have a weak influence and minimal effect on the political system.[34] Universities have even less influence on the political system. However, arguably, the political system or more precisely political symbolism has a significant influence on the universities. This influence may not always be positive. Max Weber (1946) observed the stifling effect that politics can have on research. This phenomenon does not occur because politics is capable of controlling the life of the mind. The ancient Greek Stoics already knew that was nonsensical. One can imprison a person's body but not a person's mind. Much more important are the subtle and indirect effects of political atmospherics. Certain common styles of politics have a sullen effect on the mind. These styles are ideological, moralistic, and non-ironic. They exhibit few signs of integrative complexity. They inspire priggishness and pomposity. They lack value-freedom and the kind of wit that

33 'White Rabbit' (Grace Slick), single by Jefferson Airplane from the album *Surrealistic Pillow* (RCA Victor 1967).

34 Katz and Lazarsfeld (1955); Lazarsfeld, Berelson and McPhee (1954). It was the work of Edward Shils, Talcott Parson's collaborator at the University of Chicago, which suggested this line of inquiry to Lazarsfeld.

accompanies it. The joke, like the metaphor, transports us from one idea or one value to another. Wit and analogy are conducted by the twists, turns, leaps, and jumps of the imagination (Davis 2007; Murphy 2009). The act of imagination – the act of creation – causes us mentally to 'switch' sides. This ability is indispensable to the scientist who is able thereby to imagine light as a wave and a particle simultaneously. It is not amenable, though, to the political ingénue who feels a deep urge to 'take sides' without any sense of irony. One wonders whether the triumph of the ingénue is reflected in falling rates of discovery and innovation measurable in copyright and patent registrations per capita and in the long-term decline in the production of great works per capita over the past 140 years in most areas of the arts and sciences. If so, the absence of laughter might turn out to be no laughing matter after all.

Chapter 7
Society

Imagination and the Autonomous Society

Modern economies are characterized by long waves of industrialization. It was Joseph Schumpeter who first observed that each wave is set in motion by acts of innovation and creation. Since the beginning of the industrial era, the world has experienced four of these waves. The modern world accordingly can be divided into four periods. These are the epochs of the machine, empire, nation, and globe. The most recent epoch – the global era, the communications and media age – ended in 2008–10. What began in 1950 concluded decisively, with a thud, with the onset of the Global Financial Crisis. Just as with each of its predecessors, the effects of the age of globalization will haunt us, like a ghostly trace, in perpetuity. But what is gone is gone. The power of the media age retreated, swiftly. It ended, as all long waves do, amidst a miasma of debt, speculation, and recession. In the blink of an eye, the imaginative power that underpinned the once-triumphal global knowledge economy entered into deep recession.

The future is unknowable. This means that the world now waits uncertainly for the next wave of industrialization to unfurl. It is possible to make guesses about what the next wave might contain. But if this is done, it needs to be done in full awareness that almost all social prophecies fail. The usefulness of such hypothesizing is not to spell out what will happen in the future. It is rather a prompt to better understand the nature, structure and function of the collective imagination present and past. The hypothetical future in other words helps explain what has already taken place . It helps explain how, through cycles of expansion and contraction and climactic moments of expansion-in-contraction, the collective imagination fuels the diaphragm of economies and the long-term, large-scale oscillations of social prosperity. The collective faculty of the imagination is able to play this role because the imagination is creative. That is to say, it is not discursive like reason. It does not judge. Nor does it predicate. Rather the imagination *outputs*. It creates virtual objects that are translated via production into the real objects that populate the world around us and that constitute the second nature that human beings inhabit.

The primary medium of the creation of this artefactual world, this second nature, is paradox. Imaginary creation in other words precedes material production. Like all social orders, what gives industrial modernity its power are its paradoxes. Modern societies succeed in so far as they master paradox. Social order is energized and animated by a collective imagination and the core of that imagination is paradoxical. Another way of saying the same thing is that the core of the collective imagination is topological. The simplest illustration of mathematical topology is the continuous deformation of the coffee cup into the doughnut. Topology is the study of invariance under conditions of transformation, which is also a useful definition of the imagination. The imagination grasps the similarity of what is dissimilar. Societies have to do the same. They produce the means, forces and objects of production via the inventive media of the imagination – analogy, metaphor, patterns of resemblance and contrast, and all the rest – that have the paradoxical capability of producing what is invariant and transformative at the same time.

The pivotal role of paradox as the medium of the object-creating power of the imagination means that those rare societies that are good at mastering paradox are liable to have strong economies. Such mastery of paradox is always time-limited. The paradox that 'hard' technology could be driven by 'soft' ware set ablaze for a moment the collective imagination of the 1980s. Today this idea is a cliché. Never mind that creation always ends up as cliché. What matters is that from time to time super-positional couplings, dyads, conjurations, ironies, and metaphors give rise to strange and compelling entities that energize the social imagination. It is this, the enigmatic force of the collective imagination, which animates, drives and forges large-scale aesthetic creation and scientific invention. This, in turn, conditions economic growth and social prosperity. The collective imagination is not a kind of 'group think'. It is not the big-brother society or even the big society. It is not state direction or government planning. Rather it simply echoes the reality that societies as well as individuals create, and both create through the medium of paradoxical imagining.

The distinction between individual and social imagining might be made clearer with the following example. The philosopher Aristotle imagined the automaton. This was a tool that moved itself. It did so as if a shuttle could weave and a plectrum could touch the lyre without a hand guiding them.[1] Aristotle was not the first to conceive of this in antiquity. Nor was he the last. From the myth of Pygmalion to Pindar's seventh Olympic Ode ('The animated figures stand/Adorning every public street/And seem to breathe in stone, or move their marble feet') to the experimental pneumatic and hydraulic devices of Hero of Alexandria, the ancient world was rich in models of automata. Yet this was still not an automated society. In contrast, in modernity as we understand it, whole societies, not just individuals, began to systematically imagine a world populated by such machines. Thus began the industrial age. A handful of societies on the littoral rim of north-west Europe – England and Scotland notably – in the period between 1780 and 1850 conceived the paradoxical concept of a world in which the human quality of self-motion was transferred to tools, giving birth not only to industrial machinery but also to industrial society. Individual inventors like Newcomen, Watt, Hargreaves, Arkwright, and Cartwright played a key role in this. This new world, though, did not simply turn upon their technological genius. The larger industrializing

1 Aristotle, *The Politics*, I.iv.

society also gave that genius impetus and drew it out of itself. The industrial machine flourished in societies that ruminated not only on the idea of the self-moving machine but also upon auto-motion more generally. Even romantic critics of the machine and 'accursed' industry were fascinated by self-motion. Modern societies imagine themselves as autonomous, as moving without the direction of a guiding hand. There are many, perhaps infinite, versions of the paradox of objects that move themselves and of human beings who act with discipline and yet without reference to the guiding hand, and who can brag about 'how I escaped my certain fate', as one wag put it. Images of autonomy, auto-poiesis, self-organization, self-direction, self-rule, self-determination, independence, self-government, self-reliance, and sovereignty coexist with images of auto-mobility, automation, automata, mechanization, computerization, robotics, computer-aided manufacturing, artificial intelligence, cybernetics, pattern recognition, androids and cyborgs. The modern imagination seeded the aspiration for an autonomous society and the accompanying paradoxical impulse toward ordered liberty. In this enigmatic matrix, freedom accordingly interpolates necessity while necessity is incorporated into and exists as freedom; wilful purpose aspires to general pattern while impersonal order and abstract form inspire audacious intentions. Each one of these is interjected, interposed, insinuated, imported, inlaid and inset in the other one.

What we conventionally understand as modernity subdivides into four lengthy periods (see Tables 7.1a and 7.1b). Each period lasts around 70 to 80 years. Each period has a wave-like structure. Each of these long waves overlaps with the preceding wave. The motion of these waves is paradoxical. Every act of expansion or up-turn contains the seeds or currents of contraction and downturn. Every long wave contains elements or characteristics that presage the next long wave. The ideologists of industrial modernity have typically thought of it as a world of progress. Yet the underlying paradox of modernity is that, to the extent that progress exists, and to an extent it does, progress is cyclical. Modern economies are dominated by cycles – what comes around goes around. There are the Kitchin inventory cycles lasting three to five years, the Juglar business investment cycles lasting eight to 10 years, the Kuznets infrastructure investment cycles lasting 15 to 25 years and the long Kondratieff waves lasting 70 to 80 years. Modernity does move forward, but in part it moves forward by going backwards or at least by going around.

Table 7.1a Long waves – matter and form

				Matter	**Form**	**Form**	**Form**	**Form**
Long Waves	*Eras*	*Technologies*	*Turning points**	*Material*	*Hierarchies*	*Markets*	*Networks*	*Publics*
1780–1870	Machine Industrial	Inland canal networks, industrial machines, wrought iron, water power	1815, 1848 Trough: 1790 Peak: 1810–1817 Trough: 1844–1851	Iron	Factory	Maritime	Canal	Coffee House
1850–1920	Empire	Railway networks, steamships, electrical telegraph, standardization, steel, coal	1870, 1896 Trough: 1844–1851 Peak: 1870–1875 Trough: 1890–1896 Peak: 1914–1920	Steel	Company	Imperial	Rail	Parliament
1900–1970	Nation Organization	Automobiles, electrical, urban transit and utility networks, corporate organization, mass production, telephone, wireless, oil	1914, 1922, 1945 Peak: 1914–1920 Trough: 1929–1935 Peak: 1957–1962		Corporation	National	Telegraph	Reading
1950–2010	Global Media	Electronics, television, jet engines, air conditioners, computers, Internet, plastics, fibre-optics, semi-conductor materials, nuclear energy	1968, 2001, 2008 Peak: 1957–1962 Trough: 1984–1991 Peak: 1996–2001 Trough: 2008–2010+	Plastics, fibre optics, semi-conductors	Multinational Corporation	Global	Tele-communication	Electronic

Note: *Peak and trough economic data modelled by Korotayev and Tsirel 2010.

Table 7.1b Long waves – efficient cause and knowledge

				Efficient Cause	Efficient Cause	Efficient Cause	Efficient Cause	Knowledge
Long Waves	*Eras*	*Technologies*	*Turning points*	*Aesthetic*	*Economic*	*Political*	*Values*	
1780–1870	Machine Industrial	Inland canal networks, industrial machines, wrought iron, water power	1815, 1848 Trough: 1790 Peak: 1810–1817 Trough: 1844–1851	Historical	Industrial	Command	Exchange-value	Economic
1850–1920	Empire	Railway networks, steamships, electrical telegraph. standardization, steel, coal	1870, 1896 Trough: 1844–1851 Peak: 1870–1875 Trough: 1890–1896 Peak: 1914–1920	Impressionist	Venture	Parliamentary Law	Vital-value	Symbolic
1900–1970	Nation Organization	Automobiles, electrical, urban transit and utility networks, corporate organization, mass production, telephone, wireless, oil	1914, 1922, 1945 Peak: 1914–1920 Trough: 1929–1935 Peak: 1957–1962	Abstract	Procedural Organizational	Regulation	Norm-value	Linguistic
1950–2010	Global Media	Electronics, television, jet engines, air conditioners, computers, Internet, plastics, fibre-optics, semi-conductor materials, nuclear energy	1968, 2001, 2008 Peak: 1957–1962 Trough: 1984–1991 Peak: 1996–2001 Trough: 2008–2010+	Pop-Post-modern	Distribution	Norms	Sign-value	Medial
(1990) 2010	Mega-regions?	Three-dimensional printing?	2008	Artefact?	Productive?	Patterns?	Object-value?	Pattern?

Note: *Peak and trough economic data modelled by Korotayev and Tsirel 2010.

The most profound characteristic of the first long wave, the longest of the long waves, the one that extended between 1780 and 1870, was the appearance of the self-moving tool, the industrial machine. The same period also saw extensive experiments in the conjugation of motion and space. That latter conjugation was eventually to be the defining feature of the age of empire between 1850 and 1920. Thus while the machine age in Britain and the United States saw the creation of extensive inland water-way systems, the early rail-roads and John L. McAdam's road surface, the act of metaphor, that is to say the act of transport, became the animating spirit of the age of empire. Utilizing coal as a source of its power, steam made possible the paradox of the stationary machine, the engine, which moved. The steam engine and steam ship enabled millions of people to move across the face of the earth, principally from Europe to the New World. In that fashion, for many, one's home became one's away home. To settle meant to move. Steam power and steel rails, which replaced limited-life wrought-iron rails, made this technically feasible. But first, before any technical innovation exerted its power, millions had to imagine that their home here was actually somewhere else. Such elisions proliferated. Just as the imagination melded the image of the road and the image of the rail to come up with the rail-road, so the act of conjugating writing (*graphein*) and distance (*tele*), materialized in the optical, electrical and wireless telegraph, which allowed messages to be moved for the first time almost instantly in time across space.

Like all the ages of modernity, the age of empire exhausted itself. In the case of the United States, the US Immigration Act of 1924 put an end to the vast wave of immigration from Europe that began around 1840. America's continental empire stopped, finally, at the 49th parallel. Long-dreamt plans to invade Canada were set aside. The last formal contingency plan of that kind, the 'Joint Army and Navy Basic War Plan – Red', was drafted in 1931 as part of war planning against England.[2] By the 1930s, across the world, nationalism, or in America's case isolationism, was the dominant tone of the times. In tandem, metropolitan economies with national reach challenged imperial economies. The electrification of cities facilitated this. Electrical systems (the fruit of Thomas Edison's astonishing imagination) and electric-powered machines enabled the mass production and urban transit of the Fordist age. The modern suburb, a function of transit, electrical and utility networks, emerged. The modern imaginary of auto-motion was extended, yet again, with the auto-mobile. For a time the electrification of the car was seriously contemplated, but this gave way for practical reasons to the oil-powered internal combustion engine. While the suburban metropolitan manufacturing economy steadily rose during the long wave between 1900 and 1970, in matters political the image of the nation replaced that of empire. Nation, nationalism, national self-determination, and pan-nationalism flourished during the era. Each echoed the automatism of autarchy. Nationalization, national corporatism, trade protection

2 *Joint Army and Navy Basic War Plan – Red* (Washington, D.C.: US National Archives, Joint Board, J.B. 325, serial 435–641, amended draft, 1935).

and national planning schemes were all popular. Many of the great political crises of the age were caused by the collapse of pre-modern empires under the weight of nationalism. The Austro-Hungarian, Russian, Chinese and Ottoman Empires all disintegrated, each with severe and compelling consequences. These very old empires were followed into extinction by the more modern French and British empires. However no modern imaginary and perhaps even pre-modern imaginary ever disappears completely. Each instead is sublimated. Thus empire recurs in Stalin's admix of totalitarianism and nationalism as it did in the pan-national dictatorships of the Nazi and Baath Parties, or in the empty benignity of the league of nations, as it did again with the various interventionist, multilateralist and post-colonialist currents of the more recent global era.

With each long wave, just when it appears most ascendant, it is already in descent. The era of the nation terminated with the emphatic embrace of national economic autarchy in Latin America and the triumph of movements of national self-determination in former colonies across the world. Just as national self-consciousness reached its peak in the 1950s and 1960s, it was already in recession. The global age was precipitating. It would be characterized economically by free trade and tariff reduction and politically by multilateral global organizations like the World Bank, International Monetary Fund, the World Trade Organization, the International Criminal Court, and the United Nations. In this era, international trade grew at a rate much more rapidly than the world's population did. The jet engine made possible the emergence of globe-trotting political elites. Many of the characteristic industries of the period, like airlines, the Internet, satellite and telecommunications, were literally global in nature. Not just goods but jobs, including manufacturing and service jobs, were exported across the globe. This was mirrored by the assembling of goods in plants from parts sourced all over the world. The global age was a media age, the age of the world-wide electronic reproduction and telecommunication of images, which become a big business. A global entertainment pop culture emerged while pan-religious and pan-national political extremism parodied the age's own multi-lateral, border-hopping clichés. The two coalesced in the 2001 attack on the Twin Towers in New York City. Stock schlock global entertainment images of planes crashing into buildings were rudely materialized.

The law of long waves is that whatever expands contracts. Come 2011 the most successful multi-national political-economic institution of the global era, the European Union, was in systemic crisis. The attempt to create a common currency for the European Union's disparate economies had failed. The puzzle then was – what would come next? To anyone who stands in the middle of the forest of time, that is, each one of us, little more than trees are visible. The self-understanding of an historical era comes after, not before its time. In part this is because the future cannot be known. As in quantum physics, the social observer changes what is observed – or in this case what is anticipated. Also, long waves overlap. Thus the end of one era is the beginning of another era, and so it is very difficult in situ to discern what belongs to one descending period and what to the other ascending period.

Perhaps the best approach to understanding the distinctive nature of any coming era is first to understand what each of the eras of industrial modernity share in common. The most telling thing about the history of the epoch of industrial modernity since the late eighteenth century has not been its ruptures or its breaches but rather its profound continuities. For all of its dynamism, which is vast, industrial modernity is also deeply conservative. Across two centuries its underlying structure has not changed all that much. That structure is composed of hierarchies, markets, publics and networks. The drivers of industrial modernity are aesthetic, economic, political and axiological. Modern personalities think, act and feel in terms of patterns, instruments, goals and values. The primary media of the epoch as a whole are imaginative, technological, communicative and cultural. Each of these systems, drivers, and media overlap with each other. While impersonal large-scale social action occurs on the level of cities, mega-regions, nations and global units, intimate small-scale action occurs among family, friends, peers and organizations.

The different phases, periods and long cycles of industrial modernity replicate a number of basic patterns, again and again. In each period we find new technologies that are variations on the theme of the self-moving machine. Industrial modernity began with the appearance of the self-moving stationary mechanical system, the machine. This was followed by the train, then the automobile, and then the airplane and the computer. So what is next? We can safely assume that whatever the signature technology of the fifth wave of industrialism turns out to be, it will not be the high-speed train, a concept that was minted at the turn of the twentieth century and that was first seriously tried out in the United States in the 1930s and that reached its apotheosis in Japan in 1964 with the introduction of the Shinkansen bullet train. Modernity is conservative. What it invents, it also re-invents, repeatedly. The prototype of the modern automobile was developed by Karl Benz in 1885; the mobile phone was developed in Ohio in the 1940s. Industrial eras, though, are marked by something more than re-invention. For a start, whatever the defining technology of an industrial period is, it must make the kind of difference that the railroad made when it replaced the horse-drawn wagon. In the mid-nineteenth century rail freight costs were a fifteenth of the wagon rate and a twelfth of the barge rate (Hamerow: 16). Fifty years later, rail cost a seventieth of wagon delivery (Vleck: 133). That is the type of economy that makes a real difference to human societies. To imagine what might have a comparable economic and social impact in the future is difficult and probably impossible to project. The future in that sense is unknowable. Nonetheless speculating about what such a technology might be is still interesting. It helps us understand better the era that has closed, and what it was incapable of.

So what is next? Suggestions for molecular machines or nano-machines have been around some time. In practice though, they have made less impact than was predicted. If I had to nominate a machine that might come to characterize the fifth wave of industrialism, it would be the three-dimensional printer. Like all powerful technologies, conceptually it is a contrarian machine. It is a synecdoche. Printing is minor kind of production. Three-dimensional printing merges the concepts of printing and production such that the part (printing) becomes the whole (production). In other words, production is carried out as a kind of printing rather than printing as a kind of production. Printing began as a pre-industrial technology. It was industrialized and then it was digitalized. Three-dimensional printing represents an inversion of the digital age. The dominant digital technology of the media age made it possible for real three-dimensional objects to be replicated in two-dimensional formats. From film canisters to books to newspapers to architectural models to accountant's ledger books, a massive re-mediation of material things occurred in the media age. Three-dimensional printing is an upside-down mirror of this. Three-dimensional scanning and printing processes make it possible not only to digitally scan the three dimensions of an object, but also, more interestingly, to physically print out the object in three dimensions. The virtual can now be made real, in addition to the real being made virtual. This unites together technology that began with Gutternberg (printing) with digitization (electronic scanning, emailing, and digital manipulation) with objectivation. It is the latter that is the most intriguing. It hints at a switch from an age of electronic reproduction to an age of objectivation. It suggests we might move from information to artefact and from communication to sculpture. In place of digital flows and electronic broadcasts, and instead of the wireless and the wired world, we could end up in a Pygmalion world of statues, figurines and carvings.

The possibilities of the three-dimensional printer are wide-ranging. This printing is a type of additive manufacturing. A machine, the printer, prints successive layers of material, principally today powders (plasters or resins) or liquid polymers. Biotechnology companies are developing bio-materials for printing; the printing of metals presumably will follow. Three-dimensional printing conceptually makes possible the desk-top factory. In other words it encourages a collapse of the distinction between the factory and the office. In doing so it may well transform economies of scale, making a prototype or customized-object no more expensive to produce than one of millions of a mass-produced item. In a larger sense, this points to a shift from the virtual to the real, without sacrificing the virtual. Remember that industrial modernity is conservative. What it creates, it conserves. It also creates because it conserves. When human beings create, they objectivate, which is to say they like to create objects that last. They do not just have dreams that are willow the wisp. Nor do they just think upon schemes, with their thoughts lost even to memory. Rather human beings objectivate. They work to create and externalize lasting objects that encapsulate what they ruminate about. Indeed, much, perhaps most, human thinking is objectivated outside the human mind. It is interpolated in things and spaces with physical form. The human being is by nature a maker, an artificer, a fabricator. We are artificers before we are officers. As a species, we are happiest when we produce things. We also have an impulse to produce beautiful things. These things have shape, pattern and form.

The fourth wave of industrialism, the media and global age, emphasized the power not of production but of distribution. Production was imagined under the axiological signs of distribution, delivery, supply and circulation. This was somewhat perverse, but nonetheless that was the way it was. The role of the successful state was to distribute welfare and benefits. The role of the successful company was to manage supply chains and logistics. The Internet was conceived as and functioned as a medium of distribution. The limit of the fourth wave of industrialism was experienced as the limit of distribution. The welfare state reached its fiscal limit when it began to fund distributive payments by debt. By 2010, in many countries, interest repayments on sovereign debt were monopolizing a visibly large and growing share of state spending, a self-defeating exercise. Already by 2000 and the end of the Internet boom, the limit of an economy dependent on the electronically-mediated distribution of goods was apparent. The electronic circulation of goods has its advantages. These advantages, though, cannot be sustained in the absence of new generations of durable products. This became clear when the Internet boom was replaced after 2002 in parts of the United States, Europe, and elsewhere by a mortgage boom. What was being sold was the most credulous of products. 'Sub-prime' mortgages were retailed to mortgagees who had no chance of repaying the principal of their loan. Those who wanted less fictitious investments, and yet who otherwise had little faith in industry, pumped money into the purchase of sovereign debt. Seemingly safe investment in government bonds by 2010 had in some cases turned into high risks. Governments that had accumulated too high debt levels struggled to avoid defaulting on payments to their creditors. In 2011, the European Union was contemplating paying states like Greece billions of euros to shore up repayments on the sovereign debt they had accumulated that they could never repay.

Each wave of industrialism ends in speculative booms and financial crises. Such was the ignominious end of the fourth wave of industrialism. But neither speculation nor finance is the root of the problem, though. Speculation is simply the effect of money being invested in marginal activities because there is nowhere else for the money to go, because existing industry sectors have matured and no new credible sectors have emerged. That specious instruments are created to prove that bad investments are good is the logical consequence of this. Everyone in a market seeks reassurance that the right thing has been done. That is human nature. But false confidence and irrational bravado are epiphenomena of other, deeper forces. These forces are not just monetary or fiscal, but rather are the forces of production that lie at the very heart of an economy. The greatest difficulty of industrial capitalism is its need periodically to renew its productive impulse.

The Beauty of Economy

There are many impediments to the renewal of the productive impulse. Many of those are impediments of the imagination. Two impediments are worth quickly remarking on. One is the impediment of ideology; the other is the impediment of scale. The lustre of the distributive state and the logistics firm in the fourth wave of industrialism underscored the problem of ideology. Put simply, industrial modernity routinely produces ideologies that lionize its own weaknesses. Very likely the fifth wave of industrialization, once it eventuates, will entail the same. On the other hand, lessons can be learnt. If we are entering an era of objects, a time of things, a Pygmalion age then this suggests also a return to an emphasis on work and the discipline of work.

Work, though, points to the second impediment of the imagination – that of scale. If we say a word like 'work', we immediately and naturally think of work on the small scale of individual action. We begin to anticipate that what the desktop three-dimensional printer will produce will differ from factory-scale models. We naturally talk about how the artist and the engineer will use these devices differently. Yet, crucially, the meaning of any epochal technology is not just about what individuals create or how they act. It is also about what societies create and how they act, and the switching that occurs between the small and the large scale of human endeavour. The creations of human beings are both individual and collective. The imagination is both individual and collective. We should not forget that the greatest, the most sublime, human creations are cities. Cities are accumulations of millions of units of individual makings and imaginings. Even then, the whole of a city is more than just the sum of its parts. Cities are as much works of collective imagination as they are of individual imagination. Even then, human imaginings and makings do not end with cities. We have seen repeatedly, through all of the phases of industrial modernity, the crucial influence of city mega-regions. Such regions, containing multiple cities, are invariably key centres for the creation of material wealth, social prosperity and cultural vitality. Along with cities, nations, and global structures, city mega-regions have been co-constitutive of modern spatiality.

One of the things that made city mega-regions so decisive in the epoch of industrial modernity is their ambidexterity. They are neither city, nation, nor globe yet they share characteristics of the city, the nation and the globe simultaneously. The most influential city regions in modernity have been for the most part littoral or located on river systems. After the Second World War, as the fourth wave of industrialism got into its stride, Maritime East Asia followed the classic path of the great historic portal sea regions that produced modern capitalism.[3] On the East Asian Pacific Rim, there emerged nodal centres of historically impressive growth and wealth. These were comparable with the Anglo–Scottish–Dutch

3 The role of portal regions in modern economies is discussed in Marginson, Murphy and Peters, *Global Creation*, 2010: 18–116.

North Seas ecumene in the seventeenth and eighteenth centuries, and the Boston–New York–Hudson–Great Lakes ecumene in the nineteenth century. Hong Kong and Singapore developed a per capita level of wealth similar to Japan and the United States. Taiwan and South Korea, which sit today at around 44 percent and 36 percent of the wealthiest countries' level of GNP per capita, were also remarkable success stories. After the late 1970s and the end of the Maoist dictatorship, China's coastal and delta urban regions – the Pearl Delta, the Yangtze River Delta, the Yellow River Delta-Bohai Sea, and the coastal cities of Fujian Province – began one of the greatest growth spurts in the economic history of the world.

The sprint to wealth was not uniform across Maritime East Asia, though. Seoul, Taipei, Tokyo, Singapore, Hong Kong, Beijing and Shanghai shot ahead. Manila, Bangkok, and Djakarta lagged. One way of understanding the disparities between Djakarta and Seoul, Manila and Taipei is in terms of city types. Maritime East Asia during the fourth wave of industrialism produced A-style and B-style city types. A-type cities were able to move in the direction of high concentrations of science, engineering know-how, applied art, and economic and social intelligence. Why does this matter? Look at any possible indicator of economic and social prosperity. Try anything: from education to health to infrastructure spending, from agriculture to manufacturing to service industries. What you will find is that the most reliable, consistent indicator of economic and social prosperity is 'innovation' – measured as a composite of the numbers per capita of the following: scientists and technologists in the workforce, spending on research and development, international patents registered, and research universities. In most instances the best shorthand summary index of all of these factors is the number of international patents per capita. The more of those you have, the richer you are (Porter and Stern 2001; Stern, Porter and Furman 2001). That is to say, there is a strong *outward* correlation between intellectual capital and social prosperity. Yet an important caveat applies. While knowledge is produced by creative acts, creation is not produced by knowledge. In other words, causes produce effects, but those effects do not inversely produce the cause. So, while knowledge is a measurable index of creative activity, it does not mean conversely that knowledge is the driver of creation. One of the common delusions of the fourth wave of industrialism was the fascination with the idea of 'the knowledge society'. Society, it was supposed, had passed from 'classic industrialism' to 'post-industrialism' and that the material output of the former in part was replaced by the immaterial output of the latter. Up to a point, that was correct. However, the further conclusion was not correct. This was the idea that what is produced (e.g. knowledge) is the key to explaining why some countries and some cities are highly energetic producers and others are less energetic.

In fact, knowledge does not explain the creation of knowledge, any more than it explains the creative conception of industrial artefacts. This is not to say that knowledge is not a major factor of production in modern economies. But that has been true from the beginning of the industrial era. It long preceded the fourth wave of industrialism. This is because modern industry tout court is based on science and its application. This is true irrespective of whether the industry in question is a mechanized agriculture, manufacturing, a service or a cultural industry. Without science, there is no modern industry. Modern industry is dynamic. Industry produces goods and services, while science, including the social sciences, and complemented by the arts, produces 'new generations' of goods and services – along with new generations of jobs, markets, processes, and applications. As the paradoxical expression 'new generation' suggests, these are both 'new-to-world' as well as durable and conservative. The question remains though: what is it that produces the arts and sciences that are capable of creating a venerable 'new generation' of industry? For example, the building of skyscrapers transformed not only the aesthetics of cities but also the nature of property markets and the role of architects and urban planners. The formation of 'the idea of the skyscraper' though was not a function of the property market. Nor was it a function of the existing knowledge of a profession or the existing urban law. The idea of the skyscraper redefined all of those. This should give us cause for caution on a number of fronts.

Whenever anyone turns to you and says 'look there, markets are booming', be sceptical. After the devastations of the Second World War, Germany and Japan both enjoyed a 40-year-long boom. After the ending of Maoist totalitarianism, China began a long boom at the end of 1970s. So did India in 1990. Despite much hyping, this was not unprecedented. Germany did the same between 1950 and 1990, Japan between 1955 and 1991, South Korea between 1960 and 1990. As occurred in China, 8 and 10 percent growth rates in GDP were common. The paradox of economic miracles is that they are normal. They also come to an end. Will China, which has grown rapidly for 30 years, exceed Germany's Promethean growth streak of 40 years? Perhaps, perhaps not, but the super-sized growth streak will end at some point.[4] While mega-booms are fascinating and compel the attention of observers, they are not the core of modern economies. There is a difference between a growing consumer market for pharmaceuticals and a pharmaceutical industry that produces a new drug type. The most powerful economies are not just markets with industries that employ people, but rather are economies that are capable of producing successive generations of markets, industries and jobs, and waves of industrialization. The art of modern economics is the paradoxical production of unexpected patterns and new durables. The strange translation of the unexpected into the expected has become, with the passage of time, the chief condition of economic well-being. This is because in a modern society the production of jobs – especially skilled jobs, which means high-wage jobs, and most especially the production of successive generations and types of skilled jobs, in industries we had not heard of three or five or 10 years ago – is the principle determinant of social decency. There is a simple equation: plenty

4 Weaknesses abound in China: for example the local governments who have got round limits on bond-raising by creating companies financed by loans that are excellent vehicles of patronage but that earn marginal rates of return. These are China's local capitalism's equivalent of sub-prime mortgages.

of good jobs = social fairness. This is because jobs are the most effective and efficient distributors of wealth and income. In their case, the distribution of wealth is achieved in and through the very act of the production of wealth. Nothing could be more elegant in conception or execution.

Because science lies at the core of dynamic economies that produce cumulative and consecutive generations of jobs, science is in one sense a solvent of poverty. The technologies and technicians of A-style economies create the industries that create the jobs that improve material well-being. But what is it that produces the technological power of an A-style economy? Certainly it is not education. There is no correlation between numbers in education, including higher education, and social-economic prosperity. A-style economies have educated (skilled) workforces, but so do many failed modernities such as Egypt and Russia. Indeed, in the failed modernities, education mainly produces under-employed workforces. Among other problems, these become attracted to fundamentalism, terrorism, and other messianic plagues. Education is an act of transmission. It disseminates knowledge. It does not produce knowledge. Science in contrast is productive. It produces what previously did not exist. The creative aspect of science generates unexpected ideas, systems and processes that produce the consecutive waves of industries that create successive generations of jobs and each 'next generation' of markets that confound Malthusian-style fears of over-population, over-production and under-consumption.

There is one thing about creative science. It is not achieved by piracy. It is perfectly true – copying will get you cheap drugs and cheap DVDs. The attraction of that to low-GNP-per-capita countries is perfectly intelligible. But what is logical often at the end of the day does not make good sense. That said, copyright is not the *sine qua non* of economic prosperity either. Intellectual property is an indicator of economic and social success. An indicator is a symptom but it is not the source of social and economic wealth creation. Intellectual property is an index of something other than itself. It is a social measure of originality. It is a useful, though hardly exhaustive, social metric of inventiveness. Amassing copyrights and patents is the consequence of an inventive society. The accumulation of intellectual capital, though, does not explain the origin of such inventiveness. Conversely, while copying can be a leg up to inventiveness, it is also a dire trap. The person who learns to reproduce something runs the risk of never learning the nature of the very different art of creation. Thus the question still remains: where does creative science come from?

The single most potent source of science is art – or beauty. Einstein spent a life time insisting that the things that he was captivated by were simplicity and unity. These are classic aesthetic values. Great science is characterized by the pursuit of beauty, elegance, and symmetry. Beauty, though, is still not the touchstone of creative science. Rather it is the interstitial stepping stone to that core. Creation is the unification of divergent quantities, qualities and powers. We create when we unify bitter and sweet, light and dark, large and small. Most often we do this aesthetically. We bring together what has been set asunder by establishing a point of equilibrium between polar forces or qualities. When we do this successfully, we register something like beauty or elegance. Creation spirals up out of the tension of opposites. In the act of creation, we reconcile the (seemingly) irreconcilable. We make the horrible joyful and the disgusting humorous. We make fear pleasurable and turn pleasure into work. In creation, the weakest is the strongest, the passing event lasts, and the contingent attains necessity. In all creation, that which is created originates from its opposite. Thus what is an opposite in creation is the different appearance of the same thing. In the police state, we lie to save our friend. Thus we behave well by behaving badly. That is the moral beauty of paradox. And paradox lies at the heart of creation. All beauty is paradoxical because in unifying bitter and sweet or light and shadow it equates contrary qualities, or turns a quality into its opposite. It equates thesis and antithesis, generating thereby an interesting synthesis.

There are many specific kinds of beauty – ranging from the fine arts to terraced horticulture, from machine beauty to athletic grace. Perhaps the single most important social exemplar of beauty is the city. Successful cities do what creation does. They turn shadow into light. We see this in the case of the A-style urbanism of East Asia. In some ways, a technopolis like Singapore is among the most striking modernist-apartment cities in the world. The beauty of the technopolis is not picturesque. It is not romantic. It is not a medieval or antique kind of beauty. Rather it is the beauty of an efficient modern functional order – which, all told, on a world scale is a rare and great achievement. Such cities are lucid or at least easy to negotiate. They have a rising, escalating, vertical scale that is often dramatic and sometimes compelling. The B-style cities, Djakarta, Metro Manila, Bangkok among them, were significantly less successful than the A-style cities in achieving a dynamic spiral of science, economy, and metropolis during the fourth wave of industrialism. This was not a function of size. There is no observable correlation between city size and social prosperity. Neither was it a function of resources. Many historic rich societies have begun poor – the Dutch and the Venetians are important cases in point. There is a strong argument to say that South Korea managed the transition to relative affluence precisely because it lost the resource-rich North to a totalitarian-slave regime.

The seemingly illogical pairing of scarce resources and productive economies highlights the peculiar, one might say unexpected, and most certainly paradoxical advantages of societies with a creative pulse – or rather creativity arises from this paradox. Scarcity generates abundance. From Venice to Tokyo, Hong Kong to New York often those least endowed by nature have been the best off. Underpinning this is the fact that the art of science is the achieving of more with less. This is also a potent formula for cities with millions of people. The essence of beauty, and thus also of science, is economy or what Einstein called simplicity. The economist and the technologist both aim in their different ways to achieve the most output for the least input of energy. A beautiful machine, a beautiful piece of software code, and a beautiful social system all do the same thing. Poverty and economy are curiously similar. They are both functions of less, only in the case of poverty less is not more. B-style cities have too little of the economical less – the less of artful morphological simplicity. Instead, they have too much of a hollow less – the less of chaotic busyness or entropic torpor. Megapolitan cities often massively under-employ their populations, and this is a key reason for enervating poverty. Sometimes this is socially sanctioned. Elites enjoy having the under-employed waiting around for them. These cities waste human energies, or allow them to go to waste. What follows from this are shanty towns and demoralizing poverty. In social systemic terms, the most important inputs into any economy are human energies. Effective use of such energies requires skill and thought. Social energy or dynamism, however, is generated by the tension between opposite things. Once it is created such energies require morphological shaping or patterning. That is what thought and skill does. On a social scale, B-style cities build in subtle preferences for unskilled labour instead of inventive industry. Invention discerns patterns that reduce labour. The art of science is to devise economical methods rather than apply raw power. The paradox of a modern economy is that less labour equals more jobs.

Grasping such paradoxes is important. Understanding that they are paradoxes is even more important. Ask yourself what do the industrial powers of Maritime East Asia have in common? What explains their rise during the fourth wave of industrialism? The standard answer to that question in the 1990s was 'Confucianism'. These were states that shared some kind of Confucian ethos. While Confucianism of a kind does colour the spirit of state capitalism of post-Mao China, and it does echo in the South Korean state's stress on education, it does not explain the creative pulse. Confucian capitalism is capitalism with strong bureaucratic and patrimonial traits. In contrast, the common denominator of the A-style East Asian cities including the Chinese coastal mega regions is a strong dose of Taoism (or Taoist-influenced Zen in Japan's case). What makes Taoism important is that it is a heterodox religion of paradoxes. Taoism is redolent in paradoxes.[5] This is far from trivial when we realize that paradox – the union of opposites – lies at the heart of creativity. No paradox, no creativity; no creativity, no science. The relational character of Taoism has strong parallels with the ideas of the pre-Socratics that drove the birth of ancient Greek science.[6] At the heart of pre-Socratic thought was the idea of the union of opposites. This was the antipodal fulcrum upon which knowledge pivoted.

Like philosophy, heterodox religion is full of paradox. Protestantism began with the paradox that worldly success was a sign amidst uncertainty that you would get into heaven. Thousands of sociologists are still trying to figure out that paradox. In fact, Christianity tout court is based on paradox. What is more

5 Here are a number of such paradoxes: (1) the best path of action is non-action; (2) 30 spokes of a wheel are made one by holes in a hub; (3) for a house, the good thing is level ground, in thinking, depth is good.

6 This is echoed in the relational nature of the Chinese language (Lash 2010: 221–6) which is permeated by polarities and dyads (father-son, etc.).

paradoxical than the notion of the virgin birth – or the idea of a messiah who is sceptical of his anointed followers? Indeed what is more paradoxical than the Christian desire for the death of death, or the belief that the lion with all its instinctive ferocity will lie down beside the lamb with all its dumb gentleness? The great Catholic writer G.K. Chesterton observed that paradox lies at the heart of virtue. Courage is a strong desire to live taking the form of a readiness to die. Charity is the preparedness to pardon unpardonable acts and to love unlovable people. Modesty is a kind of prostrate pride, and poverty is abolished not by the abolition of property but by the restoration of property. In a manner both consistent and paradoxical, Chesterton declared such heterodoxy to be the acme of orthodoxy. Indeed he called his principal treatise on it *Orthodoxy* (1908/2004) – a nice touch, that.

Paradox applies as much to economics as it does to morals. Take for instance the case of intellectual property, one of the newer kinds of property. It is a product of the post-Napoleonic age when copyright and patent offices appeared. What Chesterton would have made of the idea of intellectual capital is unclear. He may have appreciated the paradox of it. Intellectual property requires us to own what is common. This is a scandal in some people's eyes. But not, I think, if we also understand the more interesting feature of it, and the condition of such property – the necessity of making common what is private. After all, what is the worth of an idea without an audience, or of a patent without someone who wants to apply it? That there is an inexplicable loop at the core of societies that accumulate intellectual capital underscores the importance of religious 'mystery' to modern economies. We can give 'rational' explanations of the circle that leads from science to economy to city to science to economy to city, and so on. But the circle itself encircles strange paradoxes, such as less labour means more jobs, or fewer resources means greater productiveness, or that wealth is the key to heaven, or that science is an unending process of conception understood as virgin birth.

It is true that these paradoxes are annoying and sometimes even sound blasphemous to orthodox ears. They certainly have the aura of absurdity about them. But they also work. Is there any more potent or useful bit of economic advice than the paradox that one has to 'spend money to make money'? Modern capitalism was built on such paradoxes. Not least of all this is true of the paradox of innovation. You may have noticed that when people claim to be innovating, what they are usually doing is regurgitating. They are copying the latest trend. In point of fact, newness is normally repetition. We do what we have not done before by repeating what someone else has already done. After all, why try and reinvent the wheel? Homo sapiens is a herd creature. Yet some of the herd does march to a different drum. There is a curious human pull toward poly-rhythms. Those who 'step out of step' have an appetite to create something new-to-the-world. But this is something that is very difficult to understand because that which is new-to-the-world sits right on the paradoxical edge between what exists and what does not exist. Creation is a function of what simultaneously exists and does not exist. In a similar contrarian vein, innovation can be understood as restoration –

the eternal return of the same. We see this in the case of Einstein who 'began by returning' to Euclid as a pathway to the non-Euclidian geometries that became the foundation of his revolutionary physics. This is an example of a more general principle that virgin birth in the arts and sciences relies paradoxically on the rebirth or renaissance of great forms or universal morphologies. Thus it turns out that the most daring innovations are often the most conservative. The great howling blast of modern capitalism that appeared in North West Europe and then in North America was routinely accompanied by antique motifs, principally Hellenism and various interpretations of ancient Rome, or else revivals of the Renaissance. The greatest modernism was always accompanied by the exploration of classicism. The heights of innovation are always deeply conservative. The paradox of creation is consistent in its ironic inconsistency. The origin of anything is its opposite. When we come to speculate about what lies before us, *viz.* the fifth wave of industrialism, we should keep this in mind.

Social Class and Creative Economies

From a sociological and historical standpoint, it is an empirical truism that innovation concentrates. It clusters in defined geographical locations, most especially on the littoral rim or edge of continents – from the Mediterranean to the North Sea to the East and West Coasts of Australia and America, to maritime East Asia, and (today) to the Gulf of Mexico and the Baltic. The puzzle is, though, that even in these great portal regions, innovation concentrations appear and disappear and sometimes reappear over time. Why Italy in the fifteenth century and Israel in the twentieth century? Why the Gulf of Mexico now, but not a hundred years ago? Why Seoul today and not Manila?

The question has already been answered. The answer lies in the strange old-but-new-to-the-world of paradox. This is a very strange world indeed. It is a world in which conservative societies race ahead as radical innovators, and mercurial innovators fail to achieve anything much. The pendulum of successful modernity is pivoted exquisitely between rebirth and birth. The challenge for poor societies is to find their own paradoxical entry into prosperous modernity. The challenge for those further up the ladder is to maintain and expand the scope of their paradoxical behaviour. Each established economy has to periodically re-invent itself. This is not a leap into the unknown. Every innovation is a kind of continuity. The fund of invention though is not inexhaustible. Great cities rise and fall as do great societies. The ability to control the tense relation of opposites and to generate each thing (sweetness) out of its opposite (sourness) is demanding. Eventually things slacken. The irony and wit of creation falter. Smugness and complacency sets in.

Take the case of California. Across three long waves of economic development, its coast line produced one of the great portal economies of the world. From 1850 to 1950 California's economy and society developed in fascinating ways, animated by the mirror cities of Los Angeles and San Francisco. From 1950 to 2000, it grew to become the sixth largest economy in the world. Then in 2000, the information technology industry, which had been the corner-stone of the Californian economy since the 1980s, declined sharply. This was a microcosm of what afflicted the global economy which had entered one of its periodic phases of flagging creative energy. The information technology industry drew on a series of key inventions that dated from the 1940s to the early 1980s. Little new of enduring value appeared after that. The late 1990s was a time of promethean activity but a lot of it was hollow. Money nonetheless poured into the information industry because it had nowhere else to go. The IT bubble collapsed in 2000. This was followed by a property bubble that collapsed in 2008. As the creative pulse ebbed, state debt ballooned in California. The liberals who dominated the politics and ethos of the state promoted a programmatic mix of deficit spending, regulatory over-reach, uneconomic technologies (e.g. wind and solar energy), science-as-ideology (climate change policy) and various fantasies of 'innovation' as a way out of the sorry impasse. Holes began to appear in the highways of California. State spending on schools, universities and public pension schemes became unsustainable. Cities faced bankruptcy or dysfunctional austerity because of the untenable entitlements that had been bestowed on their retirees.

As the first decade of the twenty-first century rolled on, California's malaise echoed through American national life, indeed through most OECD countries. At its root, the malaise reflected the way in which economics and politics had been seduced by kitsch. The bankers who sold baroque financial products to guarantee sub-prime investments sold kitsch products. The investors who bought those products were hooked on kitsch finance. So also were the mortgagees who had no income and no assets to repay the loans they were encouraged to take out. So were the Clinton-era policy architects who believed that giving loans to people who had no means of repaying those loans was progressive social policy and who elbowed banks with regulations to mandate the policy. So were the financial wizards who packaged a few good mortgages with a lot of unviable ones to be sold-on to unsuspecting clients. So was the US Federal Reserve which engineered artificially low interest rates to feed the property boom. Everyone loved the feel-good kitsch. It reassured with fake and mawkish emotion.

It could do this because a kind of kitsch now percolated through the whole of the public policy system. Although the roots of this extend back into the nineteenth century, the kitschification of the political system accelerated after 1968, when a kind of liberal fundamentalism exploded in popularity.[7] Its impact was broad-reaching. It turned most public policies into parodies of themselves. Its basic premise reversed the view of millennia that individuals were capable of acts of evil while a well-ordered society was a bulwark against predatory behaviour. In this kitsch world, human beings were good and only did bad things because they

7 The term liberal fundamentalism was coined by centrist Democrats William Galston and Elaine Karmack in their 1989 pamphlet *The Politics of Evasion: Democrats and the Presidency*.

were corrupted by a repressive society. Society was bad because it mutilated the wholly good nature of individuals. Society accordingly had to be undone. But paradoxically it was to be undone by the most social of means. This was not simply Gnosticism but kitsch Gnosticism. This is why the apparent anarchy of the 1960s counter-culture turned instantaneously over-night into bureaucracy. The first step of post-modern kitschification was to transform the simplicities of law into a labyrinth of regulation. Regulation and codification, common enough in the twentieth century, reached a fever-pitch by the twenty-first century, driven by kitsch progressivism. By this point, the American federal government's regulatory codes boasted over 160,000 pages of regulations.

The economic and social cost of complying with regulations is enormous.[8] Benefits are rarely if ever weighed against costs. There is a time-cost, a labour-cost, an equipment-cost but most of all there is a common-sense cost.[9] An inordinate number of regulations are silly either in concept or unintended consequence or in the rapidity by which they date. Traditional law is much more elegant. It defines the nature of injury in abstraction. Such abstractions are then applied, in court, to specific cases. Anything that is elegant in its operation is also economical in its effect. Kitsch is neither elegant nor consequently economic. This is evident throughout the gamut of post-modern government. There were two traditional reasons that governments borrowed. One was to go to war; the other was to invest in infrastructure so as to increase the productiveness of society. Now governments borrow to fund pension schemes. Originally entitlements were paid for by tax income. More spending was made possible by greater taxable income. Greater income was a function of higher levels of business activity. In kitsch world, though, spending increasingly came to mean borrowing more or else increasing the level of taxation independent of the pitch of business activity. To borrow for purposes that are not productive, such as entitlement spending, only undermines the government's capacity to spend. This is because state spending then has to be

8 One study for the US Small Business Administration (Crain and Crain 2010) estimated the cost at 12 percent of gross domestic product, or $1.75 trillion, or $15,500 per capita. The cost to business was $8,000 per business employee and $10,500 per small business employee.

9 Consider the 2009 edition of the US federal *Manual on Uniform Traffic Control Devices*. It devised new regulations. As Diane Katz (2011) reported, these required that the 'lettering for names of streets and highways on Street Name signs shall be composed of a combination of lower-case letters with initial upper-case letters'. The upper-case letters had to be at least six inches in height, while lower-case letters had to be 4.5 inches tall. Streets with speed limits of 40 mph and over were required to have sizes of eight inches and six inches for upper- and lower-case letters, respectively. Signs for local roads with speed limits under 25 mph only needed letters half as tall as the high-speed roads. The cost of changing signs to comply with such regulations is enormous. Why require it, when a single sentence of law specifying that traffic signs be 'legible and visible' is quite sufficient. How a county enacts the law is then properly its own business and one that does not entail needless expenditure.

directed towards repaying the interest and principal on borrowings rather than financing health, education and defence. Likewise raising tax rates beyond a moderate and proportionate level simply demolishes business incentive, reducing thereby investment, business activity and consequently government revenue.

Kitsch thinking found its apotheosis in innovation policy. Of all branches of public policy, this one lends itself most to exaggeration, illusion and fakery. Almost anything, including the most puerile, can be declared an innovation. The new class of corporate, media and university intellectuals, which crystallized in 1968, was particularly apt to do this. It saw itself as transforming the world. It fantasized that it was the change-agent par excellence. Yet what changes it wrought either back-fired, came to nothing, or faded out. Its influence was world-wide, but its laboratory was California. This was a state where even Republicans were liberals. California was America's post-war star. But as liberal fundamentalism grew in power through the post-modern period, from 1970 to 2000, California began to run on empty. At first this was not visible and then the warning signs came. The dot.com technology boom collapsed. In its wake, consolation was sought, as consolation is always sought. The ageing new class intellectuals turned to what they knew best, their own image, to save the day. As the information economy fell into distress, and retrenched, the rhetoric of creativity was stepped up.

The most prominent and the most interesting of the works of new class self-affirmation was Richard Florida's *The Rise of the Creative Class*. The first edition of the book appeared in 2002. It proved to be one of the most influential books of its time. Some of the intuitions underlying Florida's study were correct. Creativity, he observed, is a key source of the value produced by advanced economies, and creative activities have a strong propensity to cluster in a small number of cities around the world. While Florida did not dwell much on historical data, his intuitions were nevertheless supported by the evidence of the past. Advanced economies of the kind that we have had for the 200 years since the Industrial Revolution are inconceivable without the continual application of technological science and inspired design to economic production, and without the creation of ever-new means of communication and transportation essential to streamlined economic distribution. The most powerful economies in part grow by becoming more efficient. Efficiencies emerge from new developments in the technology of production and in the distribution of goods, services and messages through communication networks. The most advanced economies rely on continually increasing productivity (output) per capita. The economist Robert Solow in 1956 estimated that more than 80 percent of increased productivity in the American economy was due to 'technological change' in the broad sense – including business methods and organization as well as tools and media (Bell 1973/1999: 193; Solow 1956).

Innovations have a distinctive geography. From the steam engine to the computer, railways and telegraph to the telephone and radio, from the modern office to the business corporation, the greater part of innovation has invariably been concentrated in a handful of city regions. In the case of the United States, until the mid-nineteenth century these included principally the Eastern Seaboard cities of Boston, New York, Philadelphia, Baltimore and Washington. The United States is a 'coastal nation' – meaning that its 'economic activity is greatly concentrated at its ocean and Great Lakes coasts' (Rappaport and Sachs 2003). Its social creativity mirrors this economic geography. A relatively small number of cities dominate innovation. These are as noted principally coastal cities or else near-by hinterland cities that have strong links to the pivotal littoral economy and which are typically no more than 500 kilometres from the coast (see Table 7.2). Chicago, Detroit and other Great Lakes area cities emerged as a second innovation cluster in the United States in the late nineteenth century. The California Coast incubated a third cluster in the twentieth century – San Diego through Los Angeles to San Francisco – mirrored by the Puget Sound cities of Seattle and Portland. Finally, as the twentieth century ended, yet another region, the Gulf of Mexico, was producing cities with a propensity to innovate economically and technologically, most notably the Texas triangle of Houston, Dallas and Austin, and the Floridian arc between Miami, Tampa, and St Petersburg. The littoral model is not a strict rule. The important Piedmont Atlantic region (Atlanta, Raleigh, Durham, Knoxville) is one step removed from the littoral, and the inland growth zones of the Arizona Sun Corridor and Rocky Mountains Front Range are entirely separate from it.

Table 7.2 Richard Florida's 'top 20' creative cities by geographical region

Innovation Cluster One:	Boston, Hartford CT, New York, Philadelphia, Washington-Baltimore
Innovation Cluster Two:	Chicago, Indianapolis, Minneapolis-St Paul
Innovation Cluster Three:	San Diego, Los Angeles, San Francisco, Portland OR, Seattle
Innovation Cluster Four:	Houston, Dallas, Austin
Innovation Cluster Five:	Atlanta, Raleigh-Durham
Innovation Cluster Six:	Phoenix, Denver

Richard Florida's index of the 'top 20' creative city regions in the United States (2004: 246) reflects this historical-cum-geographical pattern. What is contentious is not the picture of geo-intellectual distribution that Florida paints. Rather it is his conception of creativity. Creativity is difficult to define. A classic bad definition is the one that equates creativity with 'newness' or 'change'. Without a doubt the act of creation interpolates aspects of both 'newness' and 'change' but it is not identical with either. The invention of the telephone in the 1870s was an important episode of technological creativity. Yet what makes it important is the durability and pervasiveness of the telephone's social presence. In part this also reflects the telephone's capacity for re-invention. Whenever social theorists begin to talk seriously about creativity they end up having to grapple with the paradox of change and permanence. The greatest changes lead to the most enduring consequences. Great change is remarkably conservative.[10] Theories of creativity therefore are slippery. The topic is treacherous. In some ways it is less risky to do what Florida did. This is to side step the abstract question of 'what is creativity?' The avoidance of risk, though, has its own cost.

Rather than begin with a messy prologue musing about 'what does it mean to be creative?' Florida simply assumed that certain economies, classes and industries are creative. Further he took for granted, as if it was self-evident, that particular professions are 'super creative' – computing, engineering, architecture, mathematics, social sciences, education, library, arts, design, sports, and media (2004: 328). Likewise, he supposed that 'high tech' industries are more creative than either classic industrialism, the legacy of the nineteenth-century, or twentieth-century service industries. What makes this scenario prima facie plausible was Florida's tacit equation of creativity with knowledge. This equation allowed Florida to build on theories about post-industrial knowledge societies. Such societies, the theories allow, are constituted by economies, industries, and occupations that concentrate energies on the production of knowledge – words, numbers and figures primarily. Florida tweaked this notion by assuming a strong correlation between knowledge production and creative action.

The merits of this equation will be examined in due course. Suffice for the moment to say that a creative economy and a knowledge economy are treated as roughly the same thing from an empirical point of view. Thus, for the purposes of Florida's model, a creative economy has high levels of research and development spending per capita and high levels of patents per capita (2004: 328). Correspondingly, creative industries separate the designing of products from the manufacture of products – by outsourcing manufacturing to specialized subcontractors in foreign countries, and by focusing efforts on innovative product design (2004: 52–5). A creative workforce means growing the numbers of scientists and engineers per capita, and growing the numbers of 'bohemians' (artists, writers and performers) per capita. The most interesting tacit assumption that Florida makes is that economy, industry and workforce, together with knowledge and creativity, are all unified by the concept of the city. What this further supposes is that knowledge is not just something 'in our heads' but that it is a process of objectivation – of object making. Objects embody knowledge that has been externalized or put out into the world. Such objects may be tools or machines, books and newspapers, or, less visibly but most powerfully, cities. When we look at the long-term historical data, we are reminded that there is a strong correlation between particular cities, particular historical periods, and high levels of creativity understood as knowledge objectified in exceptional artefacts,

10 Conversely and paradoxically the greatest conservatives are obliged to be reformers. As Chesterton (1908/2004) remarked, 'all conservatism is based upon the idea that if you leave things alone you leave them as they are. But you do not. If you leave a thing alone you leave it to a torrent of change. If you leave a white post alone it will soon be a black post'.

whether these be small scale or large scale, scientific or artistic, technological or humanistic in nature.

Florida's analytic model first and foremost is constructed with an eye to explaining the distinctive dynamics of the American economy and its social and urban substrata. The United States is a world leader in research and development spending, design industrialism, and professional employment. In 1900, there were 55 scientists and engineers for every 100,000 people in the United States. In 1999 that figure had risen to 1,800 scientists and engineers per 100,000 people (Florida, 2004: 45). In the same period the numbers of artists, writers and performers rose from 250 per 100,000 to 900 for every 100,000 Americans. Small high-technology littoral states like Israel outstrip the United States. Israel has 1,350 engineers per 100,000 citizens (CNN, 1998) while the United Sates has 670 per 100,000 of population and 230 employed doctoral engineers and scientists per 100,000 of population (Oregon Progress Board, 2004). Contrast this with China and India. China graduates 49.5 engineers per 100,000 of population. India graduates 21.5 engineers per 100,000 of population. The United Sates rate is 75.3 per 100,000 of population. The Chinese definition of an engineer inflates the China figure.[11] As China's post-1990 wealth spurt continues the inflation of titles will presumably decline.

Professionals are a visible and influential proportion of the American workforce. They made up 5 percent of the working population in the 1950s; they represented 16 percent in 2002.[12] Their social impact is even greater – for example, they constitute 21 percent of voters in the United States and up to 25 percent of voters in many North-eastern states. In addition to professionals, a further 15 percent of the workforce is composed of executives, managers and administrators. Just under a third of the American workforce is made up of those in sales, technical support and administrative support (28.6 percent). The final third of the workforce is subdivided between service occupations (14.2 percent), precision production, craft, and repair occupations (10.6 percent), machine operators, fabricators, and labourers (12.6 percent) and farming, forestry, and fishing jobs (2.3 percent). Of the 30 percent plus of the workforce involved in professional and managerial work, Florida estimated that a little more than a third of them – or 12 percent of the total workforce – constituted what he called the 'super creative' core of the workforce.

The distinction between 'creative' and 'super creative' reflects the reality that somewhere between 8 percent and 12 percent of the population can usefully graduate from university with a degree (Murray 2008: 67–106). While university

11 Red Herring, The Business of Technology http://www.redherring.com/Article.aspx?a=14849&hed=US+Engineers+Undercount.

12 American Census Bureau, Major Occupation Group of the Employed Civilian Population 16 Years and over by Sex, and Race and Hispanic Origin: March 2002 and Detailed Occupation of the Employed Civilian Population 16 Years and Over by Sex and Race and Hispanic Origin: March 2002. See also Micklethwait and Wooldridge (2004: 242).

enrolments have crept up to over 30 percent of the 19 year-old age cohort in the United States and comparable societies, university education has diminishing returns for this larger group of enrolees who have difficulty assimilating a standard university arts and sciences curriculum. Many either drop out of university or graduate only to work in jobs that do not require a degree. While, at the upper limit, 12 percent of 19 year-olds might have a use for a university degree, just that does not in and of itself make them 'creative'. At best they will end up being proficient and productive professionals. This illustrates the difficulties of talking about a 'creative class'. It is so easy for the category to be inflated. Florida has a propensity to such inflation. The inclination is to include all professional and paraprofessional, administrative and management occupations, and anyone with a degree, no matter how useful or useless that degree might be, in the 'creative class'. The rationale for this is that, to do their job effectively, each of these occupations requires a degree of independent judgement. Job holders of this kind cannot just follow rules or obey orders rigidly. They have to be able to apply models or formulas or schedules, and in doing so they have to display some degree of creative problem solving, initiative, thoughtfulness, and the like. While it is true that even photocopying can be done independently and that standing over someone doing the photocopying is one of those petty tyrannies that the world can well do without, independent judgement nevertheless is not the same thing as creativity. The equation of the two is misleading.

Accompanying the growing professional-managerial class character of American society has been the export of American manufacturing abroad – to Mexico, China, and the like. America is much less a blue collar society than it was in the 1950s. What has not been exported abroad, though, has been conceptual work. Design – e.g. of PCs, cell phones, clothing, and even the plants that manufacture these goods – remains in the United States while the factories that produce the goods and the warehouses that store them and distribute them have left American shores. Conceptual work is done in offices but the economic value of such work is best represented less by tangible capital than by intangible intellectual property such as patents, copyright, trademarks and proprietary designs. The knowledge economies of advanced societies are built around intellectual property regimes.

The importance of intellectual property is not new. The writers of the US Constitution in 1789 specifically gave the United States Congress the power 'to promote the Progress of Science and useful Arts, by securing for limited Times to Authors and Inventors the exclusive Right to their respective Writings and Discoveries'.[13] Patent law was one of the principle building blocks of the American economy through the nineteenth century, securing property rights in technological innovations. The US established a Patent Commission in 1790, re-constituted

13 This is from Article 1, Section 8, Clause 8, the 'Intellectual Property Clause' or Patent and/or Copyright Clause of the United States Constitution.

as the more familiar Patent Office in 1802.[14] Key industries like the telegraph and telephony would not have developed without property rights in intellectual capital.[15] James Huebner, however, shows that the peak of registration of patents per capita in the United States was 1915, and that the patent per capita figure has been declining ever since.[16] This is in spite of the impressive absolute trends cited by Florida (2004: 45) that has the number of patents granted annually in the United States nearly doubling in the period 1900 to 1945 from 25,000 to 43,000, and tripling by the end of the century, rising to 150,000 by 1999. We should not forget though that the annual patents registered rose *ten-fold* in the second-half of the nineteenth century – from 2,000 per annum in the 1850s to 13,000 in the 1870s to 21,000 in the 1890s (Jones 1983: 297).

Many of the key industries that came to dominate advanced economies after 1820 have been based on technologies derived from science. In this respect, to draw distinctions between nineteenth-century industrialism and twentieth-century post industrialism or twenty-first-century creative industrialism is tenuous. Often what is most compelling is not how much but how little has changed in the past 200 years. Take for example the case of service industries – much is made of how, after the 1950s, service industries outpaced both rural and manufacturing industries as a source of employment. Today, as Florida and others have noted, minor occupations in health care, food preparation, personal care, many of them distinctly uncreative and unskilled, make up 43 percent of the US workforce. Cities like New Orleans, overly dependent on service class employment, suffer from deep-going social dysfunctions. It is interesting to observe, though, that in 1900 the largest single category of employment tracked by the US census was domestic service – cooks, waiters, maids, and laundresses (Gordon 2004: 165). What was once done in the home by servants is now done outside of it by the service class. Everything changes and nothing changes at the same time.

What is noticeably different today, however, is the decline of the working class – as mass manufacturing plants in cities like Detroit and Pittsburgh either have been exported abroad or else automated, while transportation and construction industries have been mechanized and modularized. Working-class occupations peaked at 40 percent of the US workforce during 1920–50. They then fell to 36 percent in 1970 and 25 percent by 1999 (Florida 2004: 45). As working-class occupations declined, they were either replaced by service occupations or by professional-managerial and administrative occupations. In a sense, American cities have tracked in two directions: they either become cities like Seattle inflected by a professional-

14 Secretary of State Thomas Jefferson, Secretary of War Henry Knox, and Attorney General Edmund Randolph were the first three members of the Patent Commission.

15 Classic examples of nineteenth-century US patents include Eli Whitney's Cotton Gin patent (US Patent No. X72, 1774); Samuel Morse's Morse Code patent (US Patent No. 1,647, 1840); Charles Goodyear's Vulcanized Rubber patent (US Patent No. 3,633, 1844); Alexander Graham Bell's Telephone patent (US Patent No. 174,465).

16 United Press International, 'Scientist: Rate of progress slowing', 1 July 2005.

managerial ethos or else cities like New Orleans inflected by a pervasive service ethos. The third option, the industrial working class city, has largely become an historical memory. Along with this, the political influence of organized labour once the backbone of the US Democratic Party, has declined. Today unions are more likely to represent the low-wage and less market-savvy end of the professional class, groups like teachers and social workers, than they are to represent blue-collar workers. In 1990 10 percent of private sector workers in the US were unionized. The figure is even less than that today.[17]

Something that Florida observed in Pittsburgh sparked his study of the creative class. Pittsburgh historically had high levels of blue-collar employment. This social constellation collapsed in the 1970s. The city, then, made a successful transition to a service economy with classic kinds of service jobs in areas like hospitality and the conference industry. Pittsburgh though was a lot less successful in expanding its professional-managerial class. Florida pointed out that this was true especially when contrasted with a case like Austin in Texas. What triggered Florida's study of the creative class is important because it signalled both the insight and the blindness of the study. The insight, reasonably enough, was that Austin had something that Pittsburgh lacked. The blindness was to context – for Austin was located in a state, Texas, which had two other cities that ranked very high on standardized measures of creativity. The city mega-region that includes San Antonio, Houston, Dallas and Austin was emerging as one of the most buoyant in the world. Yet to mention the word 'Texas' in the same sentence as 'creativity' was to violate a tacit new class cultural taboo. The essence of this taboo is that only fashionable places are creative and that fashion is defined by whether a place is politically liberal or not. In noting the forward momentum of Austin, Florida observed something significant. But by screening out the larger context of this momentum, he not only missed something of social import but also misunderstood something important about the nature of creativity.

Florida's comparison of Austin and Pittsburgh was unflattering to Pittsburgh. Florida was alerted to the case of Austin by statistical work undertaken by former University of Texas sociologist, Robert Cushing. Cushing analysed federal income records from 1992 to 2000 for Austin's *American-Statesman* newspaper (Bishop and Lisheron 2002). The analysis showed that the five-county Austin metropolitan region exported poorer people to the rest of the country and took in a more affluent cohort. The net gain for Austin in income from people coming in and going out of the metro region during that nine-year period was $4.3 billion. Other data tells a similar story. The population growth of Austin's Travis County for the period 1970–2004 was 194 percent and from 1990–2004 it was 50 percent. The figures for Pittsburgh's Allegheny County in contrast were -22 percent and -6 percent respectively.[18] The per capita personal income of Allegheny County was

17 'As recently as late 1970s, UAW was America's biggest and most influential union, with 1.9 million members. Now that's shrunk to 400,000' (Marshall 2011).

18 Stats Indiana, US Counties in Profile.

still greater than its Austin counterpart – $37,475 compared to $34,439. But Travis County experienced a 10-year per capita personal income growth of 25 percent compared with the 19 percent recorded by Allegheny County. Unemployment rates of the two were about the same in 2004. Austin had a higher poverty rate than Pittsburgh (13.9 percent to 10.5 percent in 2003). On the other hand, 40 percent of adults in Travis County over 25 years old had a bachelor's degree, the typical credential of the professional-managerial and administrative cohorts, compared with 28 percent in Allegheny County. Nine percent of Travis County's jobs were in high-wage manufacturing ($81,753 average wage) compared to Allegheny County's 6.5 percent in considerably lower-wage manufacturing ($52,543 average wage). Even more starkly, Allegheny County had 16 percent of its workforce in health and social assistance occupations compared to 8.9 percent in Travis County. These occupations rated wages around $40,000 which was below the 2004 median for American household income of $44,684.[19]

A question is begged by such data: why was a city such as Pittsburgh less successful than Austin in expanding its higher-end professional-managerial, administrative, and manufacturing occupations? This conundrum was one of the starting points for Florida's study of the creative economy. Florida's tacit assumption was that the fate of the professional-managerial class was the fate of a 'creative class'. This assumption does not bear too close scrutiny. While the percentage of professional-managerial occupations in the workforce is one sign of social prosperity (though hardly the only sign) it is not credible, given the nature of such occupations, to suppose that each of them have a substantive creative component or purpose. Thus, when we compare Pittsburgh with Austin, what Florida's empirical analysis proved most useful for was in understanding the relative capacity of cities to generate and retain higher-income occupations. There is no doubt that some fraction of those occupations is creative. It is also possibly true that the creative fraction of occupations is growing in size and social importance – though, even if it is, it remains a tiny fraction of the over-all workforce, and will always do so. The notion of a society made up of creative people is romantic nonsense. To stand still a modern economy must grow. To grow, a modern economy must create. But identifying who or what the agents of creation are is much trickier than Florida allowed. Creativity is a very rare quality, and that is a social constant. If there is a class of creative people, it is a very small one.

19 American Census Bureau, *American Community Survey*, 2004.

What is Creati

High levels of *technology*, *toleration*, and *talent* are Florida's principal empirical measures of a creative city. Of the three empirical measures of creativity, two are inputs (toleration and talent) and one is an output (technology).

The Technology Enigma

While technological advance is a good, rough-and-ready measure of creativity, creativity is not reducible to technological innovation. What makes technology creative is no different from what makes art creative or a court decision creative. Creativity ought not to be confused with the world of shiny devices. Thus digital computing had its creative moment, but is now as commonplace as the cotton mill or the rail road. What made digital computing interesting as a phenomenon was the manner in which it conflated 'real' and 'virtual' processes. The digitization of spreadsheets, film and video, newspapers, visual images, recordings, and so on, led to a mass translation or re-mediation of human activities. Each of these activities remained as they were and yet were visibly changed; they continued in existence and yet were materially transformed. The real was translated into the virtual to the point where the virtual became the real. The writer who once wrote in an analogue medium stopped entirely writing in anything but the digital medium. Digital technology ended up being no more interesting than a pen and a sheet of paper. In the moment when one could say that word processing was 'virtually' like writing (that it was writing's similitude), then the technology was, in that moment and for an instant, 'creative'. But all successful creation creates a model or pattern to be followed. At that point, the virtual reverts to being real. Technology is not creative per se.

The Myth of Talent

Neither is talent. Talent is many things. It is a mixture of competence, judgement, and understanding. But talent is not necessarily nor is it normally creative. In the second-half of the twentieth century, a university degree became a standard index of the talent of those who work with symbols of some kind – including words, numbers and figures. However, not everyone who has a degree is creative – far from it. For example, sometimes architects are creative yet most talented architects are not creative. They are simply able. Sometimes they are very able. Professional architects are good at reproducing the architectural styles and forms of the day. Often they do their worst work when they try to be creative. Not only do they not produce a new form, they usually mangle the existing forms of the day when they try to do so.

Florida was correct when he said that creativity involves the positing of new forms (2004: 5, 44). That is a good definition of what creativity is. The trouble is that talent in itself is not enough to create 'new' forms. On the other hand, it is perfectly clear that we rely more and more on the positing of 'new' forms in advanced economies and societies, though these paradoxically are new forms that endure and become in turn classic forms. We see this not only in science, technology and industry, but in art, government and business management. There is an argument to be made that advancement or progress is the social ability to produce 'unprecedented' forms that paradoxically establish powerful 'precedents', that is, durable patterns of productive activity. The thing that is less clear is how many people this involves – or under what conditions it flourishes.

The creative class by any measure is small. One of the reasons it is small is that one of the peculiar things that makes a creative act creative is that its principal end-result is a form – meaning a pattern that can be reproduced. Take for example Crick and Watson's discovery of DNA (Deoxyribonucleic acid), the medium of genetics. The creative act of theirs was to intuit that DNA was structured like a double helix. The double helix form easily reproduces in nature. One of the characteristics of successful forms is that they spread quickly. In the same way, nobody legislated that the form of the shopping mall should replicate itself everywhere in society. But, from its inception in the 1950s, the invention of the Austrian-American Victor Gruen did exactly that – with little or no prompting required.[20] The most interesting and most influential kinds of economic and social development happen in this way. Mimesis or imitation, the copying of a pattern, is a kind of communication at a distance. As social action occurs over increasing distances, including on a world scale, form-driven or model-driven development that is conveyed through imitation becomes ever-more important. This makes 'ideas people' influential but it does not necessarily mean that there are lots of them. What it does mean is that there are lots of imitators. It is possible that an above-average proportion of imitators or adopters in the early stages of the diffusion of a new form belong to the professional-managerial cohort. A classic confusion, not least on the part of the members of this class, is to confuse early adoption with creation.

The Toleration Myth

Just as talent is not a condition of creativity, neither is toleration. It is true that the historic cities where great works of art and science have been produced have typically enjoyed a significant degree of intellectual freedom. It is also true that censorious governments and moralizing societies are hostile to creativity. This is because they are hostile to wit, metaphor and paradox. But the purveyors of wit, metaphor and paradox are perfectly capable of resisting this. Take the case of the United States. It produced throughout its history a phalanx of censorious and moralistic personalities of all political stripes. Some of those who most think of themselves as 'open' personalities, for example contemporary left-liberals, often

20 The Gruen-designed Southdale Center opened for business in Edina, Minnesota in the United States in 1956.

hyperventilate with priggishness and didacticism of the most suffocating kind. And yet – despite this – for the most part intellectual freedom flourishes. Indeed often it is inspired by the actions of prigs and moralizers. It takes a dictatorship to eliminate intellectual freedom. Intolerance in contrast is more a social and cultural phenomenon than an intellectual or political one. A political conservative living in a left-liberal county in the United States will feel the social or cultural pressure of neighbours and peers but that is hardly a restraint of intellectual freedom. While it is true that there are few social types more self-righteous than the average American left-liberal, putting pressure on opinion is not the same as political dictatorship. Alexis de Tocqueville observed 'the tyranny of the majority' in America. This is the pervasive social pressure exercised by majority opinion and directed at minority opinions to get them to toe the line. Where such pressure exists, and it is common-place, it coexists in the United States with a rare degree of intellectual freedom.

The standard psychological measure of creativity is openness. 'Openness to experience' is used by research psychologists as a proxy for creativity. 'Openness to experience' is one of the five personality traits included in the standard Five Factor Model (FFM). The traits include Extraversion, Agreeableness, Conscientiousness, Neuroticism, and Openness. The Five Factor Model is a very widely-accepted psychological model of personality. In psychological studies of the regional variation of creativity, liberal American states like California always rate high on these measures of creativity because liberals habitually score high in personality tests to determine whether they are 'open to experience' or not – and as noted 'openness' is the psychologists' proxy for creativity (Rentfrow, Gosling and Potter 2008; Rentfrow 2010). Conservatives in contrast score high on agreeableness or conscientiousness. Here again we are faced with the question: 'what is creativity?' What is clear is that the answer to the question is not 'openness to new experience'. That can simply be synonymous with vacuity. In fact, to randomly or greedily acquire 'new experiences' is liable to negate the focus and discipline required for creative action. Neither is creativity simply a synonym for newness, change, and unpredictability, or for the remote, the unusual or the unconventional. It might at times overlap with or interpolate such qualities, but also in powerful ways it transcends them. The higher the level of creativity, the more an unusual act will translate itself into a typical pattern. Creativity switches the new into the durable, and change into permanence. It brings the remote near, it turns unconventionality into popular style, and it flips unpredictability into recurrence.

The personality traits of highly creative individuals range far beyond curiosity or 'openness to experience'. They include self-confidence, risk taking, high energy, interest in complexity, eagerness to cooperate, independent judgement, playfulness, sense of humour, imagination, the need for achievement, and the need for autonomy (Barron and Harrington 1981; Csikszentmihalyi 1999; Dacey and Lennon 1998; Feist 1999; King, McKee Walker and Broyles 1996; McCrae 1986). Creative individuals are both introverted and extroverted, and they have the signature ability to solve antonyms. Indeed the creative personality is syn-antonymic. Creativity is the ability to make one thing out of two things that, at first glance, seem to be completely unlike each other.[21] One of the most elementary and most powerful creative devices is metaphor. Metaphor compares two unlike things – making them one.

> 'Our life is short; our days run/As fast away as do's the sun …'[22]
>
> 'Diamonds are a girl's best friend'.[23]
>
> 'You ain't nothin' but a hound dog/Crying all the time'.[24]
>
> 'I see in this only the chaos/Of your round mirror which organizes everything/ Around the polestar of your eyes which are empty …'[25]

The toleration theorem of Florida echoes an idea that became practically compulsory in late twentieth-century American universities. This was the desideratum that we must 'recognize the other' and 'live with difference'. As a general rule, such notions were prescribed by individuals who had grave difficulty recognizing others or living with differences outside a very narrow range. In fact it is not uncommon for tolerance to become very intolerant. This is not to deny that tolerance as an ethos of getting on with people of different occupations, tastes, nationalities, races, or sexualities is a useful virtue in a modern stranger society. It means simply accepting others who are different up to a point. It is not clear, however, that toleration is a condition of creativity. That Oscar Wilde went to jail for being a homosexual was the act of an intolerant society perhaps but not an un-creative one. The jail sentence broke Wilde as a person and ended his writing career. The very same society that did this had previously recognized his genius and celebrated it. Conversely, a society that has a tolerant attitude to homosexuality is not, for that reason alone, going to produce artists of the quality of Oscar Wilde. To suppose otherwise is to misunderstand the nature of creativity.

---

21 Janet Burroway (2002) put it very well: 'The fusion of elements into a unified pattern is the nature of creativity, a word devalued… to the extent that it has come to mean a random gush of self-expression. God, perhaps, created out of the void; but in the world as we know it, all creativity, from the sprouting of an onion to the painting of Guernica, is a matter of selection and arrangement … At the conception of a foetus or a short story, there occurs the conjunction of two unlike things, whether cells or ideas, that have never been joined before. Around this conjunction other cells, other ideas accumulate in a deliberate pattern. That pattern is the unique personality of the creature, and if the pattern does not cohere, it miscarries or is stillborn'.

22 Robert Herrick, 'Corrina's going a-Maying' (1648).

23 Written by Jule Styn and Leo Robin for the Broadway stage show (later film) *Gentlemen Prefer Blondes* (1949).

24 Words and music by Jerry Leiber and Mike Stoller (1952).

25 John Ashbery, 'Self-Portrait in a Convex Mirror' (1975).

Creativity is not the tolerant coexistence of difference. Rather the act of creation is the melding of two unlike things into a single thing. It is the finding of similitude amidst difference. If one wants to understand creativity figuratively in terms of sexuality, then the appropriate metaphor is not the tolerance of minority sexualities. Rather it is the melding of male and female into one. One of the oldest images of creativity is the hermaphrodite. The characteristic note of the creative mind was struck by Sigmund Freud when he proposed the idea of the innate bisexuality of human beings. Whether or not Freud's thesis was literally true (it doesn't need to be) in a figurative sense it tells us something about the nature of creative personalities. They have a strong cognitive preference for the union of opposites. This is not the same as respect for differences, anodyne or otherwise.

One interesting question is whether the image of the creative hermaphrodite applies equally to the social mind as to the individual mind. Some of Florida's work suggests that it might. In particular he points to the way in which the American professional-managerial class internalized polar opposite values. In the second half of the twentieth century, it is noticeable that certain things that previously been set asunder came together.[26] There was a steady coalescence of bourgeois values of hard work, long hours, and time keeping with bohemian values of informality, adventure, and cultural consumption. The bourgeois and the bohemian had always agreed on at least one thing. Both had a taste for frugality. Frugality was manifest in the care-worn effort of the bourgeois individual to save and economize; and in the care-free, aesthetically-driven scrimping and poverty of the bohemian. As twentieth-century culture was industrialized and twentieth-century industry became more reliant on cultural components such as marketing, the sharp nineteenth-century divide became less emphatic and slid away.

The shift was marked sartorially by the late twentieth-century business dress code for males. The grey business suit and tie did not die out but it did make room for open-neck shirts, black skivvies, khaki pants and even occasionally blue jeans. This had a number of meanings. In some cases, it marked hedonism's triumph over Puritanism. It signalled a transition from a saving to a debt culture and from a production to consumption society. In other cases, though, what happened was more an expression of irony. It was the act of the upper classes and middle classes adopting the clothing styles of the military uniform (khaki) and of labourers (denim). The historian Niall Ferguson (2011: 240–44) wonders why it was that affluent America and Europe took to blue jeans and the Soviet Union made the wearing of them a crime. The answer to this lies in each society's predilection or not for irony. The Soviet Union was an irony-free zone. Doubtless an American executive in blue jeans at times can cut quite an absurd figure. But equally a society's ability to invert signifiers and transport them metaphorically, to compound worker and boss, civilian and soldier, hints at some kind of collective creativity. Stripped of irony, though, the same is easily turned into kitschy cliché.

26 In the United States, the phenomenon of a journalistic-artistic bohemia takes off on in the 1850s and crystallizes in the 1860s.

All metaphors end up as clichés. The proletarian fantasies of executives or the khaki-militarization of civilians are no more exempt from this than anything else. To the extent that its metaphors did not become clichés or worse, then, to that extent, it can be argued that the post-war American professional-managerial class, as a cohort, did take on some of the characteristics of a hermaphrodite class. In doing so, what it did in some measure was to reconcile what the great American sociologist Daniel Bell in 1976 called the cultural contradictions of American capitalism. Bell observed in the 1960s a society that was torn between the Puritan bourgeois heritage of delayed gratification and hard work and Romantic bohemian counter-cultural values of aesthetic hedonism and authenticity. Florida in contrast offered an image of the contemporary professional-managerial class that was simultaneously bourgeois and romantic in its behaviours. He adopted the term that the journalist David Brooks (2001) coined for this phenomenon: the 'bo-bo' or bourgeois-bohemian. This in turn was an echo of a strain that runs through Anglo-American capitalism, perhaps in part giving it its distinctive character. The mix of discipline and enjoyment, work and culture that you find in the stories of Jane Austen or in the life of Thomas Jefferson suggests deep roots of the 'bo-bo' phenomenon.

Whatever its origins may be, the American professional-managerial class is an influential social group. Its size, its income, and its political engagement make it so. Numbers, wealth and clout though are not synonyms of creativity. Classes are not for the most part creative. Middle classes, management classes, professional classes, upper-middle classes at their finest are best defined by talent and merit, not by creative action. Creation is the exception and not the rule of social life. To the extent that these classes are creative, it is because of some hermaphrodite character. They manage at times and fail at other times to achieve a synthesis of warring parts. In the rare times that this happens, the synthesis gives the class energy and drive. Yet such social action is also a harbour of illusions. The merger of hedonism and hard work is often taken as a sign by observers that members of the professional-managerial class are individually creative. In reality, though, the paradoxical synthesis of hard work and hedonism at a social level simply establishes propitious conditions for a relative handful of ingenious and inventive personalities to flourish.

Is Texas the Future?

If classes at times have hermaphrodite characteristics, so do cities. These characteristics are a context for creation. This context draws ingenuity out of human beings. It helps elicit the intangible power of invention. Creation is a form of objectivation. It is a putting out into the world. The human species inhabits a world of objects that it makes. Cities are the most intense aggregation of such objects. There is a human drive to objectivate. That much is clear. But what gets the impulse to make objects going? In part, the object-world around us does; cities in particular stimulate objectivation. But not all cities are equal in this. It is both obvious and widely observed that certain cities at certain times are especially powerful in eliciting creation. That elicitation arises from tension. A tensile environment elicits object creation. The most interesting tensile environments are inset with deep strains of contradiction.

When Richard Florida asked graduates from the University of Pittsburgh why they were not staying in Pittsburgh but going to Austin in Texas to work, he did not ask them whether they preferred a tensile environment. Yet the most notable thing about Austin is that it is a liberal pocket in a conservative American state. As the millennium turned, once powerful American liberal states like California, Michigan and New York, previously icons of industrial and post-industrial America, were in serious decline, wracked by unsustainable public debt, unemployment and the sub-prime mortgages. In contrast, Texas combined employment growth, net migrant inflow, low debt, housing affordability, and few toxic house loans. Austin was a liberal bubble in a successful conservative economy. That very success might have attracted Pittsburgh graduates. Florida resisted such a conclusion. He emphasized instead that graduates, neophyte members of the professional-managerial class, made decisions about where they wanted to live and work based first of all not on economic pragmatics but rather on the post-industrial romantic low-fidelity of bike lanes, rehabilitated housing stock, and DIY culture. Florida's paradigmatic interviewee spoke to him in these terms (2004: 217):

> I asked the young man with spiked hair why he was going to a smaller city in the middle of Texas, a place with a small airport and no professional sports teams, without museums and high-art cultural amenities comparable to Pittsburgh's. The company is excellent, he told me. It has terrific people and the work is challenging. But the clincher was: "It's in *Austin*!" "Why is that good?" I asked. There are lots of young people, he explained, and a tremendous amount to do, a thriving music scene, ethnic and cultural diversity, fabulous outdoor recreation, and a great nightlife. That's what mattered – not the symphony or the opera, which he enjoyed but would not feel comfortable attending. What's more Austin is affordable, unlike Silicon Valley, another place that offered the kinds of work he desired. He was right: Austin ranked as the fourth most affordable place for information-technology workers like him, with a pay differential of more than $18,000 over San Francisco Bay Area, when cost of living differences are taken into account.

Table 7.3 Houston, Austin, Dallas and Pittsburgh counties

	Houston	**Austin**	**Dallas**	**Pittsburgh**
	Harris County	*Travis County*	*Dallas County*	*Allegheny County*
Occupation	Manufacturing	Manufacturing	Manufacturing	Manufacturing
Average Earnings per Job	$99,478	$100,152	$75,987	$94,031
Percentage of Local Workforce	7.50%	7.50%	8.60%	5.80%
Occupation	Information	Information	Information	Information
Average Earnings per Job	$82,182	$80,811	$106,350	$69,410
Percentage of Local Workforce	1.70%	3.30%	3.90%	2.40%
Occupation	Professional	Professional	Professional	Professional
Average Earnings per Job	$80,298	$60,206	$84,509	$72,001
Percentage of Local Workforce	8.40%	9.60%	8.30%	8.20%
Occupation	Finance	Finance	Finance	Finance
Average Earnings per Job	$77,695	$61,558	$81,410	$58,584
Percentage of Local Workforce	4.50%	5.40%	7.40%	6.50%
Occupation	Government	Government	Government	Government
Average Earnings per Job	$49,014	$49,630	$51,349	$53,054
Percentage of Local Workforce	10.80%	17.50%	9.10%	9.40%
Occupation	Education	Education	Education	Education
Average Earnings per Job	$34,549	$19,221	$27,885	$36,415
Percentage of Local Workforce	1.80%	1.50%	1.40%	5.40%

Table 7.3 Continued

	Houston	Austin	Dallas	Pittsburgh
	Harris County	*Travis County*	*Dallas County*	*Allegheny County*
Occupation	Administrative	Administrative	Administrative	Administrative
Average Earnings per Job	$31,976	$28,140	$34,796	$24,140
Percentage of Local Workforce	7.60%	6.40%	8.00%	5.70%
Occupation	Arts	Arts	Arts	Arts
Average Earnings per Job	$24,283	$13,789	$32,592	$30,397
Percentage of Local Workforce	1.50%	2.30%	1.50%	2.20%

Source: Stats Indiana USA Counties in Profile (2005).

What, here, is self-image and what is cause? What explains behaviour? Is it explained by cultural motives or economic causes? As Table 7.3 indicates, there is a large information workforce in Dallas. The city in fact has a larger information workforce in per capita terms than does Austin. It also has an extensive high-art infrastructure and a net inflow of workers. It is difficult to conclude that 'the presence or the absence of the opera or the sports stadium' was the decisive factor in why industrial-turned-service cities like Pittsburgh or post-industrial economies like the San Francisco Bay Area have been outstripped economically by cities in Texas. More realistically, both Dallas and Austin along with Houston offer economically competitive, low-cost conditions that attract workers and businesses including high-end labour and industry. Low-fidelity, high-fidelity, and other kinds of fidelity is an after-thought.

Florida's economic model pivots on the following: industries cluster, creative industries cluster where talent is located and talent follows the post-industrial picturesque. This model interpolates the world view of the ageing new class of academic, media and corporate intellectuals. This class was spawned by the romantic counter-cultural shift that occurred in 1968. The new class, from inception, saw itself as creative. Its collective fantasy was that it would 'transform the world'. Yet in reality it recycled a lot of romantic clichés. The desire for innovation and transformation was a reflex of a romantic-Gnostic view that the world was a bad place. This expressed itself in the cultural pessimism of the new class and in its environmental pantheism that viewed the nature around it as both ruined and redemptive. Such formulae are periodically regurgitated in modern culture. The only thing that the new class of 1968 added to this was conceit.

Its pervasive image of itself was one of cleverness, smartness, intelligence, aptitude, brainpower and acumen. To those who it thought not smart, it condescended. The ideology of smartness has its own set of signifiers, a little like khaki pants. A 'smart person' signals smartness by their love of the industrial picturesque chic and their infatuation with the language of 'diversity', 'authenticity', and 'the environment'. It is enough that words are said. They do not have meaning in themselves. Rather they are symbols of something else, namely an arrogating smugness that deems itself in charge. The theory of the creative class assumes that if a city attracts a critical mass of such social actors, represented by masses of bicycles, progress will be self-generating. The critical mass of the smart people ('talent') will attract more of their kind ('more talent').[27] Such a pool of talent will in turn attract the kind of high technology and design-driven industries that support high-wage jobs and social prosperity. But do they?

The clear evidence from the comparison of California and Texas is that they do not. California embraced whole-heartedly the new class authenticity-diversity-environmental ideology. In many respects, this *was* the Californian ideology. It was also in practice an economic disaster. By the historic turning-point of 2008–10, California's economy, which had grown to the sixth largest in the world, was crippled by massive public debt, bad housing loans, and stifling regulation. Texas in contrast was the only American state to emerge from the 2008–09 recession with a rapid rate of growth (Merlin 2011). In 2011 it was one of only eight states to have registered a net gain in jobs after President Obama took office. It added 64,400 jobs. The United States overall lost a net 2.4 million jobs between January 2009 and August 2011. During that period unemployment in Texas peaked at 8.3 percent compared with the national average of 10.1 percent. In 2010, the Texas economy grew 5.3 percent compared with 3.8 percent for the US economy as a whole. It provided four out of five net new private sector jobs in the United States in 2006–10.[28] It had high wage growth, high levels of housing affordability, and no history of sub-prime mortgage lending.[29] This made Texas a magnet for people. Texas was the top destination for Americans moving inter-state. It gained a net 800,000 migrants in 2000 and 2010.[30] The vast majority of those came from other

27 How the most inane and silly of modern vehicles, the bicycle, became a symbol of cleverness is almost beyond explanation.

28 Source: US Bureau of Labor Statistics, June 2011 (preliminary data).

29 Texas was one of the few American states that did not have a housing crash in 2008. A third of the asset value of American housing disappeared in the resulting recession. Texas avoided this because it outlawed sub-prime lending practices. It insisted on prudential mortgage lending, adhering to a long-standing state requirement going back to the nineteenth century. Rather than seek growth from speculative housing, Texas grew its STEM economy instead. One of the things that allowed that was the affordability of housing in Texas, which made even low wages in Texas attractive. A median home in Brooklyn costs over $500,000 dollars; in Houston, it is $130,000.

30 If other Americans had not moved to Texas, its unemployment rate in 2011 would have been under 5.5 percent. Calculation by Texanomics: http://texanomics.blogspot.com/.

American states. What about California? Net 1.5 million left California (Kotkin 2010a). The urbanist Joel Kotkin observed that a vast difference in economic performance drove these demographic shifts:

> Since 1998, California's economy has not produced a single new net job … Public employment has swelled, but private jobs have declined. Critically, as Texas grew its middle-income jobs by 16 percent, one of the highest rates in the nation, California, at 2.1 percent growth, ranked near the bottom. In the year ending September, Texas accounted for roughly half of all the new jobs created in the country. Even more revealing is California's diminishing pre-eminence in high-tech and science-based (or STEM – Science, Technology, Engineering and Mathematics) jobs. Over the past decade California's supposed bulwark grew a mere 2 percent – less than half the national rate. In contrast, Texas' tech-related employment surged 14 percent. Since 2002 the Lone Star state added 80,000 STEM jobs; California, a mere 17,000.

In the simplest terms, Texas was the best performing American state economy of the new millennium because it had learnt the lesson of all successful modern economies of how to master technology-led industrialization. Texas proved its resilience by bouncing back from the 2008–09 recession with a normal level of growth. By August 2010, it was back at 97.3 percent of its peak employment. California was at 91 percent of its peak.[31] Texas was one of a handful of states that had more people employed in 2011 than at the start of the recession, up about a quarter of a million jobs.[32] Some commentators at the time rationalized this as due to soaring oil prices benefiting the nation's leading oil producer.[33] Texas added 15,000 resource extraction jobs through the recession. But the reason the mini-oil boom happened is just as instructive. This was because of new drilling methods and technologies such as hydraulic fracturing and horizontal drilling that opened up new deposits of natural gas to production and expanded the production of older oil fields.

So what is the difference that makes the difference? Why should Texas over-take California as a STEM-economy? There are political reasons why this happened. California became dominated by a coalition of Democratic machine politicians, public employee unions, and social activists. The result was a state that once spent money on the best highway and university infrastructure in the world now spent it on state pension entitlements that were funded by spiralling taxes, chronic deficits or else simply not funded at all.[34] The goal of the state became to

31 Source: US Bureau of Labor Statistics.

32 Calculation by Political Math: http://www.politicalmathblog.com/.

33 It produces 21 percent of America's crude oil.

34 As Joel Kotkin (2010b) notes, this is a pre- and post-1968 story. The Republican administration of Earl Warren in 1943–53 and the Democratic administration of Pat Brown in 1958–66 developed California's widely-admired post-war infrastructure of roads,

regulate, expand civil service employment, and to satisfy rent-seeking interests. That this happened flowed directly from the nature of the left-liberal mentality that came to reign supreme in California. There was something flawed about its nature. It lacked an in-built oscillator. It lacked a conservative corrective to its liberal impulse. There is nothing inherently wrong with fiscal deficits or public employment or public rules so long as they are limited. Californian liberalism did not understand limits. It did not understand that spending must be matched by income, that borrowing must be repaid, that the benefit of a rule must not be outweighed by the time or expense in following or implementing the rule, and the taxes which pay for public goods must not crowd out the private benefit of personal income or the ability of business to re-invest corporate income. In short, Californian liberalism had no imagination.

California's liberal intellectuals talked incessantly about the creative economy and oversaw the strangulation of one. To understand the reasons why the standard liberal authenticity-diversity-environmentalism model was destined to fail, it is useful to revisit the comparison of Pittsburgh and Austin. What ailed a city like Pittsburgh in the 1990s was not a lack of diversity or authenticity or picturesque-generating regulations. What it lacked was a tensile synthesis. Such synthesis requires a paradoxical mind-set. It requires not one frame, but contradictory frames that merge into one like Joseph Jastrow's duck-rabbit picture. Whether it is politics or economics, science or technology, it is the ambidextrous mind, both individual and social, that explains creative action. When these contradictory frames are brought into contact, when these cross-over and envelope each other, they release energy. When what runs in parallel is united in an uncanny union, then vigour, oomph and drive are released. These are the 'animal spirits' of an economy. It is not the capacity to save or the capacity to spend that is interesting but rather the gestalt of saving-spending.

---

water supply and schools. (Brown began political life as a Republican in the 1920s.) The Republican administration of Ronald Reagan, 1966–75, was a turbulent interregnum period, as the ethos of the state radically changed. The change was reflected in the administration of Jerry Brown (the son of Pat Brown), 1975–83. The politics of infrastructure development was replaced by anti-development and pro-pension politics. A coalition of environmental activists and public service unions, spurred by the ideologies of 1968, dominated the state from this point. Spending priorities changed from productive expenditure on research, training, transport and network infrastructures. Activists encumbered development with as many hostile rules as possible. Spending switched to civil service pensions and salaries. The result was that by 2010 the state of California had unfunded pension liabilities of $500 billion and the city of Los Angeles was on the edge of bankruptcy because of its pension liabilities. The universities were not exempt. The University of California retirement system was one of the largest components of the pension system. Everything had been tainted by the 1968 ethos. Accordingly the spirit of what once in the 1940s, 1950s and early 1960s had been California's great research universities, and the seed-bed of its technological moment in the sun (its IT industry) had shrivelled. Even the professors had become pensioners in waiting.

The kind of milieu that produces the creative hermaphrodite produces both the most audacious innovation and the most efficient economy. One is related to the other. Conversely what made Austin a success story in the 1990s was not its status as an enclave of liberal toleration and post-modern diversity but rather its location in a larger context of conservative anti-liberalism. While Austin rates relatively high – 23rd nationally – among large city regions on Florida's 1999 diversity index, Florida never talks about the fact that Austin is in Texas, which is not a liberal state.

Texas is an interesting case. When Florida first proposed his creative class thesis, based on an analysis of 1999 data, one of the most startling results was that three of the top 10 'creative economy' city regions in the United States were in Texas – Austin, Houston and Dallas. This was startling because Texas is still conventionally thought of as the same oil boom resources state that it was in the 1960s. This is despite the fact that, today, Texas is the only state in the US that has three cities (Houston, San Antonio, and Dallas) with populations greater than one million. California only has two. Florida's index of 'creative city regions' helps deflate many of the myths about Texas. This begs the question then how could a place such as Texas, which epitomizes in-authenticity for most American elite opinion-makers, have done so well? The answer to this simply is that romantic authenticity requires the antithesis of in-authenticity in order to generate high levels of creative action. This is the *sine qua non* of the creative hermaphrodite. What makes Texas work, as a burgeoning locus of new and re-located industries, is a state of tension. Conversely what has happened, over the long term, to Pittsburgh's Pennsylvania and more recently to Silicon Valley's California, is that they have lost the drive to unite warring opposites.

In 1960, Texas was an agrarian and oil economy. Five decades later Texas was ranked 27th among American states in per capita levels of research and development expenditure.[35] One might pass quickly over such middling performance, except that Texas has characteristics that resemble what was once true of other, now declining, economic-intellectual powerhouses in the United States. Most notably, it is a littoral Gulf Coast hugging state with massive traffic with neighbouring and

35 In 2004 Texas spent $655 per person on R&D in comparison with Pennsylvania which ranked 19th with $792 per head R&D expenditure. This was still well below states like New Mexico (2nd ranked, $2,527 per head), Massachusetts (3rd ranked, $2,233 per head), Michigan (10th ranked, $1,502 per head), and California (11th ranked, $1,469 per head). Yet there were subtle shifts in national rankings that favoured Texas over the long term. Texas' national research and development ranking had remained steady since 1987. In contrast, Michigan had slipped from 6th rank to 10th. California had dropped from 4th to 11th. Ohio had gone from 19th to 21st. New York State had slipped from 20th to 23rd. Texas was mid ranked in production of patents per capita, 21st among the American states, comparable with Pennsylvania which was ranked 22nd. Texas in 2004 generated 27.8 patents per 100,000 persons. Third-ranked state Massachusetts produced 60.9 patents per 100,000 persons. Texas was also mid ranked for the proportion of adults over 25 years old with a bachelor degree (24th) and a graduate degree (29th).

global states. The Port of Houston is ranked first in the United States in foreign waterborne commerce, second in total tonnage, and it is sixth in the world. There were times when much the same could be reported about New York, Chicago, or San Francisco. What is notable is the propensity of intellectual-economic power in history to follow portal dominance. There are many examples of this rule including London, Venice, and Amsterdam.

Texas at the turn of the twenty-first century was an interesting case study in ambivalence. The division of its labour force reflected this: in 2004, 19.7 percent of working Texans were professionals compared with 26 percent in Massachusetts and 15 percent in Nevada. 13.3 percent of the Texas workforce was in management, financial or business occupations, compared with 15.7 percent in Massachusetts and 10.2 percent in West Virginia.[36] Against this background though, what was apparent, at the county rather than the state level, was that Texas's premier urban nodes – Houston, Dallas and Austin – were outstripping older American centres like Pittsburgh in the percentage of high-wage white collar occupations (information, finance, professional, and managerial) as well as in high wage (high technology) manufacturing. What is doubly interesting to note is *how* this was being done. Texan cities tended to avoid large numbers of low-wage high-qualification occupations like teaching, arts and entertainment.[37] One of the further effects of this was to create a professional-managerial cohort that was not particularly politically and socially liberal. Texas has not encouraged occupations like acting that generally pay very little, even though Texas is now the third major centre for film making in the United States after California and New York State.[38] Compared with Pittsburgh then, the pattern in the premier Texan urban centre is a higher percentage of high-wage professional jobs and a lower percentage of low-wage professional jobs. Only in the curious case of government does this not apply. I say curious because Texan cities have a higher percentage of workers in government than Pittsburgh, yet paid at lower wage rates (offset by the lower housing costs and cost-of-living in the state).

Most commentators on Texas dwell on the fact that the state is reluctant to spend money on government. This is true. Texas is the lowest ranked state for 'per capita government spending' in the United States. It is a low tax, small government, low regulation state. The Texas state legislature only meets once every two years. The origin of this is generally attributed to the meshing of

36 American Census Bureau, 2004 American Community Survey.

37 At 17 percent, growth in annual average pay in Texas in 2005–10 was higher than the United States and higher than other large US states including New York, Pennsylvania, and California. With high numbers of under 18-year-olds and home to 1.7 million illegal immigrants, Texas also had significant numbers of low-wage, low-benefit no-health-insurance occupations. Even so, in 2010 in Harris County Texas the median household income was $50,577. In Brooklyn, it was $42,932.

38 In 2002, Hollywood in California produced 82 percent of films in the United States. By the end of the decade, the number had fallen to a third.

two forms of social idealism: Southern Baptist Scots-Irish values of individual responsibility and reliance on family rather than state and the libertarian values of small government that typify the American West. Texas bridges the social conservatism of the American South and the libertarian conservatism of the American West. Texas' low spending on government and education is not clinically fiscal. It is rather a reflection of its hermaphrodite history. It is something that both social conservatives and libertarian conservatives can agree on – if perhaps for different reasons.

At the same time, for much of the twentieth century in federal politics Texans voted for socially-conservative but fiscally-liberal New Deal Democrats, figures like Lyndon Johnson who were masters of the art of government spending. Johnson was a long-time Senator from Texas and later American President. Texas and the South were lost to Democrats after Johnson broke with the then-prevailing social conservative prejudice and supported the passage of the Civil Rights Act in 1964 ending official racial segregation in America. Johnson's Presidency simultaneously ushered in the liberal Great Society dramatically expanding government programmes like the economically unsustainable yet politically popular Medicaid and Medicare programmes. Later the iconic Republican figure of George W. Bush re-enacted the parallax politics of old Texan Democrats. He practiced the art of what might be called small state government and big federal government.

This in turn echoed a larger parallax characteristic of the state. This was for an above average percent of the Texan workforce to be employed in government in a small government state. The circle was squared because more public sector employees were paid less in a state where less was more because housing and other living costs were low.[39] As Texas successfully extricated itself from the 2008–09 recession commentators pointed out that 70,000 of the jobs created in the state were civil service jobs. The false implication of this was that the federal government's 2008 fiscal stimulus, which funded temporary state and local public sector jobs, had saved Texas. In reality those 70,000 jobs were a fraction of 250,000 jobs created in the state, the majority of them in the private sector.[40] Texas had created private sector jobs when most American states had not. Conversely when there were federal funds to expand public employment, this was done in parallel with an expanded private sector. The point is not that one happened and the other did not but rather that both happened. The effect was a Jastrow-style duck-rabbit

39 In October 2011, the median house sale price in Allegheny County, PA was $98–$120,000; in Harris County, TX it was $77–94,000.

40 Critics also sniped that a fair proportion of these jobs were low-wage service jobs, but this is a pernicious criticism. If an economy only produced high-skill high-wage jobs, it would doom to welfare a segment of the population for whom technical, managerial, or professional employment will always be firmly out of reach. One of the latent cruelties of post-industrial ideology is its condescending assumption that an economy should only produce genteel forms of work.

gestalt. The effect of this gestalt was that the net creation of jobs in Texas was positive – more jobs were created across 2008–10 than were lost.

No state in a federation is an island, though, and no nation is immune from a downturn of the global economy. A competent government can keep taxes proportionate to income. It can minimize bureaucracy. It can also avoid unfunded liabilities, debts and deficits. Doing that, a state may do better than other states comparatively. Nevertheless, in an age of global stagnation, everyone by degrees is in the same boat. Prudence alone cannot re-start growth. To do this, prudence must be married to invention. Showing an instinct to do exactly that, Texas after 2005 doubled its allocation to university research and promoted STEM education in its high schools. This though was not universally well received. Universities complained that, in their case, the linking of research funding to the commercialization of technology research was misdirected. The romance of this complaint was plain. What was implied was that science was pure while technology and commercialization were tainted. Or put otherwise: science was inventive while technology and business were not. The problem with this view though was that universities themselves had not shown much pure invention during the post-modern decades. The pot, alas, was calling the kettle black. The root difficulty of the global economy at the turning point in 2008 as its spluttered into stagnation was that the spirit of creation was exhausted across the board.

This was because of a long-term cultural decanting. The tenor of the post-modern decades from the beginning of the 1970s had been one of derivation, fragmentation, ennui, entropy, disintegration, the caricaturing of character, and the excess of signs over significance. Mannerism, narcissism, and nihilism variously provided the background texture for intellectual worlds that became consumed by the production of junk, the accumulation of redundancy, and the inflation of importance, and that found themselves suffocating in a general air of mawkishness. In this sterile era the bureaucracy of universities expanded vastly along with the numbers of students in inverse proportion to the quality and depth of the sciences and the arts. So while a small number of states in the world system acted with prudence, the same world system, as a whole, struggled to furnish the kind of durable invention necessary to provide the topology of a fifth wave of industrialization. Without that, the world was stagnant. In 2008–10, what Texas managed to demonstrate was that parallax in public policy was productive of prudence, and vice versa. Yet when one looked beyond public policy, things were not so good. The larger intellectual parallaxes, notably the duck-rabbits of science and technology, were too often absent. This absence was not hard to recognize, especially at the national level in the United States.

Chapter 8
Politics

Forty Years of Mediocrity

The year 2011 in American politics opened with a lacklustre State of Union speech delivered by an unpopular President who was the quintessential product of the post-modern age. Narrowly elected in 2008 because of the shock effect of the Global Financial Crisis, Barack Obama spent two years attempting unsuccessfully a re-tread of the 1930s New Deal. An $800 billion economic spending stimulus failed to reverse high unemployment. The federal government funded short-term public sector jobs, principally at state and local level, expecting demand to grow, the economy to grow and jobs to grow. They did not. Instead the nation's fiscal deficit ballooned. The President and Congress then committed the country long term to hundreds of billions of additional deficit spending on health care entitlements. The electorate's judgement was swift and unambiguous. The President's party, the Democrats, lost heavily in the mid-term Congressional elections. President Obama's response to the electoral verdict was not to roll back deficit or entitlement spending but rather to advocate further public investment, this time in research and technology (The White House 2011).

The President's approach reflected the two prevailing political foci of the Democratic Party. One was born of the 1930s; the other of the 1970s. One rested on the assumptions of John Maynard Keynes; the other on theories of post-industrialism. The Keynesian view supposed that economic life pivoted on demand. Yet Obama's massive spending increase in 2009–10 failed to stimulate demand. Partly this was because the American consumer, in the form of public sector employees hired under the stimulus legislation, took the government's dollar and saved it or else drew down personal debt. In lock-step, American firms also saved rather than invested. Stung by the chimeras of the IT boom, the property boom, and botched investments in government bonds and sovereign debt, companies took flight to saving, avoiding investment. As in Japan in the 1990s and elsewhere, Keynesian assumptions were scuttled. Demand was not a reflex to be set in motion by government spending. It was ultimately not a function of money but of things people wished to purchase. Only when that desire existed was production was worth investing in. In this respect the post-industrial view was closer to the point. It emphasized technological innovation. The theory was historically cogent. It observed that in modern economies growth and prosperity was closely correlated with organization and technology. Machines and electricity, for example, revolutionized modern economics. New things and new desires for those things were created. Yet in spite of the sometimes good theory, technological innovation lagged during the post-industrial era from 1970 to 2000. While the era was rife with talk about creative economies and knowledge societies, the real level of innovation declined. This has been described in previous chapters. The long-term impact of this on prosperity is evident.

The economist Tyler Cowen observed that, in the period from 1947 to 1973, inflation-adjusted median income in the United States more than doubled. Yet in the years from 1973 to 2004, it rose only 22 percent. Over the decade between 2000 and 2010, it declined. The reason for this he argues (2011b), as I have argued elsewhere, is that technological improvements in the last 40 years compare unfavourably with those of the nineteenth or early twentieth centuries:

> My grandmother, who was born in 1905, spoke often about the immense changes she had seen, including the widespread adoption of electricity, the automobile, flush toilets, antibiotics and convenient household appliances. Since my birth in 1962, it seems to me, there have not been comparable improvements.

Cowen is correct. The personal computer, a creature of the 1980s, was the most impressive artefact of post-industrial technology. Yet its social impact falls short of Joseph Swan and Thomas Edison's commercialization of the incandescent light bulb (1870s–80s), Ransom Olds, Henry Ford and Alfred P. Sloan's commercialization of the automobile (1900–30), or even Willis Haviland Carrier's 1902–06 invention of the modern system of air conditioning. The latter made possible for the first time in history an extensive commercial civilization in tropical and humid climates. Contemporary commercial power houses like Singapore and Hong Kong and now Shanghai rely on it. Air conditioning transformed the demography of America. It encouraged mass migration to the South and the realignment of its politics from Democrat to Republican. The personal computer is a useful tool. Yet so many uses of it boil down to a remediation of existing technologies. We have digital re-inventions of books, recordings, films, calculators, phones, typewriters, spreadsheets, which is not the same as the invention of those things. That there is ingenuity in this is undeniable, yet also a certain lack of imagination. The post-modern art of the post-industrial age was criticized because its recycling of the past was lame. Something of the same can be said of the technology of the age. While it is the case that in all acts of discovery there is a significant component of re-discovery, the substance of post-industrial media was heavily weighted towards the old while its rhetoric emphatically proclaimed its newness.

There is no clearer illustration of this than President Obama's 2011 State of Union address. It recommended to Congress spending on information technology, biomedical research, high-speed trains, solar and wind and nuclear energy. Innovation was the way the country made its living, it intoned. The speech was a long list of out-dated post-industrial clichés. Information technology signified innovation in 1991. Twenty years later information was a mature industry. Millions of 'personal pages' existed on the internet in 1998. That social media sites aggregated these across 2005–10 was more a function of the long-established pattern of social and economic concentration than of any mercurial innovation. As for high-speed rail, that was developed experimentally by Siemens in Germany in 1903 and developed commercially in the 1930s with the introduction of various 'inter-urban' services in the United States. The Japanese bullet train, introduced in 1964 and modelled on its American predecessor, was the peak moment of this technology. As of 2011, solar and wind energy technology was uneconomic and there was no sign that converting solar and wind energy into electric power would be economic in the foreseeable future. That said, the future is unknowable and decades of small-scale experimentation can eventually lead to a mass commercial technology. Even so, neither scientific experimentation nor commercial developments need large government investment. Commerce is perfectly capable of looking after itself; so are universities.

When governments invest strategically in the experimental unknown, thinking that it is a known quantity, they waste their money. Bio-medical research has won the lions' share of ear-marked government research funds since the 1960s. Its social appeal ('cure cancer') is undeniable and powerful. Yet while real per capita investment in medical researchers has grown massively, the significance of medical discoveries has not grown accordingly. Even though nominally numerous discoveries are made, in an age of diminished collective imagination, more investment yields proportionately fewer great insights. Science policy over-determines the scientific imagination. Governments allocate block grants to research universities to undertake curiosity-driven research and tied grants to fund specified centrally-defined outcomes. The latter is often expensive and self-defeating.

Take the case of Alexander Fleming, Professor of Bacteriology at the University of London, who discovered (or more accurately re-discovered) penicillin. His work is a perfect example of scientific contrariness. Fleming made his discovery while investigating the properties of a harmless bacteria, staphylococcus. Returning from holidays, he noticed that one of the cultures of staphylococci that he had left on a lab bench had been killed off by a fungus. The contaminant was a form of penicillin. Fleming studied the antibiotic's lethal effect on a range of bacteria. A similar effect had been observed before including by John Scott Burdon-Sanderson, Joseph Lister, William Roberts and John Tydnall in the 1870s. Fleming went a step further than his predecessors and tried to find a stable form of penicillin suitable for mass production. Eventually Fleming's idea was executed by Howard Walter Florey's laboratory at Oxford. The discovery of the first mass-produced anti-biotic was revolutionary. But, crucially, it had all occurred obliquely. Fleming had been working on how to fight Gran-negative bacteria that cause illnesses like typhoid fever. But penicillin works only against Gran-positive bacteria responsible for illnesses like pneumonia or meningitis. This underlies just how important obliquity is in discovery. In the act of discovery, one embarks with an intention to do A, but achieves Z by pursuing inspired digressions. The crucial digressions occur because the research is driven by internal curiosity, rather than by external purposes. The problem of public research policy is that it is purposive, that is, goal-rational. It enunciates objectives and grants money for their achievement. But the greatest scientific achievements come via in-direction rather than direction. One of the reasons for this is that by the time something can be enunciated as an objective, it has already been achieved at least in outline. The rhetoric of the purpose-specific research grant application requires the goal of an investigation to be elaborated. This can only be done if near-approximations of the goal have already been achieved. Discovery in such cases is then subtly re-defined as the 'filling in of gaps'.

'Filling in the gaps' became the modus operandi of the post-industrial age in the arts and the sciences. In the 40 years between 1970 and 2000, words like smart, intelligent, innovation and knowledge were used with increasing frequency as status signifiers. Yet the efficacy of the arts and the sciences declined. Smartness turned into a classic rhetorical word – in the worst sense. Such paltry rhetoric nonetheless had an attentive audience. It principally spoke to the class of university, media and corporate intellectuals, sometimes called the 'new class', which crystallized after 1968. In the alchemical era between 1964 and 1968, class lines and political alignments familiar from the 1930s were re-cast. This was true throughout the West. It was especially true in America. A new post-industrial class joined the public employee class and the various entitlement classes (both poor and middle strata pensioner classes) that grew up after the New Deal.

The voting behaviour of professors is indicative of the political re-alignment that occurred. In the American elections of 1944 the professoriate's voting pattern was closely aligned with the general population. Fifty-four percent of Americans voted Democrat; compared with 57 percent of professors. A distinct gap opened up between the two in 1948. The gap spiked in 1964.[1] A similar shift occurred in the United Kingdom, but later. There it begins in 1964. Either way, that year is a water-shed. A study of voter affiliations of 4,500 academics in 11 Californian institutions, four decades later, showed how wide the gap subsequently grew (Cardiff and Klein 2005). Sixteen percent of the professoriate voted Republican while 45 percent or more of the general population did.[2] In the 2000s in the United Kingdom, barely 1 in 10 academics voted Conservative.[3] A similar gap between the voting pattern of the professorial class and the general population

1 In successive US Presidential elections, the percentage of the general population voting for the Democrats compared with the professorial class was as follows: 57:54 (1944), 52:61 (1948), 44:56 (1952), 62:42 (1956), 78:61 (1964), 61:43 (1968), 57: 39 (1972). Data from Lipset and Ladd (1974).

2 In liberal-arts fields, the ratio was 8:1. In 2003, a large survey of American social scientists was undertaken, with 1,600 academics responding (Klein and Stern 2005). The ratio of Democrats to Republicans was likewise 8:1.

3 In the 1964 election, the UK population voted 43 percent Conservative and the UK professoriate voted 38 percent Conservative. The populace voted 44 percent Labour, the professoriate 45 percent Labour; the populace 11 percent Liberal and the professoriate 15 percent Liberal. The gap steadily widens until it becomes a chasm. In 2001, 65 percent of UK academics voted for the Labour Party; 22 percent for the Liberal Democrats. That

was evident in Canada.[4] This gap has no particular electoral significance. The new class grew along with the expansion of universities, culture industries and the research departments of corporations and financial institutions. Nonetheless the number of votes it commanded in general elections was tiny. The intellectual class dominated media chit-chat. Yet, crucially, despite its omni-presence, the media has little influence on electoral outcomes. Few media intellectuals after 1970 were Republicans yet Republicans dominated the American Presidency. In the 40 years to 2010, 29 of those presidential years were Republican. The real impact of the re-alignment of intellectuals rather was on discovery. Discovery is a function of opposition. The intellectual origin of something – its creative spark – is its opposite. Thus with a flash of insight in 1902 Willis Haviland Carrier observed the paradox that, by wetting humid air, the moisture content of air could be regulated and reduced. This observation made possible the modern air conditioner. Discovery in a collective sense relies on a social ecology that stimulates antinomy and irony of this kind. If that is reduced, then discovery will decline. The new intellectual class that crystallized in 1968 pictured itself as a creative class, yet the very terms of its existence obviated that.

The Myth of Post-industrial Politics

The media and academic class thought of itself not just as a creative class but also as a class that would change the nature of politics. One of the by-products of the conjunction of those two beliefs was an argument developed in a 2002 book by Democratic Party strategists John B. Judis and Ruy Teixeira, *The Emerging Democratic Majority*. The pair proposed that the electoral future of America's Democratic Party was tied to the post-industrialization of the country. Democrat electoral success, they suggested, increasingly correlated with places where the production of ideas and services had either redefined or else had replaced an economy dependent on manufacturing, agriculture, and resource extraction. Many of these areas were in the North and West of the United States but also in coastal states like Florida and Virginia. Republicans, they suggested, were strongest in

---

left a share of the residual 13 percent for the Conservatives. In 2001 7 percent of academics voted Conservative and 10 percent in 2005.

4 The study by Nakhaie and Adam (2008), based on data from the 1993, 1997, and 2000 elections, showed that over 40 percent of Canadian professors voted for the Liberal Party, just over 10 percent for Conservative parties (PC/Reform/Alliance), 7 percent for the Bloc Québécois, and about 30 percent for the New Democratic Party (NDP). Nakhaie and Adam found that the Liberal vote among professors was comparable to that of the population (around 41.5–46.5 percent versus 38.5–41.3 percent), the Conservative and the Bloc vote was lower than that of the population (10.8–13.3 percent and 6.9–7.9 percent versus 34.7–37.7 percent and 10.7–13.5 percent, respectively), while professors tended to vote much more for the NDP than did the general populace (28.4–30.1 percent versus 6.9–11 percent). Professors voted NDP about three times more than the general population.

areas where the transition to post-industrial society had lagged. Many of these places were in the Deep South or in Prairie States. The idea in essence was that Republicans were dinosaurs – headed for extinction.

To a degree Judis and Teixeira's thesis paralleled the work of Richard Florida. Florida though was always keen to stress his bi-partisanship – insisting that his urban sociology was useful for understanding the trajectories of both Republican and Democrat-dominated states and cities. Judis and Teixeira, in contrast, emphasized the partisan significance of creative class sociology. They argued that America's post-industrial politics were not defined by states per se but rather by metropolitan regions within states. They called these post-industrial metropolises – 'ideopolises'. These, they suggested, were the breeding ground of a 'new Democratic majority'. They steered away from older political sociologies that had identified Democrat politics with the urban core of American cities. Post-industrial society, they observed, was organized around metropolitan areas that included suburbs, exurbs and city centres.

The pair approached the question of the social composition of post-industrial cities with some subtlety. While observing the rise of professional-technical and service classes, and the decline of classic manufacturing typified by Pittsburgh steel and Detroit autos and their unionized labour forces, the two were careful to note that post-industrial metropolitan areas like Silicon Valley's Santa Clara County or the Boulder, Colorado metro region contained significant manufacturing facilities. This was not the manufacturing typical of the New Deal era style big company-big government-big union matrix, John Kenneth Galbraith's 'new industrial state'. Which is why the most successful manufacturing industries in post-industrial societies, the STEM (science, technology, engineering and mathematical) industries, which are research-and-development intensive, and include the pharmaceutical, aircraft, spacecraft, and medical industries, are prominent in small-government, minimal-union states like Texas. Like its labour-intensive predecessor in its hey-day, STEM industrialization drives high wage manufacturing. But, in its operation, less emphasis is placed on labour organization and negotiation and more emphasis is given to high technology and high productivity. Where physical manufacturing can be separated from the design of pharmaceuticals, semiconductors and so forth, jobs in such industries are liable to be exported overseas unless the productivity of local plants can compete against lower wages abroad.[5] Only a workforce with high levels of technical problem-solving and skill can deliver that. In that sense design-driven STEM manufacturing is as much a knowledge industry as are communication industries like entertainment, media, fashion, and advertising, or information industries such as searchable databases, or professional advice industries such as law and accounting.

Judis and Teixeira observed three things about post-industrial urban areas. First, professionals and technicians make up a very sizeable proportion of the workforces of post-industrial metropolises. In 2002, a quarter or so of the jobs in

5 Or wages overseas rise markedly, as in the case of China today.

Austin, Boston, San Francisco, and North Carolina's Research Triangle were held by professionals and technicians. Second, there are also large numbers of low-skill, low-wage service, administrative and support jobs in these places, a point also made by Richard Florida. In post-industrial cities, a wide income gap exists between professional and service occupations. Third, these urban areas are often closely connected to research universities. Boston's Route 128 feeds off Harvard and MIT. Silicon Valley is closely linked to Stanford and the University of California at Berkeley. Dane County's biomedical research is tied to the University of Wisconsin at Madison. The purpose of this sociology, though, was to make a political point. Namely that while many of these areas were once Republican, they had become Democrat in their partisan politics.

Judis and Teixeira offered plenty of examples of this from the 2000 US Presidential race between George W. Bush and Al Gore: Gore won Portland's Multnomah County 64 percent to 28 percent. Princeton University's Mercer County went for Gore 61 percent to 34 percent. Seattle's King County preferred Gore 60 percent to 34 percent. What followed from the exposition of such examples was the strategic proposition that post-industrialization in the medium and long term favoured the Democratic Party over the Republicans. A Democrat majority, it was predicted, would emerge on the basis of metropolitan counties that had heavy and increasing concentrations of professionals and a service class concentrated in industries patronized by the professional-technical class. On the surface of things, such an argument was persuasive. However, on closer examination, it did not stand up. As Table 8.1 indicates, there are both Republican and Democrat counties that have virtually identical post-industrial sociological profiles – with comparable high levels of formal qualifications and concentrations of professions, information-arts-education industries and high-technology manufacturing. On virtually every social measure, the counties in Table 8.1 that voted for George W. Bush and for John Kerry in the 2004 US Presidential election were almost identical. Other data confirms that there was no predisposition for voters with a bachelors' degree (the basic entry-level credential for professional and information-education-arts employment) to vote for the Democrats. In the 2004 Presidential election, 52 percent of college graduates backed Bush compared to 42 percent for Kerry (Gallup).While Obama reversed this in 2008, winning 55 percent (to 45 percent) of college voters, this was the political inverse of the Bush result in 2004, not the signifier of a fundamental shift.[6]

6 Obama's re-election strategy in 2011 (for 2012) was to target traditional Republican states that had high numbers of college-educated voters (Colorado, Virginia, and North Carolina).

Table 8.1 Democrat and Republican ideopolises 2004

Cluster One: The 'Democrat' Ideopolis					
County	*Travis*	*Mercer*	*Fairfax*	*King*	*USA*
	TX	NJ	VA	WA	
Population Size	869,868	365,271	1,003,157	1,777,143	
Median Age	32.10	36.50	37.80	37.50	
Per Capita Income – 2003	$34,439	$41,499	N/A	$45,334	$31,472
Percentage who Lived in a Different State a Year Ago	2.50%	1.70%	4.80%	2.70%	
Percentage of Population who are Foreign Born	16.00%	16.50%	26.00%	19.00%	
Occupation	Information	Information	Information	Information	Information
Average Earnings per Job	$80,811	$99,434	$111,297	$156,739	$78,059
Percentage of Workforce	3.30%	2.90%	5.20%	5.20%	2.10%
Occupation	Education	Education	Education	Education	Education
Average Earnings per Job	$19,221	$52,386	$26,994	$21,633	$28,218
Percentage of Workforce	1.50%	8.90%	1.70%	2.00%	2.00%
Occupation	Arts	Arts	Arts	Arts	Arts
Average Earnings per Job	$13,789	$14,530	$16,453	$24,514	$22,841
Percentage of Workforce	2.30%	1.70%	2.10%	2.70%	2.00%
Subtotal	7.10%	13.50%	9.00%	9.90%	6.10%

Table 8.1 Continued

Occupation	Professional	Professional	Professional	Professional	Professional
Average Earnings per Job	$60,206	$70,046	$85,250	$69, 192	$61,177
Percentage of Workforce	9.60%	9.70%	20.60%	9.00%	6.30%
Occupation	Finance	Finance	Finance	Finance	Finance
Average Earnings per Job	$61,558	$76,372	$102,841	$76,449	$66,173
Percentage of Workforce	5.40%	6.50%	4.50%	5.10%	4.80%
Subtotal	15.00%	16.20%	25.10%	14.10%	11.10%
Occupation	Manufacturing	Manufacturing	Manufacturing	Manufacturing	Manufacturing
Average Earnings per Job	$100,152	$66,131	$78,138	$79,364	$61,129
Percentage of Workforce	7.50%	3.50%	1.60%	8.20%	9.00%
Subtotal	7.50%	3.50%	1.60%	8.20%	9.00%
Percentage with Bachelors Degree	26.10%	18.50%	30.40%	26.60%	15.50%
Percentage with Graduate Degree	14.50%	15.50%	24.40%	13.30%	8.90%
Democrat	56%	61.30%	53.20%	65.00%	48.27%
Republican	42%	37.90%	45.90%	33.70%	50.73%

Table 8.1 Continued

Cluster Two: The 'Republican' Ideopolis					
County	*Harris*	*San Diego*	*Wake*	*Collin*	*USA*
	TX	CA	NC	TX	
Population Size	3,644,285	2,931,714	719,520	627,938	
Median Age	32	34	34	33	
Per Capita Income – 2003	$36,314	$35,841	$35,864	$39,941	$31,472
Percentage who Lived in a Different State a Year Ago	1.70%	2.50%	3.30%	2.90%	
Percentage of Population who are Foreign Born	22.80%	23.20%	12.80%	15.80%	
Occupation	Information	Information	Information	Information	Information
Average Earnings per Job	$82,162	$94,516	$72,639	$108,760	$78,059
Percentage of Workforce	1.70%	2.30%	3.90%	5.10%	2.10%
Occupation	Education	Education	Education	Education	Education
Average Earnings per Job	$34,549	$24,848	$22,890	$13,598	$28,218
Percentage of Workforce	1.80%	1.60%	1.70%	1.10%	2.00%
Occupation	Arts	Arts	Arts	Arts	Arts
Average Earnings per Job	$24,283	$23,654	$20,032	$15,039	$22,841
Percentage of Workforce	1.50%	2.20%	1.90%	2.30%	2.00%
Subtotal	5.00%	6.10%	7.50%	8.50%	6.10%

Table 8.1 Continued

Occupation	Professional	Professional	Professional	Professional	Professional
Average Earnings per Job	$80,298	$59,338	$63,909	$38,548	$61,177
Percentage of Workforce	8.40%	9.40%	9.00%	8.20%	6.30%
Occupation	Finance	Finance	Finance	Finance	Finance
Average Earnings per Job	$77,695	$63,105	$66,659	$51,260	$66,173
Percentage of Workforce	4.50%	4.40%	4.00%	7.60%	4.80%
Subtotal	12.90%	13.80%	13.00%	15.80%	11.10%
Occupation	Manufacturing	Manufacturing	Manufacturing	Manufacturing	Manufacturing
Average Earnings per Job	$99,478	$71,961	$73,287	$87,978	$61,129
Percentage of Workforce	7.50%	6.40%	5.00%	7.30%	9.00%
Subtotal	7.50%	6.40%	5.00%	7.30%	9.00%
Percentage with Bachelors Degree	17.90%	18.90%	29.60%	32.80%	15.50%
Percentage with Graduate Degree	9.00%	10.70%	14.30%	14.60%	8.90%
Democrat	44.60%	46.40%	48.70%	28.10%	46.65%
Republican	54.80%	52.50%	50.80%	71.20%	50.73%

Source: Stats Indiana USA Counties in Profile (2005). US Presidential Election 2004.

This is not to say there are no differences between Democrat and Republican post-industrial metropolises. But, often like the electoral margins separating them, the differences are more slender than gross. The Democrat cluster of counties in Table 8.1 shows overall a slighter higher incidence of information–education–arts employment. This occupational group is more liberal in inclination than most others. In the 2004 US Presidential race, 'Communications and Electronics' was the only US industry sector from which Democrat challenger John Kerry raised more money than the incumbent George W. Bush.[7] Most journalists and academics vote Democrat. Indeed, employees from The University of California and Harvard University were John Kerry's largest campaign contributors in 2004.[8] This is significant, though its significance can be exaggerated. Most post-industrial work is neither in the media nor the university. On the other hand – on the flip-side of what is a nuanced picture – research universities, which are a key post-industrial institution, do have an impact, though not on college graduates but on the voting pattern of postgraduates. Holders of graduate and professional degrees in the 2004 Presidential election voted 53 percent for Kerry and 47 percent for Bush. No election, though, will turn on the votes of what is a tiny group numerically.

The other visible difference between the two clusters of counties examined is government employment (see Table 8.2). The crucial difference turns not on the proportion of the workforce employed by government, which is broadly comparable, but on the level of salaries paid to government employees. It turns out that a much more traditional 'point of difference' between Republicans and Democrats, namely over the amount of government spending, may explain the politics of post-industrial counties as much as anything does. Judis and Teixeira themselves hinted at this. They began their analysis by proposing that post-industrial cities are socially liberal in ethos but fiscally moderate. Fiscal moderation was their euphemism for small government. Yet their use of it led them into a twist. As centrist Democrats they wanted to endorse fiscal restraint. At the same time, as political strategists, they wanted to demonstrate a weakness on the part of Republicans who 'have continued to espouse an anti-government credo closely identified with business and the religious right'. Such politics, they speculated, played well amongst rural Southern Baptists but not in post-industrial America. Yet this was not so evidently the case. It was not even the case that some of post-industrial America was for 'big government' and some for 'small government'. The real dividing line was not 'government' per se but rather its cost.

7 See the Centre for Responsive Politics' Money in Politics data at http://www.opensecrets.org/.

8 It appeared likely at the start of 2012 that the social media tycoons would play this role for Obama in the 2012 Presidential election, eclipsing both Hollywood and academe.

Table 8.2 Democratic and Republican counties 2004

		County				
		Travis	*Mercer*	*Fairfax*	*King*	*Average*
		TX	NJ	VA	WA	
Percentage of Workforce	Administrative	6.40%	5.10%	6.70%	5.40%	5.90%
Average Earnings per Job		$28,140	$34,984	$36,350	$38,475	$34,487
Percentage of Workforce	Government	17.50%	20.80%	13.10%	12.20%	15.90%
Average Earnings per Job		$49,630	$62,391	$67,019	$53,577	$58,154
Percentage of Workforce	Health care, social assist	7.80%	9.60%	7.20%	8.50%	8.28%
Average Earnings per Job		$44,784	$48,178	$49,777	$46,225	$47,241
Percentage of Workforce	Other services	5.50%	4.40%	N/A	5.10%	5.00%
Average Earnings per Job		$27,667	$31,121	N/A	$26,771	$28,520
		County				
		Harris	*San Diego*	*Wake*	*Collin*	*Average*
		TX	CA	NC	TX	
Percentage of Workforce	Administrative	7.60%	6.40%	7.50%	5.50%	6.75%
Average Earnings per Job		$31,976	$28,393	$28,786	$26,577	$28,933
Percentage of Workforce	Government	10.80%	19.20%	16.30%	10.60%	14.23%
Average Earnings per Job		$49,014	$53,850	$46,617	$41,880	$47,840
Percentage of Workforce	Health care, social assist	8.10%	7.40%	7.10%	6.90%	7.38%
Average Earnings per Job		$46,252	$42,481	$41,298	$46,609	$44,160
Percentage of Workforce	Other services	5.90%	5.80%	5.20%	6.00%	5.73%
Average Earnings per Job		$23,918	$22,328	$23,308	$19,665	$22,305

Source: Stats Indiana, USA Counties in Profile (2005).

The Republican ideopolises disliked exorbitant salaries and benefits. What they assumed in practice was the paradox of sizeable government with modest costs, or to stretch a point, the paradox of large government that was small. This was the kind of government that avoided what the Californian city of San Jose did to itself in 2011 – which was spend half of its budget on pensions and health benefits for its retired employees (Lewis 2011).

The Virtue of Paradox

There is nothing wrong with paradoxes in politics. Indeed, they are essential in a complex modern society like the United States. It is perfectly commonplace for American political actors not only to be liberal in some matters and conservative in others but also to subtly blend both in ways that defy straight-forward description. This is not a matter of confusion or Machiavellian hypocrisy but a necessary implication of the Madisonian structure of American politics. It was James Madison, one of the American Founders, who devised a formula that essentially guarantees that political parties have to engineer coalitions in order to win office, especially in federal politics. Madison set out the principles for this in *The Federalist Papers* Number Ten. Madison's purpose was to prevent politics being subverted by factions. Factions were groups of citizens, large or small, who were so passionate about their own views or interests that they were prepared to vex and oppress their fellow citizens.

> By a faction, I understand a number of citizens, whether amounting to a majority or a minority of the whole, who are united and actuated by some common impulse of passion, or of interest, adverse to the rights of other citizens, or to the permanent and aggregate interests of the community.

Madison observed that the division of opinion, interest and ambition, and the resulting formation of parties, led to deep animosities amongst political actors. These animosities encouraged oppressive behaviour.

> A zeal for different opinions concerning religion, concerning government, and many other points, as well of speculation as of practice; an attachment to different leaders ambitiously contending for pre-eminence and power; or to persons of other descriptions whose fortunes have been interesting to the human passions, have, in turn, divided mankind into parties, inflamed them with mutual animosity, and rendered them much more disposed to vex and oppress each other than to co-operate for their common good.

Madison proposed a remarkable solution to this problem. He said that the American republic should be an extended and representative republic. This idea went against the grain of much traditional thinking about republics. This thinking said that they should be small states and direct democracies. Madison argued that a large republic would create so many interests and opinions that incipient factions would cancel each other out. Madison reasoned that

> … the greater number of citizens and extent of territory which may be brought within the compass of republican than of democratic government; and it is this circumstance principally which renders factious combinations less to be dreaded in the former than in the latter. The smaller the society, the fewer probably will be the distinct parties and interests composing it; the fewer the distinct parties and interests, the more frequently will a majority be found of the same party; and the smaller the number of individuals composing a majority, and the smaller the compass within which they are placed, the more easily will they concert and execute their plans of oppression. Extend the sphere, and you take in a greater variety of parties and interests; you make it less probable that a majority of the whole will have a common motive to invade the rights of other citizens; or if such a common motive exists, it will be more difficult for all who feel it to discover their own strength, and to act in unison with each other.

Madison also argued that the mechanism of representation meant that fractious opinions and interests would have to be filtered through representative organs where there would be pressure on representatives to consider the greater good. The effect of this would be

> … to refine and enlarge the public views, by passing them through the medium of a chosen body of citizens, whose wisdom may best discern the true interest of their country, and whose patriotism and love of justice will be least likely to sacrifice it to temporary or partial considerations.

The effect of Madison's political model was profound. There was no proposal from any of the Founders more far-reaching in its consequences for the conduct of American politics than *The Federalist Papers* Number Ten. It's a good thing too. For America is incipiently factious. Its polemics are nasty and the temper of its opinion and interests groups often is foul. The grandeur of American politics certainly does not stem from partisan groups of all stripes who are regularly venomous and bigoted and display vindictive ill-will toward their opponents. Given half a chance, many of them employ vexatious and malicious pressure to scuttle their antagonists all the while feeling self-righteous about it. Sneering and contempt is a widespread attitude among American political factions – across the spectrum of opinion. It was Thomas Hobbes who pointed out that contempt was the first step toward faction, and that factions destroyed states. While Hobbes proposed a strong sovereign as the solution to this, Madison came up with the more ingenious and benign solution of the extended republic.

One of the most far-reaching consequences of this notion was to make it difficult for any opinion or interest group to ever create a majority in its own right. This meant that any party that sought an electoral majority, at a national level in particular, could only do this as a coalition of divergent opinion and interest. This had the further effect of reinforcing the incipient American distrust of what Alexis de Tocqueville dubbed the tyranny of the majority. Majorities are a necessary electoral artifice. They are the legal fiction that makes elections work. Yet nobody can legitimately expect 50 percent or more of Americans to agree on anything. Indeed political passions end up being directed to things that quite small percentages of the population are engaged or enraged by. The art of political parties then becomes that of weaving these groups of 10 percent or 20 percent of the population into organizations with a claim on the allegiance of at least 50 percent of the population. That is no easy task. This is especially so when fractious temperaments tempt political actors to create pseudo-majorities by pursuing venomous, nasty, and savage tactics. By its nature politics is hard fought. But there comes a point where vigorous even lacerating debate descends into vicious personal back-biting and malodorous character assassination. Contempt is an easier path than coalition but it is highly destructive. It flourishes where kitsch policies and political styles dominate.[9] These are so brittle and so shallow that they have little inherent cross-over appeal. So political actors then resort to self-defeating contempt to bull-doze their minority into a majority. Coalition-building in contrast is an art, a deft weaving of political contrasts, shades, and nuances.

In the American twentieth century, the greatest of these acts of weaving was the New Deal coalition created by the Democratic Party of Franklin Delano Roosevelt. This was a coalition of union bosses, blue collar labour, Catholics, Jews, intellectuals, and segregationists. It set the tone for American politics from 1932 to 1964. This was true even when Republicans were in power. No coalition of minorities lasts forever, though. Between 1964 and 1972, the Democratic New Deal Coalition collapsed. It did so partly because segregation could no longer be tolerated in America. If coalitions are uneasy combinations of minorities in a state of undeclared war, after 1964 and the passage of the Civil Rights Act, segregation was placed beyond the pale of any conceivable coalition. It was welcome nowhere. But this was not the only reason for the collapse of the New Deal Coalition. It also collapsed because there was an alternative. This alternative coalition was created because of the rise of left liberalism, the most vociferous ideology of the post-modern era. It grew out of the cultural wars of the late 1960s and is distinguishable

9 It needs to be stressed that this is not unique to America in the slightest. The Hobbesian problem of contempt haunts modern politics. A classic example is the brawling that befell the Australian Labor Party in 2012 as it fractured itself between two factions, one organized by an ex-leader (Rudd) and one by the extant leader (Gillard). The former practiced power by contempt behind the scenes while in office; the latter practiced it through ministerial agents who demonized their former leader in an orgy of spite and vitriol. Both factions committed themselves about equally to almost identical policy positions that were essentially a list of gimmicks virtually all of which had failed when executed. The electorate looked on bemused.

from the Cold War liberalism typical of the Democratic Party of the 1950s and early 1960s. In the same transition period between 1964 and 1972, an even more important event occurred. This was the emergence of a counter-coalition on the Republican side of American politics. The effect of this counter-coalition was to end the rule of the Rockefeller Republicans over the party. These were the political patricians, figures like Prescott Bush, whose politics were mildly liberal and 'Democrat Lite'. In their place emerged a new, massively contradictory and agonistic coalition that eventually came to consist of social conservatives, libertarian conservatives, neo-conservatives, paleo-conservatives, Republican moderates and liberal Republicans.[10]

In principle such a coalition should not work. Its constituent parts ostensibly have nothing in common. Even ambition and a taste for political success is not enough on its own to sustain such an alliance over decades. Yet, remember, that same contradictory nature applied to the Democrat's New Deal Coalition as well. So, in American politics, what is not supposed to work, works. On the other, what is supposed to work, which is the new coalition that the Democrats put together after 1968, did not work – or at least its efficacy visibly declined over time as New Deal coalition stalwarts, feeling spurned by the new look Democratic Party, began to vote Republican. There was a truth in former Democrat Ronald Reagan's apercu: I did not abandon the Democrats, they abandoned me. Between 1964 and 1972, the Democratic Party created a new coalition. This was a coalition in which college graduates replaced blue collar workers, feminists replaced Catholics, African-Americans replaced segregationists, and anti-war activists replaced the union bosses. Many blue collar workers from the New Deal coalition went over to the Republicans especially during the Reagan Presidency years. Catholics similarly gravitated to George W. Bush. In the 1970s and 1980s, the South became the New South, and numerous white Democrats came to identify with evangelicals and social conservatives. Democratic president Jimmy Carter still held onto most of the votes of America's evangelicals. By the time of George W. Bush, the evangelical vote had become predominately Republican.

In electoral terms, the Republican coalition proved to be exceptionally successful. What about the post-1968 Democrats? Their coalition did not work nearly as effectively. Its capacity to generate majorities by amalgamating minorities progressively declined over time. The two terms of the Clinton Presidency were not a counter example. Bill Clinton came to power only because, as a 'New Democrat', he created a 'Lite' version of the Republican coalition. The case of John Kerry, the Democrat contender in the 2004 US Presidential election against George W. Bush, demonstrates what happens when the Liberal Democrat rather

10 The inconclusive first segment of the Republican presidential primary in 2012 had all of these different forces on show but no candidate who crossed over by creating a coalition, There was the futurist conservative (Gingrich), the social conservative (Santorum), the corporate conservative (Romney), the libertarian conservative (Paul), but no one early on in the race who could bridge some or all these fragments.

than the New Democrat model is applied. It does not work, because it cannot work, because, simply, at the end of the day it cannot deliver enough votes, because it does not have a broad enough reach, which is another way of saying that it does not have the hugely contradictory base of the Republicans (or FDR's New Deal coalition).

The election of the liberal Barack Obama would seem to be a counter-case. Yet this is the case of an accidental President who was elected on a slender majority amidst the panic that surrounded the onset of the Global Financial Crisis in 2008. Obama won the election because independent voters who traditionally leaned Republican were disenchanted with the Bush years and unconvinced by Obama's Republican opponent, John McCain. Independents typically want small government, lower taxes, no deficits, and balanced budgets. They are for fossil fuels and against foreign interventions. On most of those counts, the Bush years disappointed them. Yet when Obama in office enacted policies, the independents were even more disappointed by those. His support nose-dived by the time of the mid-term Congressional elections in 2010. It took six years for George W. Bush's popularity to fall below 40 percent in the opinion polls. It took two-and-a-half years for the same to happen to Barack Obama.

The coalition of minorities created by the 1968 era Democratic Party – the alliance of feminists, African-Americans, activists, intellectuals, college graduates and public sector unions (i.e. graduates as pretend New Dealers) – did not stretch to a majority of the national voting population. Sometimes this coalition was supplemented or refigured as in the Clinton years. Obama did the most to refigure it. While outwardly his was a post-modern coalition of students, wealthy liberals and poor African-Americans, he supplemented this with Chicago-based labour-boss machine politics, a fossilized residue of the New Deal but one that still delivered some votes. Until Obama, Democrats who successfully ran for the presidency, including Lyndon Johnson, Jimmy Carter and Bill Clinton, were all Southerners – a bloc notably not included in the 1968 coalition. The South, once overwhelmingly Democrat, pivoted to the Republicans. The unviable nature of the 68er coalition can be usefully contrasted with the events of the Bush years. The Bush coalition snapped in 2006. Significant numbers of fiscal and libertarian conservatives (some registered Republicans, some independents) repudiated the Bush policies. Their nature and rationale was called into question. Bush was a conservative, but of a particular type. One of the principal talismans of the conservative is anti-tyranny. From Burke to Churchill, this has been so, especially for Whiggish conservatives. Bush ran in the 2000 election as anything but such a figure. It was only unexpectedly after the 2001 terrorist attack on the United States that he took on the mantle of the anti-tyrannical conservative. The consequences of this stretched the Republican coalition to breaking. That it did this reveals something interesting about conservative coalitions.

A conservative is someone who respects limits. The respect for limits exhibits itself in many different ways. One is repugnance towards tyrants. Tyranny is the antithesis of limited behaviour. The violence of the tyrant exceeds all human limits. The tyrant Saddam Hussein killed one million Iraqis to keep his regime in power and another million Iraqis and Iranians were killed in the mad war that Saddam engineered against Iran in 1980. The Bush Administration removed Saddam from power.[11] Like all momentous political actions, this decision had paradoxical consequences.[12] In removing the tyrant, it upheld limits. Yet, in order to do so, it put pressure on both fiscal and humanitarian limits. Americans were obliged to remove the armed tyrant, conduct war against the terrorists who took up the slack, and help rebuild the government and economy of a tyrannized and terrorized society. As in all wars, moral and fiscal boundaries were tested. One hundred thousand Iraqis died in the resulting civil war and more than 4,000 US troops.[13] America spent $10 billion per month in Iraq. Some conservatives found this too much.[14] Libertarian conservatives showed the least inclination to war. Fiscal conservatives grew alarmed at the growth of debt to fund the war. From 1965 to 1985 debt was 30 to 40 percent of GDP. From 1989 to 2008 it was 50 to 60 percent of GDP. The debt of the Bush years was higher than the lows of the Clinton years, but would turn out to be much lower than the dizzying highs

---

11 The steps towards this began in the Clinton era, with the passage of the Iraq Liberation Act by the United States Congress in 1998. The legislation was passed on a bi-partisan basis.

12 It also had a paradoxical rationale. Part of the justification for the removal of Saddam was to combat al-Qaeda. Al-Qaeda was a trans-national extra-territorial terrorist movement. Saddam's Iraq was a territorial state. Prima facie this was an asymmetrical even seemingly perverse choice. Yet, as Chesterton once observed, a wilderness is always best viewed through the frame of a window. It is not evident that a state like the United States is best suited to fighting extra-territorially, as the difficulties of combating al-Qaeda in Pakistan from Afghanistan was later to demonstrate. In contrast, from the invasion in 2003 through September 2007, some 17,000 insurgent terrorists were killed by coalition armies in Iraq.

13 In contrast, the civil war in 2011 to remove Colonel Gaddafi from power in Libya, in which no American ground troops participated, cost an estimated 30,000 Libyan lives (Laub 2001). Libya has a population of 6.6 million; Iraq has a population of 34.3 million. Libya's civil war death count was one per 220 persons; the comparable Iraqi count was one person per 343 persons.

14 This raises the interesting question of what a country gets for a trillion dollars. President Bush spent a trillion dollars on the Iraq War. A violent tyrant was removed from power and a fractured but semi-functioning democracy was created. President Obama spent a trillion dollars on an economic stimulus package in 2009. As of June 2011, the number of jobs lost from the time Obama took office to the bottom of recession was 4.3 million; the number of jobs added following the bottom was 1.8 million. The net loss of jobs was 2.5 million. Let us assume the fanciful: that all jobs created were created by the stimulus. Even making that generous assumption, each job created by the Obama budget stimulus cost the equivalent of half a million dollars per job. Any job creation programme that costly mocks economic rationality. From 2009 to 2011 unemployment remained stuck at 9 percent. This defied the historic pattern of post-war recessions. Usually rapid recovery occurred after 17 months of high unemployment.

(80 to 90 percent of GDP and rising) of the Obama years. Hindsight though is not a luxury afforded in politics.

Democratic politics is simple. If you do not have a majority, you do not get elected. To get a majority in America, which was designed to make that as difficult as possible, you have to create agonistic coalitions. This was precisely what the 68 generation in the Democratic Party could not do. The comparison with the era of George W. Bush is instructive. What Democrat pundits rarely understood about Bush is that he had the political instinct required to weave around all the minorities in the Republican Party, pitching here to the Protestant social conservatives on the one hand and then to upwardly mobile Catholic Latinos and then to the big city neo conservatives and then something for the libertarian constituency in the western states, and on and on. After 2006 this tenuous coalition cracked, or more accurately Bush simply stopped cultivating it. In any case, the politics of creating majorities out of the broad spectrum of seemingly incompatible or irreconcilable minorities is subtle to say the least.

The first condition of doing so is that you give a little bit of succour to each group but deny them the larger part of what they want. Let me illustrate this with some examples from Republican politics. Ronald Reagan appealed to libertarian conservatives who want low taxes and small government. In power, Reagan cut taxes, yet he also expanded government spending. He created a large government deficit as a result. Libertarians got something – tax cuts – but less than they wished out of Reagan. Essentially the same was repeated by the George W. Bush administration. The conclusion of libertarians from this experience might be that government cannot be trusted, yet the logic of politics underlying such decisions cannot be attributed to the bad faith of political leaders. Rather it has more to do with the logic of creating electoral majorities out of warring political minorities. Each coalition partner limits the others. Libertarians have views on how a Republican Presidency should conduct itself. But so do other minorities that make up the Republican Coalition and the aspirations of these bed-fellow minorities invariably contradict the libertarian conservatives. Neo-conservatives support government spending on national security. Expanding military-industrial spending (to meet the threats of the Cold War or the War on Terror) contradicted libertarian priorities to scale down the size and power of government. The military-industrial sector itself represents a sizeable voting cohort that tends to vote Republican.

Take also the case of social conservatives. They want abortion banned. Yet libertarians favour individual choice, as typically do liberal Republicans. It is not that pro-choice Republicans negate pro-life Republicans. Rather they limit the concessions that can be made to social conservatives. They end up being given a little but not much. This might be the appointment of a Pentecostal as Attorney General (John Ashcroft), or a Congressional law banning late-term abortions, or the appointment of Supreme Court judges who might (but also might not) one day support the overturning of the *Roe vs. Wade* case law.[15] Each of these measures has an appeal for social conservatives but they are not in themselves a triumph of social conservatism because other conservatives, and liberal and moderate Republicans as well, would be unhappy if that happened.

The Political Imagination

Here we see Madison's design at work. It is difficult for a minority to ever get more than a consoling slice of its agenda implemented. There are too many other minorities to check mate it. But for coalitions to work, each of the minorities must concede something to their allies. Check mate by itself is a recipe for paralysis and civil war. So the formula of 'something but not everything' applies. The politics of minorities in alliance with strange bed fellows is an incremental politics. The minorities advance their cause a little here, a little there, but mostly in ways that minimize outright strife between the coalition partners. The key thing in democratic politics is the trans-valuation of values. This has been true since Aristotle observed that the middle ground – in Aristotle's time, the middle class – was essential to a stable constitutional regime. The middle ground is where paradoxical exchanges between agonistic partners occur. Each transforms the other. Understanding the nature of these paradoxical exchanges is difficult because we do not really understand the nature of political 'logic'. In traditional discursive or propositional logic, contradictory statements are governed by the law of the excluded middle. That is not the case in politics. Politics is governed by the law of the included middle. We can make moral statements such as 'abortion is wrong' or 'a woman's right to choose is fundamental' – and presume one or other to be right. Economists can propose that 'more government spending is good' or 'increasing government spending is bad', and suppose that one negates the other. In politics, though, we cannot assume that one statement either invalidates the other or excludes the other. This is not to say that politics is relativistic. Indeed politics is the least relativistic of all human modes of experience. Politics requires decisions, and decisions exclude many alternatives. But, at the same time, politics is also filled with ingenious syntheses – with syn-antonyms. These negotiate seemingly irreconcilable positions. Politics is the art of finding the paradoxical middle ground between agonistic positions. I do not mean that politics is the act of splitting the difference. It is not a bargain like 'you want $100,000', 'I want to give you $60,000', let us split the difference, and 'call it $80,000'. Serious issues of morality or public policy cannot be dealt with in such a cavalier manner. Yet they do have to be subject to subtle and paradoxical syntheses all the same. If not, then democratic politics is inconceivable.

---

15 Such an overturning would have the effect of permitting different American states to regulate abortion as they each saw fit – some might then keep the status quo, others might limit abortion, others might liberalize the law, and so on.

This is true not just of the partners within a coalition that constitutes the base of a political party. It is doubly true of the electorate as a whole. To illustrate, let us again take the case of American Presidential politics since 1964 and the relative lack of success of the Democratic Party in that era. Observers point out that even when the Democratic Party lost contests, it still returned near majorities. That is consoling for the losers, but it misses a fundamental dimension of the political experience. In order to secure a majority under Madisonian conditions, a party must be effective in capturing the paradoxical middle of a society. The paradoxical middle of a society is not simply the group of voters in the political centre that will change their vote with a little extra convincing. The paradoxical middle of the electorate is the group of voters for whom the subtle synthesis and the strange political 'logic' of the included middle is attractive. These are voters who are sceptical of capital-I ideologies. This does not mean that ideologies have no influence on them. But they are more persuaded by interesting positions that reconcile the irreconcilable.

To illustrate this, I'll take some examples from *One Nation, After All*, a study of American middle class attitudes by the liberal American political scientist Alan Wolfe (1998). The phenomenon of the paradoxical middle percolates through the interviews with participants in the study. It characterizes a good part of the moral-political reasoning of the interviewees. Wolfe himself notes the conservatives who oppose the values of the 1960s and yet who use the 1960s-style language of social transformation (283). Others elsewhere have observed the converse: liberals whose views are coloured by 1960s romanticism and yet who embrace the Protestant work ethic in their jobs. This may sound schizoid and in some cases it is. But equally it is a testament to the power of the synthetic logic of politics. This synthesizing produces the union of opposites. Wolfe provides many practical examples of this at work: interviewees who cautiously approve of America's open borders but who resist bi-lingual policies and strongly support English as a national language (154). There are interviewees who disapprove of unregulated illegal immigration – it is disorderly. Yet they accept the illegal immigrant who works hard and learns English (152). There are those who disapprove of homosexuality yet who also disapprove of discrimination against homosexuals and expect homosexuals to be accorded fundamental human respect (80). There are interviewees whose conservative Christian views incline them against women working but whose other libertarian views trump their Christian views (104). The paradoxical middle leans towards cautious support for the welfare state leavened by doubts about the corrosive effects of long-term welfare on character and personal responsibility (14). Most of Wolfe's interviewees were adamant that people sometimes need help but they also worried about a life spent perpetually on welfare. Most saw a role for government and taxes in providing social welfare but most also did not want a welfare bureaucracy to entirely replace voluntary charity and the moral obligations to help others (201). No right to welfare negated the welfare recipient's personal responsibility to seek work (204–5).

Alan Wolfe is a liberal. His contextual analysis of his interviewees tends to suggest that liberal views win out over or at least moderate conservative views. But in fact many of the interviewees operated with two sets of views simultaneously. Such mind-sets are not unambiguously liberal or conservative. The judgements they make are ambidextrous. The conclusions they come to are synthetic in nature. The structure of these judgements reflects what Hannah Arendt called political judgement. A way of understanding what is peculiar about political judgement is to consider the philosopher Immanuel Kant's three great critiques of reason, morality and art. These encompassed three distinctive domains of human experience – science, ethics and aesthetics. Late in his life Kant also wrote a series of brilliant political essays. He failed though to develop these into a Fourth Critique. Had he worked on a Critique of Politics he would have encountered the problem of understanding judgements much like the ones that we have encountered here.

Late in her life also, Hannah Arendt began to work on something like a Critique of Politics. Her starting point for this was Kant's third critique. In her *Lectures on Kant's Political Philosophy* (1982) she puzzles about the nature of the public's use of reason and the distinctive nature of what she calls political 'judgement'. To explain this, let us assume that, about any given subject, a number of standpoints or views exist. We have one view of things and others have another, perhaps several other, views of the same thing. We know that such views clash. A social conservative view of abortion or gun control is not the same as one held by a liberal. Politics must invalidate, negate or reconcile views. This is so because no matter how many views or opinions there are of things, there can only be one set of laws for a state. To get from many views to one law is difficult. The notion that people can do this by argument is fallacious. Arguments can convince others who share a premise. But the most serious and most interesting political conflicts arise as a result of divergent premises. In lieu of argument, people also try vexatious behaviour to establish the truth of their views. Contempt is a classic strategy, widespread in American society. Sneering, disdain, scorn, derision, condescension and hatred are typical fractious behaviours aimed at political opponents. They may have the effect of rallying one's political friends, but they have only a polarizing and mobilizing effect on one's enemies. The expectation, in energizing those of like mind through fractious rhetoric, is of garnering an electoral majority and commanding the laws in that way. But Madison's idea of an enlarged republic made this virtually impossible to achieve in practice. This left as practically the only option, the hope of forming an electoral majority by capturing the paradoxical middle.

Arendt took from Kant the idea that political judgement was a kind of enlarged mentality. It followed other kinds of judgements and incorporated them selectively. In one of his thought experiments, Kant spoke of taking one of his own judgements and viewing it impartially from the standpoint of others. By doing this, a third view would emerge that improved upon the initial insight that he had (1982: 42). Arendt added that this impartial standpoint was not the result of some higher standpoint that would settle the dispute by being above the mêlée.

Rather judgement was an enlargement of one's own thought in order to take into account the thoughts of others. Neither viewpoint was negated as if there was a 'right' opinion and a 'wrong' opinion. But to say there was no simple 'right' or 'wrong' did not imply the rule of relativism where every view was valid. Political judgement assumes that views can be broadened, not that every view is valid.

Judgement, though, is the wrong word to use to describe this. To enlarge one's own thought to take account of the views of others requires imagination rather than judgement. One of Arendt's most interesting observations in her reading of Kant is that, in politics, we enlarge our own thoughts by representing to ourselves what is absent: *viz.*, the views of others. We might start with the opinion that government welfare is the default system in a functionalized society for helping others in need. Then we imagine another view: that work has an ethical value and that people have a personal responsibility to look for work. If, in imagination, we mesh those two views, we end up with a public policy not far removed from the welfare reforms of President Clinton in the 1990s. The particular example is not important except as small illustration of the 'logic' of the political imagination.

Here we see the creative dimension of politics. The imaginative aspect of politics is not just the ability to represent what is absent. It is also the ability to synthesize two views that are contradictory or clashing. It is the capacity to make one coherent view out of two contrary views. Imaginative action is not easy, though it is not impossible either. Not everything can be bridged in the imagination. A key to such bridging is the ability of human beings to see relationships amongst things that look at first glance to be unlike each other. Important to this is the analogical imagination. What possibly could libertarian small government and liberal large government have in common? This type of question stretches the analogical and synthetic part of the human imagination. Demands for small and large government are contrary. Surely they have nothing in common? They may have virtues, but these are incompatible virtues. We can choose one or the other but not both. But then analogical reason says, well what about 'waste in government'. Even large government can be slimmed to eliminate waste. Small government in this manner contributes to the improvement of large government. By eliminating semi-corrupt 'ear-marks', for example, small government makes big government work better.

We can take this a step further though – noting, as we go, that small and large are relative concepts. Conservatives consequently often talk about limited government rather than small government. Limited government has many meanings. One of the meanings of limits is something that is not excessive or out of proportion. The notion of the limit is an aesthetic concept. It suggests shapeliness. That which makes something shapely or aesthetic is not whether it is absolutely large or small but rather that its size is in proportion. Thus there is an eternal question of whether the size of government is proportionate to the other parts of society. Today total government spending in the United States is 39 percent of GDP. This compares with 17 percent in Singapore, 20 percent in China, 30 percent in South Korea, 34 percent in Australia, 43 percent in Germany,

47 percent in the United Kingdom, 50 percent in Belgium, and 53 percent in France.[16] Military and medical technology in real terms is more expensive than it was in the nineteenth century. Levels of public education likewise have risen. Thus fiscal demands on government are greater. But so are the sizes of country GDPs in real terms. Absolute measures, whether of demand, expectation or expenditure, cannot answer the question: at what point is government large enough? The most reliable answer rather is bound up with 'a sense of proportion'. From the first stone axe of the hominid to the most sophisticated economies, things work best when they are shaped proportionately. Good proportion generates sound equilibrium. This is the equilibrium of unlike parts. What makes societies effective is the same thing that makes artworks beautiful. It is when their contrasting parts, like dissimilar sizes, are proportionately configured. One can think of this in metrical terms. Thus if the size of government spending (b) stands to the size of the country's GDP (a) as a golden ratio, then 'a + b / a' equals 1.6. On that model, fixing public finances at a level that does not exceed the value of 36 percent of GDP would yield an ideal proportion. It would take an intellectual discipline that does not exist (aesthetic economics) to demonstrate what kinds of ideal proportions work best under what circumstances. Nevertheless it is a plausible intuition that if a government spends a sum that is the equivalent in value to more than a third of the country's GDP, then the government's expenditure risks being out of proportion.

Once again it must be stressed that it is not the example that is important but rather the structure of the political imagination. Bridging between concepts of small and large is typical of the mastery of paradox required of good political imagination. Paradox produces a coherent relationship between contrary qualities or things. The person who criticizes the unfettered crossing of borders by illegal migrants but is also happy for those same migrants to become citizens if they work hard, buy a house and behave well thinks in paradoxical terms – literally in terms of parallel or dual opinions. It is the ability to see some likeness in unlike opinions that successfully translates variegated opinions into singular political decisions and then into public policy. Analogical or metaphorical reasoning turns oppositions into appositions. As Stevan Harnad (1982) argued, an apposition is not a proposition. (Does it make sense, he asks, to 'deny' that 'Night is a blanket'?) Rather an apposition is a judgement of radical similarity. It reveals structural congruities to which our normal propositional system is blind. An apposition is not bounded in the same way that a normal proposition is. It is not subject to the bivalent logic of 'true' or 'false', 'right' or 'wrong'. Nevertheless, it must be emphasized that this is not a kind of relativism. Appositions still announce moments of truth in politics. They still state the right thing to do. An apposition simply reveals congruities that we haven't previously seen but that we readily grasp when they are pointed out to us. An apposition does this by placing two things (night, blanket) in juxtaposition or proximity and drawing out what they have in common. The commonality may be very surprising.

16 *Wall Street Journal* 2011 Index of Economic Freedom.

Appositional thinking is essential for the formation of successful electoral majorities under Madisonian conditions. Appositional reasoning is the invisible glue that binds agonistic minorities into effective political coalitions. The consequence of coalitions with insufficient appositional stickiness or insufficient appositional breadth is persistent failure to capture the all-important paradoxical middle ground of politics. A clear example of this failure is the US Democratic Party after 1968. In the heady years between 1964 and 1968, it radically reconstructed its political base. The new coalition it built of college graduates, intellectuals, anti-war proponents, feminists, Jews, and African-Americans replaced the successful but doomed New Deal coalition of union bosses, blue collar workers, Catholics, Jews, intellectuals and segregationists. There was foresight in this new coalition. It correctly anticipated the increase of college-educated professional-managerial employees in America and the corresponding decline of blue collar employment. However this coalition over-relied on the college-educated cohort. It did this in the sense that too many of the other parts of the 1968 generation coalition were cut from the same cloth as the college-educated cohort. If it was a Venn diagram, then the over-laps between the Democrat-voting college-educated, anti-war, and feminist cohorts were far too extensive. This coalition lacked sufficiently divergent, appositional fragments. Its parts were too often too similar in nature to force the kinds of appositional thinking required to capture the paradoxical middle of the Madisonian republic.

Notably it lacked a religious fragment. In a society with the highest church attendance in the West, much higher than in comparable countries, this coalition felt almost as uneasy with the once influential Catholic cohort as it did with the now pariah segregationists. This relieved the need of Democrats to think appositionally about sensitive hot button issues for church goers in America. It should be emphasized that thinking appositionally is not the same as agreeing with one's opponents. To demonstrate the difference, look at the case of the appositionally rich Republican Party since 1968. It drew both Catholics and Southern evangelicals away from the Democratic Party to its ranks. A significant number of these voters were anti-abortion. Yet other Republicans were pro-abortion including Ronald Reagan who as California Governor signed into law one of the most liberal abortion laws in America. A classic appositional strategy to bridge this seemingly unbridgeable gap was the Republican Congress' approval in 2003 of a law banning late-term abortions. This was on the one hand an 'abortion ban' yet it also appealed to right-of-centre libertarians whose endorsement of an individual's right to choose is off-set by a strong sense of individual responsibility and who wondered about the sense of responsibility of someone who waits to the third trimester to make a termination decision. In the other direction, appositional thinking began to subtly change the terms of the debate over the US Supreme Court's decision *Row vs. Wade*, which held that a presumed constitutional right to privacy overrode the power of individual states to ban abortions. From conservatives there was acknowledgement not that the original decision was right but that it was now settled law, or at least precedent worthy of respect, or simply that it was the law around which so much of American life circulated that to over-turn it would have such de-stabilizing consequences that these had to be carefully weighed against the substantive moral arguments against abortion. In 2004 and 2005, when hearings were held for the confirmation of conservative Catholic Republican judicial appointments to the US Supreme Court, this appositional logic stole the thunder from Democrat criticism of the appointees. Ironically, the 'liberal feminist progressive' *Row vs. Wade* was being refigured as a symbol of the conservative preference for stability.

Another element missing from the 1968 generation Democrat coalition was the military. The military is a major social entity in America. Its size alone makes it an electoral force.[17] Military industrialism is one of the principal drivers of the American knowledge economy. Military bases are key parts of many American state economies. The size and the high technology power of the US military have a lot to do with the fact that America is a classic republic in the tradition of Rome or Venice. The United States, on the other hand, is a modern democracy. As Alexis de Tocqueville observed, democracies have little enthusiasm for war. America has both the temperament of a republic and a democracy. It is both inclined and disinclined to war. This is once again why apposite thinking plays an important role in American politics. There is a delicate path to be walked between militarism and anti-militarism, as if these were two extremes around a presumptive American Aristotelian mean. The difficulty that the Democratic Party has had since 1968 has been finding this mean. The prior New Deal coalition produced a brilliant generation of Cold War liberals who devised the policy and practice of the containment of Communism. Containment was a middle path between imperialism and pacifism. It had its own contradictions which eventually caused it great difficulties. Military containment of Communism in Vietnam had no clear political objective. There was no imperative for a democratic Vietnamese republic. In this circumstance, Vietnamese nationalism trumped American power, leaving Lyndon Johnson's Democratic administration in ruins. From that point in time pacifists and anti-interventionists gained the moral upper-hand in the Democratic Party, though not in Congressional spending. The military-industrial economy remained the unspoken indispensable component of American post industrialization. But the pacifism and isolationism of a key segment of the Democratic Party's political base diluted its national security policy thinking in lieu of any serious appositional strategies. The Republicans inherited some of these same problems when the Nixon administration, and its Secretary of State Henry Kissinger, redoubled the fatal policy of supporting murderous military regimes and dictatorships in the name of containing Communism.

It was disenchanted Democrats who turned these policies around. A decisive group of Cold War Democratic intellectuals switched parties in the Reagan era. Many had been associated with the defence hawk Senator Henry (Scoop) Jackson who had fought a rear-guard action against rising Democrat pacifism and

17 There are 1.4 million active US military personnel and another 1.4 million reservists. There are 16 million members of American labour unions.

isolationism in the decidedly anti-war era of the late 1960s and 1970s. This group pioneered a new type of conservatism. The neo-conservatives conceived a third way between militarism and pacifism. Democracy served as a middle term between the two. If America's national security required the use of arms against enemies and military alliances with friends, the antithesis of pacifism, then the obverse of militarism would be a preference for democratic friends and the preparedness to use arms to progress democracy around the globe. This policy began to emerge in 1984–86 when former Democrat, Reagan appointee, and Assistant Secretary of State for East Asia Paul Wolfowitz played a key role in the United States decision to pressure the Philippine dictator Ferdinand Marcos to resign power (Mann 2004: 127–37). The result was not only the restoration of Philippine democracy but also the triggering of a process of liberalization in East Asia over the next decade – leading to the historic democratization of South Korea and Taiwan. As deputy Secretary of Defense in the George W. Bush administration, Wolfowitz was central to the conceptualization and prosecution of an analogous strategy to use military power to transform Iraq from a dictatorship to a democracy and thereby trigger broader regional liberalization. Only the post-1945 democratization of Germany and Japan were comparable to the scale of regime change in East Asia and the Middle East.

Neo-conservatism was a classic product of appositional thinking. It allied the strong military power of a classic republic to the goal of promoting anti-militaristic democracy. The Democratic Party after 1968 was good at producing oppositional thinking, but generally poor at producing appositional approaches. The principal exception was the Presidency of Bill Clinton. Clinton's self-conscious 'New Democrat' politics was cautiously appositional in style. It was not as overtly appositional as its counterpart in the United Kingdom, but not as artificially either. Tony Blair's 'New Labour' contrived an unsteady mix of old domestic welfare state policies and new global interventionism. Clinton on the other hand captured and held the paradoxical middle of American politics in a way that his successors Al Gore, John Kerry, and Barack Obama failed to do. The difficulty of appositional politics is that it runs against the grain of the stock-in-trade oppositional politics of political parties that compete against each and that do so by assuming that their opponents, not least their opponents in their own party, are contemptible. Why would anyone enlarge their mentality to take into account of the ideas of iniquitous foes? It is true that me-too-ism is a sign of a lack of backbone. Yet being un-ironic, narrow-minded, sneering at opponents and engaging in vexatious campaigns against them is no better. Contempt and disdain produce comforting feelings and disabling politics.

Too Clever by Half

The 2004 US Presidential campaign produced a torrent of contempt and disdain. The volume of 'Bush hating' commentary was staggering. It ended with Bush winning the first clear majority of any presidential candidate since George H.W. Bush's win in 1988 – so much for the vexatious campaigning of the Michael Moore, MoveOn.com, and other 1968 ethos bailiwicks. It is difficult to over-estimate how much this politics of contempt helped in the re-election of George W. Bush. Every dollar contributed by billionaire George Soros to defeating Bush, and every dollar spent by fans of Michael Moore's anti-Bush propaganda documentary, was in effect an additional dollar added to the Bush campaign chest – such is the paradoxical nature of political campaigning.

It is true that George Bush was an awkward public figure, easily ridiculed. But such ridicule cut both ways. In democratic politics a certain self-deprecating bumbling is attractive to the general populace. The intellectual class hates it. It raises their hackles. It offends their self-image. They imagine themselves to be the cleverest of the clever. To be anything but clever is to be unworthy. Yet as anyone who ever watched Peter Falk's shambling television detective Columbo at work, which includes most Americans, should know, the clumsy and ungainly comic figure can hide real intelligence. Ronald Reagan understood this. He presented himself as the amiable dunce. Bill Clinton did something similar. He had the good ol' boy act down pat. Bush's command of the persona of the dolt was no less impressive. Each of these comic personas mocked the intellectual class. Reagan and Bush were pilloried without mercy by the intelligentsia. Clinton was tolerated to a greater extent because of his party affiliation. But he was not loved in the way that Barack Obama was by the professoriate and corporate intellectuals. They adored him when he appeared on the national political stage. He was their candidate. His presidency was professorial in style. It displayed no hint of shambling shtick. It personified and expounded an ideology of cleverness to the nth-degree. It mocked and admonished ignoramuses. And it fell out of favour with voters with the speed of a bullet.

The clearest lesson to be learnt about James Madison's design for the American Republic is that factious politics is self-defeating. This is not to dismiss partisan politics or to confuse them with fractious behaviour. A democratic republic is partisan in nature. Its politics is competitive. But competition can be narrow-minded or it can be broad-minded. Broad-minded party politics is creative. Its thinking is analogical and appositional. Some of its best practitioners are apostates. They leave the fold of one party for the opposing party, but in doing so they bring with them some of the values and assumptions of the old party into the ranks of the new party. One of the signs of the weakness of the 1968 generation Democratic coalition is how few apostates it attracted. Republican strategist Kevin Phillips is one. Hilary Clinton, a teenage supporter of Barry Goldwater, is another. This is nothing compared to the stream of apostate Democrats that the neo-conservatives brought to the Republican Party. Apostates are important to appositional thinking. As David Bromley et al. observe (1983: 156), apostasy occurs in a highly polarized situation in which an organization member undertakes a total change of loyalties by allying with one or more elements of an oppositional coalition.

It is difficult to think of a better description of the neo-conservatives or a better explanation of why they stirred such bitter ideological polemics. Contempt for apostates is always stronger than contempt for loyalists. Yet apostates are suited to appositional politics, because by definition they have moved from one political pole to another and are in a position to adapt old values to new values. The neo-conservatives did this when they married liberal internationalism and democratic values to conservative defence and national security values. It is difficult to think of a more audacious political marriage in the last hundred years with the possible exception of the apostate Tory-turned-Liberal Winston Churchill's alliance with Lloyd George to create the British (contributory) welfare state. Thus George W. Bush's embrace of neo-conservatism became a singular example of American political apostasy. He campaigned in 2000 as an opponent of nation building. But the success of his Presidency in the end hung on the success of regime construction in Iraq and its flow-on effects to the broader Middle East, a story still in the making.

Apostasy is not simply the preserve of political leaders or intellectuals. Some voters are apostates as well. Exit polls for the 2004 election showed some interesting examples of this.[18] Looking at the vote by party identification, 11 percent of registered Democrats voted for Bush and 6 percent of Republicans voted for Kerry. It is notable that this border crossing happened in both directions – towards the Democrats and towards the Republicans – but it favoured the Republicans overall. Table 8.3 breaks this border-crossing voting down by regions.[19]

18 Source: CNN.com Election 2004. http://www.cnn.com/ELECTION/2004/pages/results/states/US/P/00/epolls.0.html.

19 Source: CNN 2004 US Election Exit Polling. http://www.cnn.com/ELECTION/2004/pages/results/states/US/P/00/epolls.0.html.

Table 8.3 Contrarian voters

US Contrarian Voting 2004 Presidential Election				
US Voters by Education				
Percentage with College Degree	26%			
Percentage with Graduate Degree	16%			
US Voters by Party ID		Contrarian Voting		Contrarians as Percentage of Partisan Voters
Democrat	37%	Democrats Voting for Bush	11%	4.07%
Republican	37%	Republicans Voting for Kerry	6%	2.22%
Independent	26%			
Contrarian Total				6.29%
United States by Region				
East				
Voters by Education				
Percentage with College Degree	26%			
Percentage with Graduate Degree	22%			
Voters by Party ID		Contrarian Voting		Contrarians as Percentage of Partisan Voters
Democrat	41%	Democrats Voting for Bush	11%	4.51%
Republican	30%	Republicans Voting for Kerry	12%	3.60%
Independent	30%			
Contrarian Total				8.11%
South				
Voters by Education				
Percentage with College Degree	27%			
Percentage with Graduate Degree	14%			

Table 8.3 Continued

Voters by Party ID		Contrarian Voting		Contrarians as Percentage of Voters
Democrat	35%	Democrats Voting for Bush	14%	4.90%
Republican	42%	Republicans Voting for Kerry	4%	1.68%
Independent	22%			
Contrarian Total				6.58%
West				
Voters by Education				
Percentage with College Degree	28%			
Percentage with Graduate Degree	17%			
Voters by Party ID		Contrarian Voting		Contrarians as Percentage of Partisan Voters
Democrat	34%	Democrats Voting for Bush	8%	2.72%
Republican	36%	Republicans Voting for Kerry	7%	2.52%
Independent	30%			
Contrarian Total				5.24%
Midwest				
Voters by Education				
Percentage with College Degree	22%			
Percentage with Graduate Degree	15%			
Voters by Party ID		Contrarian Voting		Contrarians as Percentage of Partisan Voters
Democrat	37%	Democrats Voting for Bush	9%	3.33%
Republican	38%	Republicans Voting for Kerry	6%	2.28%
Independent	35%			
Contrarian Total				5.61%

There is no evidence to suggest that apostate voting is a reflex of post-industrialization. This is clear if we use the numbers of voters with college and postgraduate degrees as a proxy for post-industrialization (see Table 8.4). The percentage of voters with degrees varies from region to region in the United States. If we compare these figures with voter apostasy, there is no correlation between increasing levels of post-industrial credentialing and the propensity to cross the borders between political parties. Once again, one of the things that this cautions against is the too-ready identification of smartness with wit and of post-industrial credentialing with imagination. The post-modern era assumption that creativity equalled smartness equalled university credentials equalled voting for the political party that identifies itself with graduates was deeply flawed. There are many, too many, steps in this equation, and along the way it loses efficacy. The failure of Barack Obama's professorial presidency underscores this. Imagination is much closer in nature to irony than it is to cleverness. There is something shallow, and often stupid, about cleverness. As the English playwright Tom Stoppard once put it: 'You can persuade a man to believe almost anything provided he is clever enough …'[20]

Table 8.4 Contrarian voting and education

2004 US Presidential Election	Voters with Graduate Degree	Contrarians
East	22.00%	8.11%
West	17.00%	5.24%
National	16.00%	6.29%
Midwest	15.00%	5.61%
South	14.00%	6.58%
	Voters with College Degree	**Contrarians**
West	28.00%	5.24%
South	27.00%	6.58%
East	26.00%	8.11%
National	26.00%	6.29%
Midwest	22.00%	5.61%

That the post-industrial age has spawned a huge managerial-professional class in the United States is unquestionable. That university degrees are a preparation for entry to this class is not to be disputed. That the professorial style became influential enough to bestow a presidential style is interesting. Yet each of these facts can be easily over-interpreted. They are ultimately much better understood in the light of the distinction that Thomas Hobbes drew between judgement and wit. Judgement, he reckoned, had to do with the making of distinctions.

20 Tom Stoppard, Professional Foul (1977).

Wit had to do with finding similarities between things that were not alike. Kant tried to reconcile these two in an omnibus concept of judgement. But most people, despite efforts like those of Hannah Arendt, see judgement as invariably involved in the drawing of distinctions – whether between good and bad, useful and useless, or whatever. Higher education refines judgement. In doing so, it produces large numbers of managers and professionals who routinely deliver expert judgements. It also produces a small army of academics who draw endless distinctions between concepts, themes, disciplines, fields and bodies of knowledge. The faculty of wit on the other hand has a less visible but a more potent and ultimately a much more important role in society. It is not that the modern university produces witless people, though often it does. It is not that judgement is not of use in organizations, publics and markets, though sometimes it obscures rather than clarifies what needs to be done. At the end of the day it is simply that wit is the great medium of the imagination and the indispensable intellectual virtue of an imaginative society. Without wit, all the distinction in the world is empty.

References

Alvarez, G.C. 2009. *Study of the Effects on Employment of Public Aid to Renewable Energy Sources*. Instituto Juan de Mariana, Universidad Rey Juan Carlos: Móstoles. Retrieved from http://www.juandemariana.org/pdf/090327-employment-public-aid-renewable.pdf. Accessed 6 October 2009.

Arendt, H. 1958. *The Human Condition*. Chicago: University of Chicago.

Arendt, H. 1963/2006. *Eichmann in Jerusalem: A Report on the Banality of Evil*. London: Penguin.

Arendt, H. 1982. *Lectures on Kant's Political Philosophy*. Chicago: University of Chicago Press.

Aristotle. 1991. *The Art of Rhetoric*, translated by Hugh Lawson-Tancred. London: Penguin.

Aristotle. 2004. *The Nicomachean Ethics*, translated by J.A.K. Thomson. London: Penguin.

Australian Productivity Commission. 2011. 'Carbon Emission Policies in Key Economies'. *Productivity Commission Research Report*, May. Retrieved from http://www.pc.gov.au/__data/assets/pdf_file/0003/109830/carbon-prices.pdf. Accessed 9 October 2011.

Avery, O.T., MacLeod, C.M. and McCarty, M. 1944. 'Studies on the Chemical Nature of the Substance Inducing Transformation of Pneumococcal Types'. *Journal of Experimental Medicine* 79(2), 137–58. Retrieved from http://profiles.nlm.nih.gov/CC/A/A/B/Y/_/ccaaby.pdf. Accessed 23 December 2010.

Barron, F. and Harrington, D.M. 1981. 'Creativity, Intelligence, and Personality'. *Annual Review of Psychology* 32, 439–76.

Bell, D. 1973/1999. *The Coming of Post-Industrial Society*. New York: Basic Books.

Bell, D. 1976/1996. *The Cultural Contradictions of Capitalism*. New York: Basic Books.

Bellow, S. 2001. *The Adventures of Augie March*. Introduction by Christopher Hitchens. London: Penguin.

Benjamin, A. 2000. *Architectural Philosophy*. London: The Athlone Press.

Benjamin, W. 1996. 'On The Program of the Coming Philosophy', *Selected Writings: Volume 1 1913–1926*. Harvard: Harvard University Press.

Berger, P. 1997. *Redeeming Laughter: The Comic Dimension of Human Experience*. Berlin: Walter de Gruyter.

Bishop, B. and Lisheron, M. 2002. 'Why a City Thrives: A Mix of Open Minds', *American-Statesman*, 31 December. Retrieved from http://www.statesman.com/specialreports/content/specialreports/citiesofideas/1231cities.html. Accessed 9 October 2011.

Bloom, A. 1988. *The Closing of the American Mind.* New York: Simon and Schuster.

Boldrin, M. and Levine, D.K. 2008. *Against Intellectual Monopoly.* Cambridge: Cambridge University Press.

Boyd, R. *The Australian Ugliness*. Melbourne: Cheshire.

Bromley, D.G., Shupe, A.D. and Ventimiglia, J.C. 1983. 'The Role of Anecdotal Atrocities in the Social Construction of Evil' in *Brainwashing Deprogramming Controversy: Sociological, Psychological, Legal, and Historical Perspectives*, edited by Bromley, D.G. and Richardson, J.T. Lewiston, NY: Edwin Mellen Press, 139–60.

Brooks, C. 1947. *The Well-Wrought Urn*. New York: Harcourt.

Brooks, D. 2001. *Bobos in Paradise: The New Upper Class and How They Got There*. New York: Simon and Schuster.

Burke, K. 1989. *On Symbols and Society*, edited by J.R. Gusfield. Chicago: University of Chicago Press.

Burroway, J. 2002. *Writing Fiction*. London: Longman.

Cardiff, C. and Klein, D.B. 2005. 'Faculty Partisan Affiliations in All Disciplines: A Voter-Registration Study'. *Critical Review: An Interdisciplinary Journal of Politics and Society* 17(3&4), 237–55.

Carlsson, B., Acs, Z.J., Audretsch, D.B. and Braunerhjelm, P. 2007. The Knowledge Filter, Entrepreneurship, and Economic Growth. *CESIS Electronic Working Paper Series*, Paper 104. Retrieved from http://www.infra.kth.se/cesis/documents/WP104.pdf. Accessed 15 May 2009.

Carnegie Foundation for the Advancement of Teaching. 1989. *The Condition of the Professoriate: Attitudes and Trends*. Princeton, NJ: The Carnegie Foundation for the Advancement of Teaching.

Carroll, J. 2007. *The Existential Jesus*. Melbourne: Scribe.

Castoriadis, C. 1984 [1978]. *Crossroads in the Labyrinth*. Cambridge, CA: MIT Press.

Castoriadis, C. 1987. *The Imaginary Institution of Society*. Cambridge: Polity Press.

Castoriadis, C. 1997a. *World in Fragments*. Stanford: Stanford University Press.

Castoriadis, C. 1997b. *The Castoriadis Reader*. Oxford: Blackwell.

Castoriadis, C. 2007. 'Notes on Some Poetic Resources', in *Figures of the Thinkable*. Stanford: Stanford University Press, 21–46.

Cecil, G. 1931. *Life of Robert, Marquis of Salisbury* Volume III. London: Hodder and Stoughton. Retrieved from http://www.archive.org/stream/lifeofrobertmarq03ceciuoft/lifeofrobertmarq03ceciuoft_djvu.txt. Accessed 9 October 2011.

Chargaff, E. 1971. 'Preface to a Grammar of Biology. A Hundred Years of Nucleic Acid Research'. *Science* 172, 637–42.

Chen, S. 2009. 'Dirty Reality behind Solar Power'. *South China Morning Post*, 10 September.

Chesterton, G.K. 1902/2008. *Twelve Types*. London: Echo Library.

Chesterton, G.K. 1908/2004. *Orthodoxy*. New York: Dover.

Chesterton, G.K. 1915/2008. *All Things Considered*. Sioux Falls, SD: NuVision.

Chesterton, G.K. 1924. Column. *Illustrated London News*, 19 April.

Churchill, W.S. 1899a. *The River War: An Historical Account of the Reconquest of the Soudan II*. London: Longmans, Green and Co.

Churchill, W.S. 1899b. *Savrola: A Tale of the Revolution in Laurania*. London: Longman.

Churchill, W.S. 1909. *Liberalism and the Social Problem*. London: Hodder and Stoughton.

Churchill, W.S. 1930/1947. *My Early Life*. London: Odhams.

Churchill, W.S. 1932. *Thoughts and Adventures*. London: Odhams Press.

Churchill, W.S. 1933/2002. *Marlborough: His Life and Times, Book One*. Chicago: University of Chicago Press.

Churchill, W.S. 1939. 'George Bernard Shaw', in *Great Contemporaries*. London: Odhams, 31–42.

Churchill, W.S. 2004. *Never Give In! The Best of Winston Churchill's Speeches*, edited by W.S. Churchill. London: Pimlico.

Colebatch, T. and Lahey, K. 2009. 'Melbourne's Population Hits 4 Million'. *The Age*, 23 September.

Conquest, R. 1986. *Harvest of Sorrow: Soviet Collectivisation and the Terror-Famine*. New York: Oxford University Press.

Cook, P. 2002. *Tragically I Was An Only Twin: The Comedy of Peter Cook*. London: Century.

Cowen, T. 2011a. *The Great Stagnation*. New York: Penguin.

Cowen, T. 2011b. 'Innovation is Doing Little for Incomes', *New York Times*, 29 January.

CNN. 1998. 'Israel as High-tech Hub'. Retrieved from http://www.cnn.com/SPECIALS/1998/netanyahu/high.tech/. Accessed 20 October 2006.

CNN. 2004. *US President National Exit Poll*. Retrieved from http://www.cnn.com/ELECTION/2004/pages/results/states/US/P/00/epolls.0.html. Accessed 20 October 2006.

Crain, N.V. and Crain, W.M. 2010. *The Impact of Regulatory Costs on Small Firms*. Small Business Administration Office of Advocacy.

Csikszentmihalyi, M. 1999. 'Implications of a Systems Perspective for the Study of Creativity' in *Handbook of Creativity* edited by R.J. Sternberg. Cambridge, UK: Cambridge University Press, 313–35.

Dacey, J.S. and Lennon, K.M. 1998. *Understanding Creativity: The Interplay of Biological, Psychological, and Social Factors*. New York: Jossey Bass.

Davis, P. 2007. *Shakespeare Thinking*. London: Continuum.

Dylan, B. 2004. 'The TV Guide Interview' with Neil Hickey, in *Younger Than That Now: The Collected Interviews with Bob Dylan*, edited by J. Ellison. New York: Thunder's Mouth.

Einstein, A. 1935/2007. 'The World as I See It', in *The World As I See It*. San Diego, CA: The Book Tree.

Empson, W. 1947. *7 Types of Ambiguity*. New York: New Directions.

Feist, G.J. 1999. 'Autonomy and Independence', in *Encyclopedia of Creativity*, Volume One, edited by M.A. Runco and S. Pritzker. San Diego, CA: Academic Press, 157–63.

Ferguson, N. 2011. *Civilization: The West and the Rest*. London: Penguin.

Fichte, J.G. 1794–95/1982. *The Science of Knowledge*, edited by Peter Heath and John Lachs. New York: Cambridge University Press.

Florida, R. 2002. *The Rise of the Creative Class*. New York: Basic Books.

Florida, R. 2004. *The Rise of the Creative Class*. Second edition. New York: Basic Books, 2004.

Foerster, H.V. 1995. 'Interview with Heinz von Foerster' by S. Franchi, G. Güzeldere and E. Minch. *Stanford Electronic Humanities Review* 4(2), June. Retrieved from http://www.stanford.edu/group/SHR/4-2/text/interviewvonf.html. Accessed 27 August 2006.

Freud, S. 1919/2011. 'The "Uncanny"', in *The Standard Edition of the Complete Psychological Works of Sigmund Freud, Volume XVII (1917–1919), An Infantile Neurosis and Other Works*. London: Vintage.

Gallup. N/D. 'Election Polls – Presidential Vote by Groups'. Retrieved from http://www.gallup.com/poll/139880/Election-Polls-Presidential-Vote-Groups.aspx#2. Accessed 10 October 2011.

Gao, X. 2004. *Soul Mountain*. Sydney: Harper, 2004.

Galston, W. and Karmack, E. 1989. *The Politics of Evasion: Democrats and the Presidency*. Washington, D.C.: Progressive Policy Institute.

Gerster, R. 2009. 'Little Boys and Fat Men: Humanising "the Bomb" in Atomic Museums in the US and Japan', *Communications Seminar Series*, Monash University, 5 October.

Gilbert, M. 1975/1990. *Winston S. Churchill Volume IV: 1917–1922*. London: Heinemann.

Gilbert, M. 1991. *Churchill: A Life*. New York: Henry Holt.

Gordon, J.S. 2004. *An Empire of Wealth*. New York: Harper Collins.

Graham, J., Haidt, J. and Nosek, B.A. 2009. 'Liberals and Conservatives Rely on Different Sets of Moral Foundations'. *Journal of Personality and Social Psychology* 96, 1029–46.

Gruenfeld, D.H. 1995. 'Status, Ideology and Integrative Complexity on the US Supreme Court: Rethinking the Politics of Political Decision Making'. *Journal of Personality and Social Psychology* 68, 5–20.

Habermas, J. 1984. *The Theory of Communicative Action Volume One*. Boston: Beacon Press.

Haidt, J. 2008. 'What Makes People Vote Republican?' *The Third Culture*, 9 September. Retrieved from http://www.edge.org/3rd_culture/haidt08/haidt08_index.html. Accessed 10 August 2009.

Haidt, J. 'Conservatives Live in a Different Moral Universe – And Here's Why it Matters'. *Mother Jones*, 27 April. Retrieved from http://www.motherjones.com/politics/2009/04/conservatives-live-different-moral-universe8212and-heres-why-it-matters. Accessed 10 August 2009.

Haidt, J. and Graham, J. 2009. 'The Planet of the Durkheimians, where Community, Authority and Sacredness are Foundations of Morality', in *Social and Psychological Bases of Ideology and System Justification*, edited by J.T. Jost, A.C. Kay and H. Thorisdottir. New York: Oxford University Press, 371–401.

Hall, P. 1998. *Cities in Civilization: Culture, Innovation and Urban Order*. London: Weidenfeld and Nicolson.

Halsey, A.H. and Trow, M.A. 1971. *The British Academics*. London: Faber and Faber.

Hambridge, J. 1926/1967. *The Elements of Dynamic Symmetry*. New York: Dover Publications.

Hamerow, T.S. 1983. *The Birth of a New Europe: State and Society in the Nineteenth Century*. Chapel Hill: University of North Carolina Press.

Hamilton, R.F. and Hargens, L.L. 1993. 'The Politics of the Professors: Self-identifications, 1969–1984'. *Social Forces* 71.

Happer, W. 2011. 'The Truth about Greenhouse Gases'. *Briefing Paper* No 3. London: The Global Warming Policy Foundation, August. Retrieved from http://www.thegwpf.org/images/stories/gwpf-reports/happer-the_truth_about_greenhouse_gases.pdf. Accessed 22 August 2011.

Harder, B. 'Universe Reborn Endlessly in New Model of the Cosmos', *National Geographic News*, 25 April, 2002. Retrieved from http://news.nationalgeographic.com/news/pf/33922717.html. Accessed 25 September 2011.

Harnad, S. 1982. 'Metaphor and Mental Duality', in *Language, Mind and Brain*, edited by T. Simon and R. Scholes. Hillsdale NJ: Erlbaum, 189–211.

Hastings, M. 2009. *Finest Years: Churchill as Warlord 1940–45*. London: HarperPress.

Hazlitt, W. 1818/2004. 'On Wit and Humour', in *Selected Essays of William Hazlitt 1778 to 1830*. Whitefish: Kessinger.

Hegel, G.W.F. 1812–1816/1969. *The Science of Logic*, translated by A.V. Miller. Amherst, NY: Prometheus.

Heller, A. 1979. *A Theory of Feelings*. Assen: Van Gorcum.

Heller, A. 1982. *A Theory of History*. London: Routledge and Kegan Paul.

Heller, A. 1985. 'Rationality and Democracy', in *The Power of Shame*. London: Routledge, 251–84.

Heller, A. 2005. *Immortal Comedy: The Comic Phenomenon in Art, Literature and Life*. Lanham, MD: Rowman and Littlefield.

Hitchens, C. 2001. 'Visit to a Small Planet', *Vanity Fair*, January. Retrieved from http://www.vanityfair.com/politics/features/2001/01/hitchens-200101. Accessed 9 October 2011.

Hitchens, C. 2004. 'The Adventures of Augie March', in *Love, Poverty, and War: Journeys and Essays*. New York: Nation Books.

Hitchens, C. 2004. 'Scoop', in *Love, Poverty, and War: Journeys and Essays*. New York: Nation Books.

Hitchens, C. 2010. *Hitch-22: A Memoir*. Sydney: Allen and Unwin.

Hitchens, C. 2011. 'From Abbottabad to Worse', *Vanity Fair*, July. Retrieved from http://www.vanityfair.com/politics/features/2011/07/osama-bin-laden-201107. Accessed 9 October 2011.

Hobbes, T. 1968. *Leviathan*. London: Penguin.

Hobbes, T. 1972. *Man and Citizen*. Humanities Press.

Holroyd, M. 1991/1993. *Bernard Shaw: The Lure of Fantasy 1918–1950*. New York: Vintage.

Huebner, J. 2005. 'A Possible Declining Trend for Worldwide Innovation'. *Technological Forecasting and Social Change* 72, 980–86.

Hughes, R. 1994. *Culture of Complaint: The Fraying of America*. New York: Warner Books.

Jacobs, J. 1969. *The Economy of Cities*. New York: Random House.

Jacobs, J. 1984/1986. *Cities and the Wealth of Nations*. Harmondsworth: Penguin.

Jenkins, R. 2001. *Churchill*. London: Macmillan.

Johnson, P. 2009. *Churchill*. New York: Penguin.

Jones, M.A. 1983. *The Limits of Liberty: American History 1607–1980*. Oxford: Oxford University Press.

Jones, R.V. 1993. 'Churchill and Science', in *Churchill*, edited by R. Blake and W.R. Lewis. Oxford: Clarendon Press, 427–42.

Judis, J.B. and Teixeira, R. 2002. *The Emerging Democratic Majority*. New York: Scribner.

Kant, I. 2003. *Critique of Pure Reason*, translated by Norman Kemp-Smith. Basingstoke: Palgrave-Macmillan.

Kant, I. 2007. *Critique of Judgement*, translated by James Creed Meredith. Oxford: Oxford University Press.

Katz, D. 2011. 'A Year of Regulatory Abuse', *The Foundary*, January.

Katz, E. and Lazarsfeld, P.F. 1955. *Personal Influence: The Part Played by People in the Flow of Mass Communication*. Glencoe, IL: Free Press.

Keegan, J. 2002. *Churchill*. New York: Penguin.

Ker, I. 2011. *G.K Chesterton: A Biography*. Oxford: Oxford University Press.

Kenner, H. 1947. *Paradox in Chesterton*. New York: Sheed & Ward.

Kierkegaard, S. 1841/1985. 'Johannes Climacus, or, De omnibus dubitandum est' in *Philosophical Fragments, Johannes Climacus*. Princeton: Princeton University Press.

Kierkegaard, S. 1859/2009. *Concluding Unscientific Postscript to the Philosophical Crumbs*. Cambridge: Cambridge University Press.

King, L.A., McKee Walker, L. and Broyles, S.J. 1996. 'Creativity and the Five-factor Model'. *Journal of Research in Personality* 30, 189–203.

Klein, D.B. and Stern, C. 2005. 'Professors and their Politics: The Policy Views of Social Scientists'. *Critical Review* 3 and 4, 257–303.

Koestler, A. 1964. *The Act of Creation*. New York: Dell.

Korotayev, A.V. and Tsirel, S.V. 2010. 'A Spectral Analysis of World GDP Dynamics: Kondratieff Waves, Kuznets Swings, Juglar and Kitchin Cycles in Global Economic Development, and the 2008–2009 Economic Crisis'. *Structure and Dynamics* 4(1), Article 1.

Kotkin, J. 2010a. 'California Suggests Suicide; Texas Asks: Can I Lend You a Knife?' *Forbes.com*, 15 November.

Kotkin, J. 2010b. 'The Golden State's War on Itself'. *The City Journal*, 8 August.

Krushelnycky, A. 'Stalin's Starvation of Ukraine – Seventy Years Later, World Still Largely Unaware of Tragedy'. Retrieved from http://www.ukemonde.com/news/rferl.html. Accessed 28 May 2011.

Ladd, E.C. and Lipset, S.M. 1975. *The Divided Academy: Professors and Politics*. New York: McGraw-Hill.

Lash, S. 2010. *Intensive Culture*. London: Sage.

Laub, K. 2011. 'Libyan Estimate: At Least 30,000 Died in the War'. *San Francisco Chronicle*, 8 September. Retrieved from http://www.sfgate.com/cgi-bin/article.cgi?f=/n/a/2011/09/08/international/i004907D85.DTL. Accessed 25 September 2011.

Lazarsfeld, P., Berelson, F. and McPhee, W. 1954. *Voting*. Chicago: University of Chicago Press.

Lewis, M. 2011. 'California and Bust'. *Vanity Fair*. November.

Lightman, A. 2006. *The Discoveries: Great Breakthroughs in 20th-Century Science*. New York: Vintage.

Lipset, S.M. and Ladd, E.C. 1974. 'The Myth of the "Conservative" Professor: A Reply to Michael Faia'. *Sociology of Education* 47(2), 203–13.

Locke, J. 1997. *An Essay Concerning Human Understanding*. London: Penguin.

Machlup, F. 1962/1973. *The Production and Distribution of Knowledge in the United States*. Princeton: Princeton University Press.

Nakhaie, R. and Adam, B. 2008. 'Political Affiliation of Canadian University Professors'. *Canadian Journal of Sociology/Cahiers canadiens de sociologie* 33(4).

Mandel, M. 2009. 'The Failed Promise of Innovation'. *US Business Week*, 3 June.

Mann, J. 2004. *Rise of the Vulcans: The History of Bush's War Cabinet*. New York: Penguin.

Marginson, S. 2007. 'The Global Positioning of Australian Higher Education: Where to From Here?' *The University of Melbourne Faculty of Education Dean's Lecture series*, 16 October. Retrieved from http://www.cshe.unimelb.edu.au/people/staff_pages/Marginson/MarginsonDeansLecture161007.pdf. Accessed 10 August 2009.

Marginson, S. 2009. 'Providers Rule the Roost'. *The Australian Financial Review*, 3 August.
Marginson, S. and Rhoades, G. 2002. 'Beyond National States, Markets, and Systems of Higher Education'. *Higher Education* 43, 281–309.
Marron, D.B. 2010. 'America in the Red'. *National Affairs* 3.
Marshall, W. 2011. 'Labor and the Producer Society'. *Policy Brief*, Progressive Policy Institute, August.
McCrae, R.R. 1987. 'Creativity, Divergent Thinking, and Openness to Experience'. *Journal of Personality and Social Psychology* 52, 1258–65.
McLuhan, M. 1936. 'G. K. Chesterton: A Practical Mystic'. *Dalhousie Review* 15(4), 455–64.
Mead, G.H. 1934. *Mind, Self and Society*. Chicago: University of Chicago Press.
Menninghaus, W. 2009. 'On the 'Vital Significance' of Kitsch', in *Walter Benjamin and the Architecture of Modernity*, edited by A. Benjamin and C. Rice. Melbourne: re.press.
Merlin, J. 2011. 'In Texas, Perry Outshines Obama'. *Investor's Business Daily*, 12 August.
Micklethwait, J. and Wooldridge, A. 2004. *The Right Nation: Why America is Different*. London: Penguin.
Morris, C. 1744/1947. *An Essay towards Fixing the True Standards of Wit, Humour, Raillery, Satire, and Ridicule,* with an introduction by James L. Clifford. Los Angeles: Augustan Reprint Society. Retrieved from http://www.gutenberg.org/files/16233/16233-h/16233-h.htm. Accessed 16 October 2011.
Moyes, J. 2011. 'Dictator Chic: Gold, Murals, Objects in Their Image'. *Daily Telegraph*, 27 August.
Murphy, P. 2001. *Civic Justice*. Amherst, NY: Prometheus.
Murphy, P. 2006. 'American Civilization'. *Thesis Eleven: Critical Theory and Historical Sociology* 81, 64–92.
Murphy, P. 2009. 'The Power and the Imagination: The Enigmatic State in Shakespeare's English History Plays'. *Revue Internationale de Philosophie* 63(1), 41–65.
Murphy, P. 2010a. 'Creative Economies and Research Universities', in *Education in the Creative Economy: Knowledge and Learning in the Age of Innovation*, edited by M.A. Peters and D. Araya. New York: Peter Lang, 331–58.
Murphy, P. 2010b. 'The Limits of Soft Power', in *Complicated Currents: Media Production, the Korean Wave and Soft Power in East Asia*, edited by D. Black, S. Epstein and A. Tokita. Melbourne: Monash E-Press, 15.1–15.14.
Murphy, P. 2011. 'From Information to Imagination: Multivalent Logic and System Creation in Personal Knowledge Management', in *Personal Knowledge Management: Individual, Organisational and Social Perspectives*, edited by G. Gorman and D. Pauleen. Aldershot, UK: Gower Publishing, 43–58.
Murphy, P., Marginson, S. and Peters, M. 2010. *Imagination: Three Models of Imagination in the Age of the Knowledge Economy*. New York: Peter Lang.
Murray, C. 2003. *Human Accomplishment*. New York: HarperCollins.

Murray, C. 2008. *Real Education*. New York: Three Rivers Press.

Nicholson, H. 1940. 'Elizabethan Zest for Life'. *Spectator*, 17 May.

Nietzsche, F. 1878/1994. *Human, All Too Human*. London: Penguin.

Nietzsche, F. 1886/1973. *Beyond Good and Evil*. London: Penguin.

Nisbet, R.A. *The Sociological Tradition*. London: Heinemann.

Oregon Progress Board. 2004. *Oregon Business Plan 2004 Competitive Index*. Retrieved from http://www.oregon.gov/DAS/OPB/docs/Reports/CI_Final.pdf. Accessed 25 September 2001.

Patterson, O. 1991. *Freedom: Volume One, Freedom in the Making of Western Culture*. New York: HarperCollins.

Parsons, T. 1970. *The Social System*. London: Routledge and Kegan Paul.

Penrose, R. 2010. *Cycles of Time*. London: Bodley Head.

Peters, M., Marginson, S. and Murphy, P. 2009. *Creativity and the Global Knowledge Economy*. New York: Peter Lang.

Popper, K. 1959. *Logic of Scientific Discovery*. London: Hutchinson.

Porter, M.E. and Stern, S. 2001. 'Innovation: Location Matters'. *MIT Sloan Management Review*, Summer.

Rappaport, J. and Sachs, J.D. 2003. 'The United States as a Coastal Nation'. *Journal of Economic Growth* 8, 5–46.

Rentfrow, P.J., Gosling, S.D. and Potter, J. 2008. 'A Theory of the Emergence, Persistence, and Expression of Geographic Variation in Psychological Characteristics'. *Perspectives on Psychological Science* 3(5), 339–69.

Rentfrow, P.J. 2010. 'Statewide Differences in Personality: Toward a Psychological Geography of the United States'. *American Psychologist* 65(6), 548–58.

Riedl, B. 2010. 'Federal Spending by the Numbers'. *Heritage Special Report*, 1 June. Retrieved from http://www.heritage.org/Research/Reports/2010/06/Federal-Spending-by-the-Numbers-2010. Accessed 9 October 2011.

Rose, N. 2009. *Churchill: An Unruly Life*. London: Taurus.

Rothman, S., Lichter, S.R. and Nevitte, N. 2005. 'Politics and Professional Advancement among College Faculty'. *The Forum: A Journal of Applied Research in Contemporary Politics* 31(2). Retrieved from http://www.bepress.com/forum/vol3/iss1/art2/. Accessed 10 August 2009.

Sachs, J. 2005. *The End of Poverty: Economic Possibilities for Our Time*. New York: Penguin.

Samuelson, R. 2011. 'Obama's Empty Evasion'. *Washington Post*, 27 January.

Sartre, J.P. 2010. 'A New Mystic', in *Critical Essays*. London: Seagull.

Schelling, F.W.J. 1841/1989. 'Notes of Schelling's Berlin Lectures: Philosophy of Revelation by Friedrich William Joseph Schelling', in S. Kierkegaard, *The Concept of Irony with Continual Reference to Socrates* together with *Notes of Schelling's Berlin Lectures*. Princeton, NJ: Princeton University Press.

Schumacher, E.F. 1973. *Small is Beautiful: A Study of Economics as if People Mattered*. London: Blond and Briggs.

Schumpeter, J. 1911/2008. *The Theory of Economic Development*. New Brunswick, NJ: Transaction.

Scruton, R. 1983/1998. *The Aesthetic Understanding: Essays in the Philosophy of Art and Culture*. South Bend, Indiana: St. Augustine's Press.
Scruton, R. 1998/2007. *Modern Culture*. London: Continuum.
Shapiro, R. 2011. 'A Former Clinton Official on How Obama Isn't Doing Enough for the Economy'. *The New Republic*, 26 August.
Shepherd, G. and Shepherd, G. 1994. 'War and Dissent: The Political Values of the American Professoriate'. *The Journal of Higher Education* 655, 587–614.
Silverberg, G. and Verspagen, B. 2003. 'Breaking the Waves: A Poisson Regression Approach to Schumpeterian Clustering of Basic Innovations'. *Cambridge Journal of Economics* 275, 671–93.
Simonton, D.K. 1984. *Genius, Creativity and Leadership*. Cambridge, MA: Harvard University Press.
Sims, P. 2010. 'Councils Pay for Disabled to Visit Prostitutes and Lap-dancing Clubs from £520m Taxpayer Fund', *Mail Online*, 16 August. Retrieved from http://www.dailymail.co.uk/news/article-1303273/Councils-pay-disabled-visit-prostitutes-lap-dancing-clubs.html. Accessed 9 October 2011.
Sloterdijk, P. 1987. *Critique of Cynical Reason*. Minneapolis: University of Minnesota Press.
Small, M. and Shayne, V. 2009. *Remember Us: My Journey from the Shtetl through the Holocaust*. New York: Skyhorse.
Smart, J. 2005. 'Measuring Innovation in an Accelerating World: Review of "A Possible Declining Trend for Worldwide Innovation"'. Acceleration Studies Foundation. Retrieved from http://www.accelerating.org/articles/huebnerinnovation.html. Accessed 10 August 2009.
Smith, A. 1776/1970. *The Wealth of Nations*, edited by A. Skinner. Harmondsworth: Penguin.
Solow, R.M. 1956, February. 'A Contribution to the Theory of Economic Growth'. *Quarterly Journal of Economics* 70, 65–94.
Steiner, G. 1971. *Tomorrow, in Bluebeard's Castle: Some Notes Towards the Re-definition of Culture*. New Haven: Yale University Press.
Steinhardt, P.J. and Turok, N. 2007. *Endless Universe*. New York: Doubleday, 2007.
Stern, S., Porter, M.E. and Furman, J.L. 2001. *The Determinants of National Innovative Capacity*, September. Retrieved from http://www.mbs.unimelb.edu.au/HOME/JGANS/STERN/Determinants%20of%20NIC%20-%20Fall%202001.pdf. Accessed 25 September 2011.
Suedfeld, S. and Tetlock, P. 1977. 'Integrative Complexity of Communications in International Crises'. *Journal of Conflict Resolution* 21, 169–84.
Suedfeld, P., Tetlock, P. and Streufert, S. 1992. 'Conceptual/Integrative Complexity', in *Motivation and Personality: Handbook of Thematic Content Analysis*, edited by C.P. Smith. Cambridge: Cambridge University Press.

Swallow, J. 2011. 'Bin Line Sales Double Nation Average after Plastic Bag Ban'. *The Advertiser*, 22 August. Retrieved from http://www.adelaidenow.com.au/bin-line-sales-double-nation-average-after-plastic-bag-ban/story-e6frea6u-1226119243127. Accessed 9 October 2011.

Tacey, D. 2009. *Derrida, God and the Revenge of Nature*. Derrida Day conference paper.

Tetlock, P.E. 1984. 'Cognitive Style and Political Belief Systems in the British House of Commons'. *Journal of Personality and Social Psychology: Personality Processes and Individual Differences* 46, 365–75.

Tetlock, P.E. 1986. 'Integrative Complexity of Policy Reasoning', in *Mass Media and Political Thought*, edited by S. Kraus and R. Perloff. Beverly Hills: Sage.

Tetlock, P. 1998. 'Close-call Counterfactuals and Belief-system Defenses: I Was Not Almost Wrong But I Was Almost Right'. *Journal of Personality & Social Psychology* 75, 639–52.

Tetlock, P.E., Bernzweig, J. and Gallant, J.L. 1985. 'Supreme Court Decision Making: Cognitive Style as a Predictor of Ideological Consistency of Voting'. *Journal of Personality and Social Psychology: Personality Processes and Individual Differences* 48, 1227–39.

Theall, D.F. 2006. *The Virtual Marshall McLuhan*. Montreal: McGill-Queen's University Press.

Tierney, J. 2004. 'Republicans Outnumbered in Academia, Studies Find'. *New York Times*, 18 November.

Uren, D. and Hohenboken, A. 2009. 'Business is Booming among Cafe Society'. *The Australian*, 7 August.

Vleck, V.N.L.V. 2002. 'Delivering Coal by Road and Rail in Britain', in *Famous Fables of Economics: Myths of Market Failures*, edited by D.F. Spulber. Oxford: Blackwell, 122–42.

Watson, J.D. 2007. *Avoid Boring People and Other Lessons from a Life in Science*. Oxford: Oxford University Press.

Watson, J.D. and Crick, F.H.C. 1953. 'A Structure for Deoxyribose Nucleic Acid'. *Nature* 171, 737–8. Retrieved from http://www.exploratorium.edu/origins/coldspring/ideas/printit.html. Accessed 23 December 2010.

Waugh, E. 1937/2000. *Scoop: A Novel about Journalists* with an introduction by Christopher Hitchens. London: Penguin.

Waugh, E. 1937/2005. *Scoop* with an Introduction by Ann Pasternak Slater. New York: Knopf, 2005.

Weber, M. 1946. 'Science as a Vocation', in *From Max Weber: Essays in Sociology*, edited by H.H. Gerth and C.W. Mills. New York: Oxford University Press, 129–56.

White House, The. 2011. *Remarks by the President in the State of Union Address*, United States Capitol, Washington, D.C. Retrieved from http://www.whitehouse.gov/the-press-office/2011/01/25/remarks-president-state-union-address. Accessed 9 October 2011.

Wimsatt, W.K. and Brooks, B. 1957. *Literary Criticism: A Short History*. New York: Vintage.
Wolfe, A. 1998. *One Nation, After All*. New York: Penguin, 1998.

Index